I0223095

WAKE-UP CALL

WAKE-UP CALL

Policing, Privilege, and Reclaiming Our
Unalienable Rights

LARRY BEARG

AVANT PRESS

WAKE UP CALL Copyright © 2019 Larry Bearg
All rights reserved. No part of this publication may be
reproduced, distributed, or transmitted in any form or by any
means, including photocopying, recording, or other electronic
or mechanical methods, without the prior written permission of
the publisher, except in the case of brief quotations embodied in
critical reviews and certain other noncommercial uses permitted
by copyright law.

ISBN 978-1-7336399-4-1

First Printing in 2019
Published in the United States by Avant Press

For all those who have been humiliated, abused, and injured at the hands of law enforcement, and for those many police officers who strive to do an impossible job with grace, respect, and dignity.

And for Michelle B. and Jay G., who helped me see beyond my class and race privilege and discover honor and honesty in the most unlikely places.

In memoriam, Morris Gross, QC, and beloved uncle.

CONTENTS

HOW TO READ
THIS BOOK

Technology, specifically the ubiquity of cell phone cameras, has made this book possible. Without the thousands of videos of citizen/police interactions recorded by both citizen witnesses and police dash and body cameras, the troubling nature of policing in the United States would be exiled to the realm of hearsay and rumor.

Even with these videos, most citizens remain unaware of the legally sanctioned abuses taking place all around them. This is particularly true if you are white, college-educated, and living a middle-class existence. Yet you certainly don't have to be black, brown, or impoverished to experience police abuse of power or to understand that these abuses ultimately impact us all.

While these videos are not definitive in establishing police misconduct, they raise fundamental questions about the ways in which citizens and police interact on a daily basis.

This book is written to be read without seeing these recordings, but viewing these recordings will provide the reader with a more visceral appreciation of the casual violence and abuse of power that occurs daily between law enforcement and our fellow citizens.

All the recordings referenced in each chapter are listed at the back of the book and can be found on Youtube.com by simply searching the name of the identified person.

This book addresses issues in law enforcement (the police), not criminal justice in general, which also includes the courts (prosecutors, defense attorneys, judges, and juries), and prisons and jails (including the system of fines, bail, sentencing, and punishment). These other parts of the criminal justice system deserve their own examination and have been written about by others.

The issues described in this book are first and foremost citizen issues, by which I mean they are not issues best left to experts. They are issues which demand input from and control by all of us, in our communities. As such, I encourage you to continue your own exploration of these issues in your particular community, in whatever way suits you, whether it is talking to neighbors, joining a community group, writing letters to the editor, doing more reading, voting, or running for office yourself! Change happens whether we wish it or not. Change we want can happen when we become in engaged in the process itself.

PREFACE

U.S. soldiers killed in the Iraq war, 2003 — 2014:
4,491[1]

U.S. civilians killed by police, 2003 — 2014:
11, 521 (estimated)[2]

Every year, police kill more than 1,000 U.S. citizens. Of those, an estimated 21 percent (200 people) are unarmed. If you search on You Tube under police killings or police brutality and you watch one of these videos, you will be shocked. But with the advent of social movements such as Black Lives Matters, and extensive news coverage of some of these killings, most of us will not be surprised.

You might also conclude, as I did until recently, that such events are the exception rather than the rule — that the police are there to protect our property and our physical safety while upholding our rights. Many, if not most cops, *want* to "serve and protect," but the police culture in which they work and live makes it almost impossible to do so.

What rights am I referring to? Rights so basic that you may not have conceived of them as rights:

- The right to not be shot and killed because the police thought you were reaching for a gun when you were reaching for your wallet to show them your ID (which they requested).
- The right to walk down the street without being stopped, questioned, and frisked, with your ID demanded, simply because of your age, gender, how you dress, or the color of your skin.
- The right to drive your car without being pulled over for no reason, questioned, ordered out of your car, searched, handcuffed, physically assaulted, and your car searched — all without your consent.
- The right to be safe in your own home and not have the police storm it, guns drawn, based on some unsubstantiated anonymous tip, and then have your bank accounts emptied, and home and car seized, before you are ever charged with a crime, or *never* charged with a crime. (Good luck getting your home, money, and car back).

These scenarios may sound like some Kafkaesque nightmare found on a conspiracy-theory website, but each of them happens in the United States on a daily basis.[3] Even more disturbing, the rights at stake in each of these scenarios were brought before the Supreme Court to determine if citizen freedom should prevail or police power should take precedence. In every case, the police were given the power, and often very broad power, over these very basic citizen rights. Unfortunately, and tragically, most of us are not even aware we have lost these rights. I certainly wasn't.

Until 2015, I was oblivious to the loss of my rights. After all, I am white, well-educated, middle class, and middle income. Except for one other instance (which I will relate later), the only interactions I had with the police was an occasional speeding ticket.

Then the police knocked on my door. That changed everything. I was stunned to learn that the rights I thought I had were gone and I never even knew it. Being white probably resulted in fewer of my rights being violated, but as I eventually learned, the police had every legal right to violate my rights as they saw fit, no matter my skin color. Rights that should belong to *all of us* now belonged to none of us, white or black. Stunned by this experience, I was compelled to understand how this had happened, why, and what I could do to regain my rights.

What I found was a fascinating and complex history of good intentions and bad decisions made into law, ultimately rendering our most sacred rights moot and meaningless in the face of burgeoning police powers. Yet, despite this tragic loss and its impact on millions of Americans, I found many examples from real-life police forces around the country who have far better relationships with their community, who are recognizing citizen rights, and in concert with their communities, helping them regain and protect those rights.

So while many of our most basic rights have been lost, there is both hope and action afoot to regain our rights and heal the rift between communities and the police sworn to serve them. Once you understand how precious these rights are and how they have been lost, I hope you will step forward and act to protect your unalienable rights for yourself and future generations of Americans.

INTRODUCTION

We hold these truths to be self-evident, that all men are created equal, that they are endowed by their Creator with certain unalienable Rights...
—Declaration of Independence

Some things are so unexpected that no one is prepared for them.
—Leo Rosten (American Humorist)

If once you forfeit the confidence of your fellow citizens, You can never regain their respect and esteem.
—Abraham Lincoln

Busted

On January 25, 2015, I was busted for growing medical marijuana. At that moment, I was thrust into the bizarre, surreal, alternate universe known as the U.S. "justice" system, which too often is anything but.

By November 9, 2016, adult recreational cannabis use would be legal in California, but even in liberal wine-loving Sonoma County, the district attorney and the local sheriff still imagined that arresting small-time medical marijuana growers was somehow an effective crime-fighting strategy. Of course, growing medical marijuana was supposedly legal in California, but the laws were so murky that the police were happy to shut down any marijuana operation, effectively putting you out of business because they confiscated all your equipment and medicine, emptied your bank accounts, and if you were really unlucky, seized your car and house. Then they handed the whole mess off to the district attorney's office, letting them figure out if what you were doing had been legal after all. ("Oops, sorry about that! No, we won't give you back your equipment, money, or car.")

I knew people who had been arrested for growing pot, and they had always made it sound like a walk in the park. No big deal. But I didn't experience it that way. My treatment was unfair, unjust, and most significant and worst, unnecessary. It was punitive for the sake of being punitive. It served no larger purpose. The cops who arrested me were rather nice for the most part, except for one who took great pleasure, he said, in parading me handcuffed out on the street for all my neighbors to see. "You're giving them quite a show," he sneered. And then there was the detective who, aside from any crime I might have committed, seemed much more interested in whether I owned my own home and the amount of my mortgage.

But beyond the psychological damage they inflicted on me, and the ethical breaches of the arrest, was the concrete damage. They took away the essentials of my life so that the actual punishment I received was meted out long before I was even charged, let alone tried and found guilty of anything. The warrant to seize evidence for my alleged illegal activity was so general that the police took my driver's license, credit and debit cards, and checkbooks, and emptied out my bank account with a court order, all in less time than it took my wife to bail me out of jail — about ten hours. Rather than being innocent until proven guilty, I was guilty until proven innocent. I couldn't even buy a cup of coffee, pay my bills, buy food for myself and my children, or put gas in my car to take my kids to school. I had been rendered destitute. It was demeaning. It was humiliating. It was embarrassing.

I hadn't been convicted of anything. But I was most certainly being punished. And the system didn't care. There was no one to appeal to. No one to call and say, "This isn't right." I didn't think this was America. Not the America I thought I lived in, in which justice meant you were presumed innocent and only punished following a determination of guilt, not preceding it.

When I was in grade school, each morning began with a recitation of the Lord's Prayer: "Our Father, who art in heaven, hallowed be they name. Thy kingdom come, thy will be done, on earth as it is in heaven." It then continues, "Give us this day our daily bread, and forgive us our trespasses, as we forgive those who trespass against us."

Forgiveness. Compassion. Kindness. This is what I had learned growing up. This is what I thought my county offered. This is what I couldn't find at all in my encounter with the police, nor in the police experiences of others. Just straight-up punishment well in advance of any consideration of one's guilt or innocence.

One year and $17,000 in legal fees later, I pled guilty to two misdemeanors of being in possession of more than an ounce of cannabis. I received three years' unmonitored probation, after which my record would be expunged. And they kept all my equipment and the $15,000 they took from my bank accounts.

Compared to many other so-called offenders, I got off easy, which sounds preposterous, but only to those who have no idea how many of our civil rights have been eroded and even seized from us — not unlike my bank accounts and my other possessions.

Fortunately, I had a loving and caring wife who had money and a credit card, which she used to pay the bail bond company to bail me out of jail.

I had parents who could loan me money for an expensive defense attorney who specialized in marijuana arrests (there were so many of them, he had a booming business). I could have pleaded not guilty and gone to trial, but that would have cost an additional $10,000. *Why give this corrupt system more money and more of my time?* I thought. I took the deal.

I could have just gotten angry and bitter over my own personal misfortune. And for a time, I did. But very quickly I became obsessed with the notion that this wasn't about me at all. This was about something much larger.

I started searching for answers online. Dramatic and obvious instances of police abuse were easy to find on YouTube. But what was stunning was how *many* there were. And most of them never made the nightly news. By then, the police killings of Michael Brown in Ferguson, Missouri, Walter Scott in Charleston, South Carolina, and the choking-to-death of Eric Garner in New York were front-page news. Did my relatively mild police encounter connect in any way to these much more dramatic and tragic events? I started reading.

Further research showed me that most of these episodes resulted in the officer being cleared of any wrongdoing. How was *that* possible, I wondered? I was no lawyer, but understanding the law seemed imperative if I was going to have any hope of unraveling this mystery. In all of these cases, I kept seeing references to the Fourth Amendment, so I started poring over books on the Constitution, which inevitably referenced specific Supreme Court cases. I spent months reading cases decided by the court, working to connect them to my own experience and that of others I had read about. There was obviously a huge disconnect between what I thought were my rights as an American and reality. There had to be some crucial information I was missing, as were many other Americans outraged by the violent deaths at the hands of the police that kept showing up in the news.

Ultimately, I realized this was about people inflicting injustice on other people just because they could. It was gratuitous. It was unnecessary, it was unjust, and it was immoral. And I had to find out how and why this was possible, here in America, because it was so much the opposite of the America I had lived in and believed in until my arrest.

Early on, I came across an interview with Richard Goerling, a Hillsboro, Oregon, police lieutenant writing about the need for mindfulness training for police officers. Of the tendency of cops to act badly, he wrote: "Talk to your neighbors and friends and most of them have horror stories about their encounters with the police." [4]

I wasn't black. And as far as I knew, none of my friends and acquaintances had had run-ins with the police. But I asked anyway and was stunned by what they told me. I bought a tape recorder, sat down, and they told me their stories. These encounters made me feel marginally better about my treatment but more concerned than ever about the deterioration of our law enforcement agencies, even our judicial system. It also furthered my confusion. If it wasn't just racism that was driving police abuses, what else was it?

Jill — Driving Home From Her Dad's Funeral

Jill's father had just died and she was driving back from Oklahoma, the family home, to Maryland, where she was living with her army officer husband. Her father had left her a modest inheritance, and she used part of it to buy herself a new car, a Volkswagen Cabriolet convertible, which she was driving at the time. Somewhere along Interstate 70 in Missouri, she was pulled over because the tag — she didn't yet have her license plates — was on the side of the car instead of the rear. She had her dog with her, a beagle, and her car was packed full of family heirlooms she had received from her father.

As she told the officer who pulled her over, because it was a convertible she couldn't very well put the tag on the rear window. If the top was down, you wouldn't be able see it. She also explained that she was driving back home to Maryland from her father's funeral and that no, the car wasn't stolen. It was her car. She had just bought it.

The officer ordered her out of the car and instructed her to remove the dog and put him on a leash. She protested, saying she had done nothing wrong. The officer's tone changed. He asked her if she was hiding something in the car. She wasn't.

"Go walk your dog down the highway," he told her.

Minutes later, more police cars showed up.

"They are going through my car. They got everything out of my car. Thank God I didn't have a gun in my car."

But they didn't stop there.

"Then my seats come out. Then the door panels come out. Then the dash comes out. Then they take the tires, they take the wheels- off. They took my whole fucking brand-new car apart on the side of the highway. Then they left me They left me with the car strewn in pieces on the side of the highway in Missouri, at dusk. Just left me. I had no drugs. I got no ticket. I was just accosted by the police. I had every single right violated. I felt like I had been emotionally raped by about eight officers. I hired an attorney to go after the police for violating my rights. Nothing. Nothing happened."

That Jill actually hired a lawyer to pursue a case against the officers is unusual in and of itself. Most of us would have neither the time, the energy, nor the resources to mount such a fight even if we felt wronged. But the question that bothered me most was that *nothing happened* despite her efforts. Why did nothing happen? Why, when our rights are obviously (to us) violated, are these violations not addressed, never acknowledged, and certainly not punished. Is it simply a case of an entrenched bureaucracy protecting its own from receiving justice? Is it that, as in my case, protecting one's rights has become so expensive and time consuming that justice is a "luxury good" available only to the relatively well-off? Is our entire premise — that our rights have been violated — wrong? Do we really not have the rights that we think we have? I didn't have the answers, but I needed to find them.

Tom — Driving Home from Work One Evening

Tom was on his way home from work when he was pulled over. He was seventeen, had grown up in Sonoma, and was starting a career in the trades. He had struggled in school, but he knew how to build things; even at seventeen he could build just about anything, fix any machine, diagnose a plumbing or electrical problem. That made sense. Books didn't.

He was driving his '64 El Camino, returning home from a job. The cargo bed was loaded with all of his tools. The officer told him he pulled him over because his reverse lights were on. Tom explained to the officer that in this old car, the reverse lights had a manual on/off switch and he had forgotten to flip the switch after he had backed up to leave his job.

By then, however, the officer was more interested in all the tools in the back of his truck. "Obviously," Tom recounted, his voice dripping with sarcasm, "this young kid [referring to himself] couldn't own thousands of dollars' worth of tools. The cop accused me of stealing the tools, but I didn't confess since they were all mine. But he seemed convinced I'm lying. So he orders me out of the car and shoves me to the ground and puts his boot on the back of my neck."

By this time, more officers had arrived, and began tossing Tom's tools out of the back of his truck into the field where he was lying, apparently hoping to find some tools marked with someone else's name. There were none.

"After fifteen minutes or half an hour – I don't remember how long it went on for – they decide there is nothing stolen and they leave. So it's dark by then and I pick up the tools that I can find and I go to a pay phone and call the sheriff's office."

The sheriff's office insisted their officers would have never done that. Tom didn't have the officers' names or badge numbers because it was dark, and as he explained, "My face was in the mud." But they insist he must have been mistaken.

The next day he returned and collected the rest of the tools that he couldn't find in the dark the night before. "But they lost a respectful citizen," he said. "I always was a law-abiding citizen and that began my career of having no respect for organized law. And it continues today. It's a total intimidation game. It's bullying."

Surprise!

If you are white, and I hadn't told you otherwise, you might assume that the people in the preceding stories are African-Americans. After all, most of us are aware of the consistent and long-standing bias in law enforcement against African-American men — everything from the rate at which they are incarcerated compared to the general population to racial profiling in the execution of so-called "community policing" which encourages police to stop and frisk citizens (in primarily black neighborhoods) even if they have not committed any crime.

Yet that is not the whole story. Far from it. And as angry as I was about my treatment by the police, I was more consumed with understanding this painful relationship between law enforcement and our communities than with simply laying blame. So I challenged myself — and I am challenging you, the reader, to examine your assumptions and beliefs about policing, but also your role in a system of law enforcement in which we are all participants, knowingly or unknowingly. What is the responsibility we have in shaping the legacy we leave our children when it comes to our rights, our freedom, and the law?

What do you make of our "white" experiences at the hands of the police? You could chalk up our experiences as exceptions to the otherwise fair and equitable application of the law. You might also cynically use our experiences to illustrate that the police don't single out people of color for mistreatment — that they are equal opportunity abusers. So why should you (a black person) expect "special" consideration?

I've heard both of these responses and they demand answers. Are these reports and the many others you can read about or view online exceptional situations, or illustrations of broader and more widespread policing issues? If the latter is true, are these violations of our rights worse now than twenty years or fifty years ago? Perhaps things were getting better and my deep misgivings about the state of police/community relations were ill-founded. But if not, it was my obligation to speak up and stand up for my beliefs.

It would be oh-so-convenient to be able to pull up a Bureau of Justice Statistics (BJS) study to confirm that we are in a full-blown law enforcement crisis, but no such study exists. In fact, the Bureau only began collecting data on use of force by police officers in 1995, and those studies are limited in their collection of data, flawed in their design, and say nothing about all the violations of citizen rights where use of force was *not* used, such as Tom's and Jill's stories. Given the lack of good data on rights violations, it is more useful to look at how citizens *feel* about the police. Do we trust the police more or less right now? Do we believe they are there to protect us or to harm us? The answers to those questions, it seems to me, are as good an indicator of whether there is a citizen/police relations problem as any study documenting greater or fewer specific acts of police misconduct.

A recent Gallup poll[5] shows that confidence in the police is at about 57 percent in the general population and has hovered between 52 and 63 percent over the past 25 years, but that it is declining among minorities and people under the age of 34, presumably because these groups are most likely to have encounters with the police. That 43 percent of the general population does not have confidence in the police certainly seems like cause for concern. That substantially more than half of minorities and those under 34 years of age do not trust the police, and that this trust is declining, makes for a crisis of confidence, albeit a slow-moving crisis, more akin to gradual climate change than a sudden hurricane. It is the gradual, almost imperceptible loss of our rights, coupled with the increasing visibility of those losses in the form of citizen cell-phone videos and police body cameras, which is bringing the crisis into sharper focus. That those who are most likely to come in contact with law enforcement have the least trust in law enforcement strongly suggests that citizen/police relations are fraught. But the question that kept resonating for me is why these relations are fraught. Are police not respecting our constitutional rights, or are we mistaken about what our rights really are?

The second point which suggests that the police treat both blacks and whites with equal disregard is simply not borne out by the numbers. Michelle Alexander's masterful book, *The New Jim Crow,* lays out the racial differences in everything from arrests for marijuana possession to sentencing to differences in criminal charges filed for similar crimes. Malcolm Holmes has written extensively on the use of force in minority communities relative to their white counterparts.[6]

All this still begs the question: Are the police violating our rights, whether we are black or white, or do we not in fact have the rights we presume? If the police are simply violating our rights, then we need to insist on making police more accountable for their misdeeds. But if we have lost our fundamental rights, it is incumbent on us to reclaim those rights, lest we and our children and their children lose what we cherish: American freedom.

Each of the incidents I have described may seem minor, insignificant, and merely unfortunate against a backdrop of police shootings of young African-American men, which have become a flashpoint for both news coverage and federal reviews and investigations by the Justice Department. But it is the continuum on which these seemingly unrelated incidents lie that paints a picture of a crisis in law enforcement in America which impacts *all* citizens. The problem of police power, and state-sanctioned greed and violence, is not relegated only to African-Americans.

If it were, we might be upset that these fellow Americans are unfairly targeted in this way, which they are. Or, in our apathetic times, we might just shrug and think that there is nothing the rest of us (the 87 percent of us who are not African-American and the 63 percent[7] who identify as "white") can do to change this institutional racism. Or that the problem of many African-Americans' continuing poverty and the associated crime are the driving force in these high rates of incarceration for African-American men. Again, what can we, as individual citizens, do in the face of such a long-standing, complex, and intractable issue which doesn't impact us directly, if at all?

The undeniable racism present in American law enforcement is a not an anomaly within an otherwise fair system of law enforcement. It is a tragic *side effect*. It is also the most obvious and visible symptom of the equal potential for law enforcement to subject *anyone* to abuse of power, which impacts all citizens, whether we are aware of it or not.

If you think that because you are not African-American you do not need to worry about law enforcement violating your rights, taking your property without due process, and in general having no regard for the day-to-day sense of fairness and respect that you enjoy in the United States, then you — like me, Jill, and Tom — are in for a shock.

The fear of law enforcement that African-Americans know every day is a fear that we should all share because we are all equally vulnerable to these violations, though not equally subject to them. What were basic rights have, over the past fifty years, turned into privileges selectively granted by the police, most often and most obviously to those of us with white skin color. These privileges, when it comes to my relationship with the police, are so expected by me that they are largely invisible — like being able to walk down the street without being stopped and frisked, being able to drive anywhere and not be pulled over because I "look suspicious," and simply walking around a store without being followed as a potential shoplifter. Yet given the laws as they now stand, and as the experience of countless white folks confirm, the police are willing and able to enforce the same version of "black justice" upon us. This is nothing like what we — the 87 percent of Americans who are not black — would expect or imagine from what we see on TV. What I thought were my rights are now privileges granted to me at the discretion of law enforcement.

That law enforcement often applies the laws differently to people of color than to white people is disturbing, shameful, and given America's long struggle with race, not at all surprising.

That the laws themselves no longer resemble any of the rights I thought I had as an American is shocking in the extreme.

What I discovered by way of research and in interviews with police, attorneys, politicians, and "perps" was that our freedom, our rights, and the fair and equal application of law are in jeopardy for all of us. If we want a country that reflects the way most of us try to live our lives day-to-day, the way in which we try to treat our family and friends, the way in which we raise our children, and the way in which we imagine our legal system is supposed to work — with compassion, fairness, honesty — then the way law enforcement is currently conducted in this country needs to change. And the only people who can change it is us.

Nobel Peace Prize winner, author, and memoirist Elie Wiesel wrote: "There may be times when we are powerless to prevent injustice, but there must never be a time when we fail to protest."[8]

Law enforcement is not the problem, but it is a symptom

of a much deeper problem. That problem is our abdication of our responsibility to maintain our rights, which we claim to value above all else. Today, some of us look at the police and see honorable public servants with a few bad apples acting badly. Others see a dysfunctional culture of abuse and violence. Rarely if ever do we connect any of those judgments to our own lack of civic engagement. *My* lack of civic engagement!

Though I resisted heading down this path, my understanding of these issues eventually required me to examine my own behavior and responsibility for the way I and others are policed. In my experience, it is *always* easier and more psychologically satisfying (in a primitive way) to find others to blame for whatever problems one may encounter in life. Yet, as a psychologist by training, and someone who finds the role of victimhood ultimately self-limiting (though pretty darn gratifying in the short-term!), I needed to look at my part in this cop/citizen dance of power vs. freedom, respect vs. safety, rights vs. authority. More than just the politics of being "tough on crime" or the policies of policing, I needed to understand the deeper psychological and social factors at play in the wildly opposite reactions many Americans have to instances of police uses of power — when that exercise of power seems to go well beyond the bounds of moral and legal propriety.

Certainly, my seven years of working with mentally ill young adults informs my thinking, as does my twenty-three years of parenting and twenty years of launching and operating a variety of businesses. That I am white, middle income, and middle class — and not by training or profession a social activist or an attorney — has allowed me the freedom to examine these issues without a lot of preconceived notions and to make connections among the areas of politics, psychology, and ethics that might otherwise be left unexamined. Although my "citizen layperson" understandings may lack nuance, I believe they have value by virtue of my willingness to assume that my constitutional rights as a citizen — indeed, my constitutional *obligation* as a citizen — *demand* that I take on these issues, and form my own thoughts and opinions on them so that I can fully participate in maintaining the "Sacred Honor" described in the Declaration of Independence, to which we as Americans are all heir to. Yet it is up to each of us to choose to take up that task, or let others determine our present and future for us. My wish is that you will join me in exploring the idea of being an "American" in relation to our rights and freedoms, and how they intersect with police powers and our desire to be safe and secure, yet free, in our day-to-day lives.

Many in law enforcement already sees all the rest of us as "the enemy." Most police forces include in their mission a version of the motto "To serve and protect." They are supposed to be serving and protecting us, the community. But increasingly, they view themselves as serving and protecting themselves against the rest of us. We are the "bad" guys and they are the "good" guys.

Ultimately, there is no us and them. There's only us. Moreover, we, the citizens of our communities, have empowered the police to act the way they do. We have authorized the police to interact with our fellow community members in a way that is oftentimes abusive, insulting, or disrespectful at best, and at worst, results in loss of livelihood, loss of property, loss of health, or as we have seen all too often now, loss of life.

Are there violent criminals out there who need to be arrested and put in prison to keep the rest of us safe? Absolutely. But if the police do not distinguish in their interactions with the community between the relatively small number of truly "bad" people who may, in fact, be threatening officer safety, and the rest of us, we lose what we value most in our country – the rule of law, and the fairness and respect that we all believe we deserve until proven otherwise.

How does the power, violence, and greed of law enforcement present itself in our lives? What are some of the causes of it? What role do we play? And what might we do to change it? These were the questions I was driven to answer, and the answers, despite innumerable surprises, that drove me to action.

Let's start by looking at the contradictions inherent in policing and daily life in America.

CHAPTER
ONE

Neighborhood Bully

*Perhaps it is only human nature to inflict suffering on anything
that will endure suffering, whether by reason
of its genuine humility, or indifference, or sheer helplessness.*
—Honoré de Balzac

*If you are neutral in situations of injustice, you have chosen the
side of the oppressor. If an elephant has its
foot on the tail of a mouse, and you say that you are neutral,
the mouse will not appreciate your neutrality.*
—Desmond Tutu

Are Police Killings Just the Tip of the Iceberg?

On July 17, 2014, Eric Garner was choked to death by police as he repeatedly told them, "I can't breathe; I can't breathe." Moments before, he had pleaded with them to leave him alone and, as they attempted to handcuff him, he politely asked, "Please don't touch me."[1] The City of New York paid the Garner family $5.9 million to settle their wrongful death lawsuit. The officer who choked Garner was never charged.

On May 19, 2011, Dwight Harris, a disabled homeless person, was parked in his wheelchair outside a Washington, D.C., subway station. He was drinking some malt liquor, according to police, but was otherwise committing no crime. Without warning, two transit police officers pulled him out of his wheelchair and slammed him to the ground, face first, each officer landing partially on top of him. Then they handcuffed him as he lay cut and bleeding on the sidewalk, and charged him with resisting arrest and assaulting an officer. This was all caught on a cell-phone video[2] by his friend, Lawrence Miller, who confronted police and asked them why they had done this to Harris. Miller was then arrested for inciting a riot and assaulting a police officer. All charges against both men were dropped and both were awarded undisclosed cash settlements for lawsuits they filed against the police. No criminal charges were ever brought against the officers involved.

On June 2, 2013, in Gardena, California, an unarmed young man, Diaz Zeferino, was shot dead by police after he received multiple differing orders from various officers to either "raise his hands" or "don't move." Zeferino first raised his hands, then lowered them, then raised them again before he was shot. The police were responding to a report of a robbery, which was actually the theft of a bicycle. They had stopped two other young men on bicycles who were, in fact, trying to locate the stolen bike. Zeferino, thirty-four years old, showed up after the initial stop and was trying to explain to the police that these two friends were trying to find the stolen bicycle and were not the thieves. He was under the influence of alcohol and speed. The confrontation was recorded by dashboard police cameras.[3] The City of Gardena paid the Zeferino family $4.7 million in a lawsuit settlement.

American policing in is crisis, brought about in large part by the ability of ordinary citizens to capture such incidents on their cell phones and bring them to public attention through the internet. While these dramatic videos do not prove policing is worse now than in past years, the resulting scrutiny has made it clear police in America kill more citizens each year as a percentage of the population than in any other comparable country.[4] Perhaps the best and most obvious comparison is Canada, which is most like the United States in language and culture, with constant exposure to American companies, products, movies, technology, and the like. Twenty-six percent of Canadians own guns[5] compared to thirty-seven percent of Americans.[6] Yet police in the U.S. kill citizens at four times the rate they do in Canada, adjusted for the differences in population.[7] Whatever the particulars of each of the above cases may be, the larger picture reveals an approach to policing in the United States which results in far more deadly encounters for citizens. Other countries, with all their similarities and differences compared to the U.S. and to each other, have one thing in common. Nearly all seem to have found a way to have fewer deadly citizen/police encounters. What makes us so different?

The common police responses to these dramatic incidents of police violence are usually one of two types. One response: "The officers were following proper procedures and did as they were trained to do under the circumstances," which inevitably and rightly calls into question the procedures and policies they are being taught, as well as the legality of said policies. The other common response: "The officers involved were 'bad apples.' The rest of the department is made up of good cops." This is, in fact, most likely true. But it belies another question: How did these "bad apples" manage to maintain a police career among all of the "good cops." And how is it that police in other countries and some police departments here in the United States, working in comparable neighborhoods (adjusted for income, crime levels, gun ownership, and the like), manage to kill citizens at far lower rates or not at all?

In his recent book, *To Serve and Protect*, former Seattle Chief of Police Norm Stamper violates the "thin blue line" of police silence and offers a blunt assessment of his former colleagues: According to Stamper, police today are "as violent, racist, and dishonest" as police have been since the 1960's.[8]

This description by itself suggests a deeper and more fundamental problem with the very culture of policing, more than individual police officers. It also suggests that these police killings are not isolated problems in an otherwise exemplary agency, but are instead the worst manifestations of a larger dysfunctional culture coupled with procedures and policies which lead to these terrible outcomes.

Before we consider policy, let's examine culture. What is the "culture of policing" in America? How did this culture come about and why should we care about changing it?

Why "Bullies"?

The deaths and assaults described above make it difficult to describe police officers as bullies. Such a term seems impossibly mild and perhaps irresponsibly gentle when we are talking about people's lives lost at the hands of police.

For most of us, the word "bullying" is a term of childhood

and schoolyard experiences. For those of us who have been bullied or have bullied, the word has a uniquely resonant emotional ring: direct, primitive, and vulnerable. Being bullied is terrifying and bullying someone is to feel the worst part of yourself on public display - at least to the victim, yourself, and perhaps other witnesses as well. As someone who has been bullied and, on occasion, bullied others, this description of police abusing their power seemed to capture the essence of the experience on both sides of the interaction. During my arrest, I had that utterly doomed feeling of helplessness in the face of a bunch of officers who held all the cards. I was one person and they were five or six. The way they treated me, the tone of their voices, being led here and there in handcuffs all led to the inevitable conclusion that whatever rights I thought I had had no purchase here. And, of course, it was then, in that situation, that I most needed to understand my rights so I could defend and protect myself against an over-reach of the already immense power granted to these officers of the law. Yet, the implicit message was: I'd best just submit to whatever they might inflict or suffer much worse consequences. They knew the rules of the game and I did not. And, more importantly, they were not about to share with me what those rules were. Better for me to feel at their mercy, which I did.

While the idea of police acting as bullies held emotional resonance for me, I needed to understand if that concept as it has been defined and studied by scientists over the past forty years applied more generally to the wide range of fraught confrontations between citizens and the police that, once I started looking, seemed so ubiquitous. What did it mean to be a bully in the context of policing?

Bullying is defined as "the systematic abuse of power."[9] As such, bullying is no longer limited to the schoolyard but is identified at work (often called "harassment"), between spouses (called "abuse"), and in prisons. "Bullying" is a way of interacting with others in which the more powerful person or persons use their position of power – whether physical, hierarchical, social, and/or legal – to abuse those with less power. The abuse can be physical, but it can just as easily be emotional and psychological or a combination of all three.

When we think about policing in this context, it becomes immediately apparent that we have granted law enforcement officers extraordinary powers that the rest of us do not have. In fact, and problematically, we have accorded law enforcement the power to engage in behaviors that we have made illegal for the rest of us to engage in – physical violence, lying, the taking of private property without consent – in the name of preventing those very same behaviors! Just a simple statement of this paradoxical state-sanctioned authority is psychologically daunting:

"We grant you, the police officer, authority to use violence, to lie, and to steal, to prevent violence, lying and theft."

Of course, when the police use violence it is called "use of force" and justified as preventing harm to the police or the community. When the police lie, it is called "deception" and is justified as a method to establish the guilt of a suspected criminal. And when police steal, it is called "asset forfeiture," and is justified as depriving suspected criminals of their suspected profits.

If these powers were used only under such circumstances, who could object? If the police exercised their extraordinary powers in good faith and made an occasional error in judgment, it would be unfortunate, but understandable. But when police actively, repeatedly, and frequently abuse their powers against our communities, all under the guise of "protecting themselves," there is a clear abuse of power in which they no longer "serve and protect" us but instead "serve and protect" their own power and position. This is the essence of bullying.

The Problem of Power

The fundamental problem with being accorded this type of power is a lack of corresponding responsibility in its use. Norm Stamper, the former Seattle police chief, observes that many officers seem to believe that their power is only meaningful if they can abuse it,[10] and given such license, it is all too easy to do so.

It would take a person of astounding moral character not to cross the line of abusing such immense power instead of using it only to "serve and protect," the motto of many of our law enforcement organizations. In fact, the text of the President's Task Force on 21st Century Policing reaches back two thousand years to quote Plato on the role of policing in a democracy and the character of those who police: "In a republic that honors the core of democracy, the greatest amount of power is given to those called Guardians. Only those with the most impeccable character are chosen to bear the responsibility of protecting the democracy."[11]

We are asking police to wield immense power while simultaneously having the strength of character not to abuse that power. It would be hard to maintain "impeccable character" under the best of conditions, but the conditions in which our police operate are far from the best. It seems fair to say that they have failed us in this regard. We, in turn, have failed them.

We can condemn the police in their failure in a way that excludes them as members of our communities, demonizing them, and using language that makes them the "other," or we can use language that is descriptive but continues to consider law enforcement as part of our communities, even though today's police officer sees himself as separate, alone, unappreciated, and under threat, except by fellow cops. While nobody likes a bully – except maybe other bullies – we generally view bullies as troubled, in need of psychological and emotional help, but certainly within the realm of the "us" that we consider members of our community. So, my use of the word "bully" is intended to keep the police "inside" rather than banishing them as "outside" to the nether world in which they already see themselves residing.

Use of Language

Brien Farrell, formerly an attorney for the City of Santa Rosa in Sonoma County, California, spent twenty years defending police officers in cases involving the use of excessive or deadly force. In the wake of the 2013 shooting death of Andy Lopez, a thirteen-year-old boy, Farrell was invited to sit on a task force on community policing and local law enforcement. Lopez had been carrying a toy gun that police mistook for a real weapon. This shooting took place in October 2013, before the death of Michael Brown and the Black Lives Matter movement. The task force's webpage described its job as intending to "address... important issues necessary for community healing."[12]

The task force, composed of various stakeholders in the community, included a representative of the sheriff's department, the department that had shot Andy. Part of their work was to hold public meetings in which members of the community could express their concerns about local law enforcement.

Farrell describes how in the first couple of meetings several community members stood up and called the police "murderers," referring to the Lopez killing, even going so far as to describe the sheriff's office representative as a murderer. According to Farrell: "He could not take the personal attacks on him. ...It just turned out that when people yelled "murderer" at him and were figuratively spitting in his face when they were at the microphone, and almost accusing him of murdering Andy Lopez, or covering up the truth or validating the shooting, he was put in a corner in a lousy situation."

"After that," says Farrell, "he virtually never spoke. He was monitoring. I was glad he was listening. But he didn't engage. ...We didn't make any progress having a community conversation about what are the problems law enforcement faces and how have they tried to solve them and what support would they like to be able to do their jobs better. And what questions do they have for us.[13]"

The task force's final report stated: "The overriding theme of the recommendations is to achieve change in the relationship between the Sheriff's Office and the community."[14]

But with the sheriff's representative basically AWOL because of the way he was treated by some community members, what healing or change in relationship was possible? Should the sheriff's department have taken the anger directed at them and continued to actively engage in the process? Of course. But so often we can't rise above the worst in ourselves. We shut down. We are defensive. We literally cannot hear what is being said. It's too threatening to our sense of self. The police are no different, despite their formidable powers.

Language matters. Describing police as bullies also means that we must consider our responsibility in creating and supporting a dysfunctional culture of policing. If police are part of "us," we have to take some ownership of the very behavior we find so objectionable. It is always more comfortable to blame "them" over there. It lets us off the hook from taking either responsibility or action. But if we do that, we have no recourse when "they, over there" turn their dysfunctional use of power on "us, over here." What will we say then?

The other component of using the word "bully" is that it

creates a different story than the one that we continue to tell ourselves on the news, in the streets, and at our dining-room tables. Because bullying describes a range of behaviors, it allows us to consider policing in a larger context. In this light, the use of lethal force by police is not a stand-alone problem in need of reform, but an inevitable and natural result of a range of behaviors of which lethal force is just the most obvious, dramatic, and newsworthy. Without considering the entire scope of law enforcement, we end up demanding cosmetic change in discrete areas instead of lasting change of an entire system.

Former Seattle police chief Norm Stamper sums it up by ascribing the source of police misconduct as a deeply entrenched and widespread systemic problem which is only getting worse.[15]

That's the bad news. The good news is that with the rise of social media, more citizens, political leaders, *and* some police departments are embracing the need for dramatic and permanent change in the way they do business.

Policy vs. Culture

For the past forty-five years, the American public has enthusiastically endorsed the political rhetoric, and the policies that followed, of being "tough on crime." To be less than tough on crime was a political suicide pill.

Unpacking all the assumptions, misconceptions, and fear that have led us to embrace a "tough on crime" approach to law enforcement is beyond the scope of this book. Suffice it to say, we are now questioning this approach because of its unacceptably high cost in blood – mostly the blood of black and brown Americans[16] – and treasure – mostly at the expense of the middle class, which pays to house more prisoners per capita than any other country in the world.[17]

"Tough on Crime" has also failed to reduce crime, though crime has indeed gone down, but for other reasons,[18] and we now have many other proven criminal justice options[19] that are more successful and far less costly. So, what is wrong with our policing, and why should the 63 percent of Americans who count themselves as white, most of whom are *not* in jail, care? The answers, I believe, reside in a closer examination of the roots of the problem.

In the wake of the Michael Brown shooting in Ferguson, Missouri, and the birth of the Black Lives Matter movement, President Barack Obama appointed a task force to study current policing in the United States and to come up with recommendations for "twenty-first century policing."

The report is masterful in all it does *not* say, but it is easy enough to read between the lines. As the task force memorably puts it: "Organizational culture eats policy for lunch." The report continues: "Any law enforcement organization can make great rules and policies...but if the policies conflict with the existing culture, they will not be institutionalized, and behavior will not change."[20]*

On the other side of the argument is Radley Balko, a longtime reporter on law enforcement for *The Wall Street Journal* and other publications. In his book, *Rise of the Warrior Cop*, his entire premise is that the excesses of policing are largely driven by policies that either permit or actively encourage cops' worst tendencies. "And policy," he reminds us, "is ultimately made by politicians."[21]

So where does the problem lie? Is it bad policy or bad culture?

The answer is both. Policy *and* culture need to be changed, and each influences and changes the other. There is no one-way cause and effect. Certainly it is possible to change policy

---

* The report is still a political document in that it studiously avoided commenting on President Obama's ongoing support for federal policies that reward law enforcement's warrior culture – specifically supplying police with military equipment and funding for drug arrests at the expense of all other types of criminal activity.

without it impacting the culture, but when changes in policy *and* culture reinforce each other, amazing things can happen!

With the recent public attention on policing, several police chiefs have stepped forward to describe how they have managed to change the culture in their departments. What becomes apparent is that a change in basic and often unspoken assumptions and values usually occurs from the chief down (often as a result of public pressure and involvement), and that these value changes are then put into action through a combination of policy and procedural changes, retraining, and leadership by example by those at the top. It is neither simple nor quick, and is often subject to resistance, but it has been successful in departments around the country.[22]

Bad Policy Reinforcing Bad Culture

Federal policies, with their focus on punishment for crimes rather than prevention or rehabilitation, have directly and indirectly promoted a culture of violence and bullying in local law enforcement. Radley Balko exhaustively details how the federal government's war on drugs/war on crime has created policies that provide strong financial and public-relations incentives for local police departments to engage in aggressive, excessive, and violent use of force to show they are "tough on crime." In return they are rewarded with money and materiel, reinforcing the existing culture.

In *The New Jim Crow*, Michelle Alexander details government "tough on crime" policies resulting in the astounding increase in America's number of prisons and prisoners (more than any other country in the world, as a percentage of population) and the billions of dollars spent on keeping those prisons full at the expense of taking care of our poor, our young, our uneducated, and more recently, our middle class. This has created a permanent, and growing, underclass of Americans. But again, those policies emerged out of an embrace by the majority of Americans that these sorts of policies and the tactics they engendered were acceptable ways of treating our fellow citizens as way of keeping the rest of us safe.

Policies can be very difficult to change, however, entwined as they are with all sorts of special interests. Police and correctional officer unions are hugely powerful in protecting the status quo, and many elected officials have a vested interest in the jobs and dollars generated by prisons in their districts. Cultural changes can happen much more quickly, in some cases, and Radley Balko cites several examples of police departments that resisted federal policy inducements to change their cultures to one of hyper-aggression and bullying and, even more revealing, each of those examples he provides showed reduced levels of crime.[23]

Bad policy does not inevitably result in bad policing if decision-makers at the local level refuse to participate in such policies. There is no need to wait for or expect policy changes to fix longstanding cultural problems in police departments. We can begin changing the police culture even if the changes fly in the face of current policy incentives and then work to align the incentives with the new culture.

Richmond, California, Police Chief Chris Magnus (now chief of police in Tucson, Arizona) arrived in town in 2006. At that time, Richmond was one of the most violent, crime-ridden small cities in the country. It had a largely poor minority population with an unemployment rate of 17 percent. In 2006 alone, police had shot and killed six Richmond residents.

Magnus focused on changing the culture of Richmond policing against the backdrop of federal policies that incentivized law enforcement across the country with additional funds and military equipment in the ongoing "war on drugs." Magnus declined. Instead he focused on building ongoing relationships and programs with all parts of the community, designing *with* the community rather than applying policies to the community in a top-down fashion. This resulted in major changes in the entire culture of policing in Richmond and changed the relationship between the police and the community for the better. The apparent result: Richmond has had only one instance of lethal force killing by police since 2007 - and violent crime and crime in general is at an all-time low in the city.[24]

Conversely, bad policies create and reinforce a dysfunctional bully culture which incentivizes officer abuses. Former L.A. narcotics detective Dave Dodderidge described the incentives individual police officers operated under during his time at the LAPD:

"Every month they look at your recap. What did you do that month? How many tickets did you write? How many felony arrests did you make? How many misdemeanor arrests did you make? How many traffics [traffic stops] did you do? How many street stops? How many field interviews did you do? You have to keep those things up. If you don't keep those things up, then they have a talk with you. They think that you're not doing your job. You're really pushed that way."[25]

More recently, in March 2016, a group of minority police officers at the New York Police Department (NYPD) filed a lawsuit alleging the use of arrest quotas (the state banned such arrest quotas in 2010) and discrimination against officers who objected to the illegal use of quotas. In an interview with twelve of the officers, the officers described the system.[26]

Officer Derek Waller: "Those officers, who at the end of the month don't have those arrests...they are pressured to find something. You might not see nothing. You find something. You go hunting, like you go bounty hunting for an arrest. You lock up some old guy, some homeless guy. Someone who is riding their bicycle on the sidewalk, someone who is spitting, and you bring him in."

Unidentified Officer: "We are the predators and they are the prey. The worst thing you can have is a police officer that needs an arrest for the month."

Officer Edwin Raymond: "It's something coming from the top that trickles its way down.

Unidentified Officer: "We refuse [to make arrests for a quota] and so we are retaliated against."

Officer Felicia Whitely: "Because you are not harassing people, you are being punished. It doesn't make for a great work environment because they want you to harass people."

Officer Ritchie Baez: "The community is suffering the most because of the pressure, the quota. Because the police department is like a whore pretending to be a lady."

Officer Adhyl Polanco: "In the culture of the department, we are the rats, the rats that speak out. It takes a lot of guts from a rat to stand where we stand, knowing that our careers are basically over the second we speak against such a mafia. Because the police department is a mafia. It's a big organized mafia."

Instead of such quotas, imagine if we had crime incentives similar to the wellness plans now being rolled out by health insurance companies. Health insurance providers have discovered that it is much cheaper to help people stay healthy than it is to treat and heal them after they get sick. So, they now provide both patients and doctors with financial incentives to exercise, to eat healthy, to stop smoking. What if we gave more money to police departments based on lower crime rates *coupled* with lower arrest rates, instead of basing their funding on higher crime rates and more arrests?

For every dollar they save on arrest and detention, they receive a portion to put towards further crime prevention efforts. Might that not change police culture to one of crime prevention, rather than criminal detention?

I have to think so.

Scapegoating Individuals Instead of Changing the System

Even now, the media and the public continue to focus on individual police actions and holding individual police officers accountable for acts of violence against unarmed and non-aggressive citizens. In most of these cases, the officers involved are never held accountable because of the extensive and extraordinary legal protections given to police. These protections go far beyond what the Constitution provides for the rest of us, making them less responsible for their use of immense powers, rather than more. This is one more way that policies, in the form of laws, encourage a culture of police violence.

But as the President's Report implies in its roundabout way, the problem is not fundamentally with individual officers, though there are bad individual cops to be sure. The problem is with police culture on a broad scale, in the context of policies which encourage bad policing. This discussion of a dysfunctional police culture is one of the hard truths that few in the media or any public official wants to acknowledge for reasons that are psychologically complex.

In a PBS NewsHour report, Mark Konkol, a Chicago-based, Pulitzer Prize-winning crime reporter commented on the 2014 shooting death of Laquan McDonald. McDonald was shot sixteen times by Officer Jason Van Dyke as he was walking away from the police. Generally, police are trained to use lethal force *only* when they believe they, or other citizens, are in mortal danger. In this case, Officer Van Dyke was charged with murder.

Konkol said about the Chicago Police Department: "There are a lot of good cops on the department. I would say the overwhelming majority, ninety to ninety-five percent. There's been stories written that there are a few officers that are troubled, but overall the police department has a generational problem. this thin blue line of silence within the department. The culture of law enforcement isn't trusted."[27]

This reporter has been critical of the police, but reading this comment you might think that the only thing wrong with the Chicago Police Department is a few bad apples and a cultural code of silence that is protecting these troubled officers.

Former Seattle Police Chief Norm Stamper suggests that the 'few bad apples' theory does not explain the current levels of police misconduct.[28] The entire barrel is rotten, says Stamper, and it has been for quite some time.

The "optics" problem with this is as insidious as it is subtle. If the barrel is bad, then by implication, all the apples, or in this case, *all* the police officers, must be bad by virtue of their contamination in this "bad barrel."

The subtlety of separating out the vast majority of "good" police officers while at the same time indicting the entire culture of policing in which they work makes for distinctions that are lost in the sound-bite news cycle that dominates media today.

On the one hand, Konkol is most likely quite right in saying that ninety to ninety-five percent of Chicago police officers are "good cops," meaning that as individuals they are honorable human beings doing a difficult job with personal integrity. But they are also working within a culture that promotes violence, abuse, and humiliation of those they are sworn to serve and protect. So, one problem is how to assign "blame" to a system without blaming all individuals working within that system. And, second, if you don't hold individuals accountable, how will the culture ever change?

Furthermore, a "bad culture" implicates not just the rank and file, but the supervisors, sergeants, police chief and/or county sheriff, and even local politicians insofar as they are responsible for appointing the chief of police. As the colorful cliché goes, "Shit flows downhill." Leaders in law enforcement and political office would rather see themselves and their agencies as having a successful and healthy culture. Any problems, therefore, are presented as stemming from a few "troubled individuals" who, once removed, will confirm that all is well within the organizational culture, protecting the leaders of these organizations from any direct responsibility or accountability. They can continue business as usual.

It's the System

The fallacy of such denial has been vividly shown in the now infamous Stanford Prison Experiment, conducted by Phillip Zimbardo back in 1971. To summarize, Zimbardo took a group of Stanford students and randomly divided them into "guards" and "prisoners." He then created a mock prison in which to evaluate how they conformed or rejected the roles assigned to them. In Zimbardo's telling, there was some assumption that "free will" would prevail and that these otherwise normal students would not take on the authoritarian attributes of prison guards and the prisoners would not take on the "victim" role. Instead, the opposite result occurred. The guards became so cruel and abusive and the prisoners so traumatized that the experiment was ended after three days instead of the scheduled full week.

In his more recent book, *The Lucifer Effect: Understanding How Good People Turn Evil*, Zimbardo is unequivocal, describing a social structure which brings out the worst in people will inevitably result in even 'good' people committing horrible acts when they are immersed in 'total situations' "that impact human nature in ways that challenge our sense of the stability and consistency of individual personality, of character, and of morality."[29]

In the intervening forty-five years since this experiment took place, it would be nice to think we had taken some of its lessons to heart, but Zimbardo details how the relatively recent torture of Iraqi prisoners by American soldiers in the Abu Ghraib prison in Iraq was blamed on a handful of "rogue solders," according to General Richard B. Meyers, Chairman of the Joint Chiefs of Staff.[30] In Zimbardo's view, it was much more likely that the context of the situation and the system which created that context led to the abuses, which the army was now trying to cover up.[31]

It is often easier and more expedient for those in power to sacrifice a few low-ranking individuals than to take responsibility for a discredited culture which authorized and condoned the behavior in question, however tacitly.

The Biology of Blame

Finally, there is our desire to decide, unequivocally, who is the good guy and who is the bad guy. Blaming systems and cultures is inherently unsatisfying because there is no "bad guy," or to put it another way, when everyone is bad, no one is bad. And if you can't find someone to blame, how do you fix the problem and achieve justice?

Assigning specific personal blame is borne out of a real biological need. For millions of years our ancestors had to make immediate decisions about what was dangerously life threatening and what was not. There was no time to analyze whether an attacking predator or rival was acting on behalf of a broader system. The primitive part of our brains recognized the specific threat against the background of the larger environment and took whatever action was deemed necessary to survive. For all our cerebral sophistication, that ancient part of our brain still reacts to perceived threats in the same way, even when the situation at hand requires a more nuanced approach. If we want to go beyond feeling the self-righteous satisfaction that all the bad in the world resides in that one person or persons, we will need to quell that primitive first reaction. It takes significant emotional intelligence to set aside those primitive but powerful feelings and consider a more complex response than the urge to strike out and lay blame.

While individuals make up cultures, cultures can and do change without all of its members participating in the change. This may offend our sense of justice and our need to make clear distinctions between good guys and bad guys. But it offers the possibility of "restorative justice" in which the perpetrator makes amends and by so doing can return to the modified culture as a member in good standing – and the victim receives acknowledgement of and/or compensation for the pain and diminishment she has suffered.

Warrior or Bully?

In his chronological look at the transformation of America's police departments over the past fifty years, Radley Balko describes the process of turning Norman Rockwell's iconic "Officer Friendly" into an "increasingly armed, increasingly isolated, increasingly paranoid, increasingly aggressive police force,"[32] partially armed, funded, and even trained by the U.S. military.

In the President's Report on 21st Century Policing, one task force member asked the rhetorical question: "Why are we training police officers like soldiers? ...The soldier's mission is that of a warrior: to conquer [the enemy]. ...The police officer's mission is that of a guardian: to protect. ... Soldiers come into communities as an outside, occupying force. Guardians are members of the community protecting from within."[33]

Reverting police officers from warriors back into guardians could radically transform law enforcement. But even describing police officers as "warriors" is perhaps too generous by half. The "warrior" culture also embodies traits such as honor, integrity, and respect. The U.S. Army describes it this way: "in The Soldier's Code, we pledge to treat others with dignity and respect while expecting others to do the same. ...Honor is a matter of carrying out, acting, and living values of respect, duty, loyalty, selfless service, integrity and personal courage in everything you do"[35]

The code does not say treat only your fellow soldiers with respect and dignity. Nor does it suggest denying respect and dignity to those you believe "might" be the enemy.

The Police Code of Ethics expresses similar expectations: "...my fundamental duty is to serve mankind; to safeguard lives and property; to protect the innocent against deception, the weak against oppression or intimidation and the peaceful against violence. ...I will enforce the law courteously and appropriately without fear or favor, malice or ill will, never employing unnecessary force or violence..."[34]

In all of the citizen/police confrontations I have described, even after the police ascertained that no crime had been committed, the police continued to abuse, insult, and humiliate their fellow citizens. These examples of abuse, both physical and psychological, and the ultimate death of several of these citizens, do not reflect the respect and honor of the warrior's code or the police code of ethics. They describe a "bullying" culture rather than a "warrior" culture. The question which always arises is: Do these cops show up with these types of personalities already in place or does becoming a police officer simply bring out these personality "potentials" that we all have to a greater or lesser degree?

Much psychological testing has been done on police officers. The one trait that continually ranks higher than in the population at large is "authoritarian personality" which is defined as a state of mind or attitude characterized by a belief in absolute obedience or submission to one's own authority, as well as the administration of that belief through the oppression of one's subordinates.[35]

There is precious little of the Guardian ethos in such personality attributes. What is equally informative about this trait is that it often shows up after officers have been on active duty for several years,[36] suggesting again, that their behavior and personality can change in response to the culture they find themselves in. Norm Stamper, who started off his police career as a rookie patrolling the streets of San Diego, acknowledges his own rapid transformation from naïve rookie to cynical veteran, describing how, as a rookie cop, his adherence to the officers Code of Ethics lasted about as long as "it took for the ink to dry on our signatures at the bottom of the swearing-in form."[37] He adds that officers that abuse their power have been taught to do so by fellow officers "in the locker room or in the front seat of a patrol car."[40]

Dave Dodderidge, the twenty-one-year veteran of the LAPD, says about the cop ethos: "There are a couple of mottos that police officers have. The first one is, I was told, 'Cops don't get wet and they don't go hungry.' Of course, we did get wet and we did go hungry at times. The second one was you always go home at night. That's number one. You go home at night. You are number one, okay? And you know, I'm not sure I always agreed with that. The whole purpose of becoming a cop is that sometimes you put yourself in a dangerous situation for the betterment of the public. You have to do that. A good cop will. So, there are times, yeah, when I could have shot people, but I didn't. And other cops I knew, didn't also."[38]

This ethos of "make it home," quickly and easily comes into conflict with an officer's duty to "serve and protect" the rest of the community, notes Stamper.[39]

What comes across here is that to be a "good cop" requires you to resist a culture that put you, not the community you are sworn to protect, first. To be a good cop requires that you go against the prevailing culture of "You Always Go Home At Night."

Patterns of Bullying

Other indirect types of research are also indicative of a police culture of bullying. One would think that off the job, in the safety of their homes and family, police officers would find little need to assert their authority through violence. Yet police officers engage in domestic abuse at rates two to three times that of the general public[40] and, as previously mentioned, domestic abuse is now classified as a form of bullying behavior. It is the systematic abuse of power over someone who is demonstrably weaker. What could be the cause of this higher than average rate of domestic abuse among police? The obvious answer is that many officers "take their work home with them," and are unable to turn off the cultural influences that their work lives entail.

A more sophisticated exploration of why police officers have such high rates of spousal abuse comes from the work of sociologist Diane Vaughn, who describes what she calls "the normalization of deviance" in which unacceptable behaviors gradually become acceptable. Vaughn conducted her study on the culture at NASA leading up to the Challenger Space Shuttle explosion. What she discovered was that the risk assessment of certain shuttle parts, initially classified as unacceptably high, were, slowly over time, changed to be acceptable and then finally became part of what industrial psychologists call a "script."

The "script," once in place, makes certain behaviors and standards unquestioned parts of a "new normal." At that point, those operating within the new cultural "normal" are not just acting as if these "deviant behaviors" are okay; they really believe they are acceptable. They are no longer deviant. Everyone "drank the Kool-Aid," as it were. As Jerry Unseem writes in *The Atlantic*, about Volkswagen engineers knowingly reprogramming their diesel engines to give false positives – results meant to evade pollution laws – this phenomenon brings "to mind Orwell's concept of doublethink, the method by which a bureaucracy conceals evil not only from the public but from itself."[41]

Applied to police officers, if bullying becomes the "new normal" at work, and an acceptable and appropriate way to interact with people, it is not surprising that many officers would continue with such behavior in the private parts of their lives – that is, with their families, because this behavior is now scripted into their daily behavior. They see it as "normal."

Lying as a Form of Bullying

Although we tell our children that lying is wrong, they, and we, become proficient at lying at a very early age,[42] and we continue to do it throughout our lives. Studies have shown that we all lie every day.[43] We lie for different reasons at different times. Sometimes we lie to make others feel better about themselves – "No, you don't look fat in those jeans" – and, of course, we lie to make ourselves look better – "No, I didn't eat the last piece of cake." So, is it any surprise that police also lie on a regular basis? Perhaps not.

The difference, though, is that when police lie it can ruin entire lives, sending innocent people to jail or even to their deaths. Thus, we place a very high value on police honesty and, with people's lives at stake, we expect them to tell the truth.

Yet at the same time, police are instructed that lying in the service of upholding the law is perfectly reasonable and, in fact, encouraged.

As outlined at the law enforcement website, Policelink.com, "Out of necessity...[police] interrogation relies extensively on duplicity and pretense. An investigator may exaggerate his confidence in the suspect's guilt, establish a misleading reason for the interrogation, such as needing to establish the circumstances that led up to the crime, display feelings of sympathy and compassion toward the suspect that are far from genuine, and, in some cases, falsely tell the suspect that evidence exists which links him to the crime."[44]

While the general public may lie on a regular basis, there are few of us who do not feel a twinge of regret at our falsehood, no matter how small or how good our intentions. In law enforcement, however, lying is not only tolerated, but encouraged and practiced as a beneficial and necessary technique. So, is it any wonder that, despite the premium placed on police truth-telling, when it comes to evidence they collect, the circumstances of an arrest, and the behavior of a suspect, all of this approved lying can easily bleed over into these other areas?

Scandals involving officers lying in court, manufacturing evidence, and confirming each other's false statements are so common as to be unremarkable these days, and these are only the cases that we know about. As San Francisco Police Commissioner, Peter Keane, wrote in the *San Francisco Chronicle:* "One of the dirty little not-so-secret secrets of the criminal justice system is undercover narcotics officers intentionally lying under oath. It is a perversion of the American justice system that strikes directly at the rule of law. Yet it is the routine way of doing business in court rooms everywhere in America."[45]

Why do the police lie? Keane's short answer is the textbook definition of bullying: "The first reason is because they get away with it. They know that in a swearing match between a drug defendant and a police officer, the judge always rules in favor of the officer. Often in search hearings, it is embarrassingly clear to everyone - judge, prosecutor, defense attorney, even spectators - that the officer is lying under oath. Yet nothing is done about it."[46]

Norm Stamper concurs, saying that in his professional experience cops make a habit of lying, while knowing full well their lies are putting innocent people in jail or even resulting in their deaths.[47]

They lie because they can – and because we let them.

Bullying as Cowardice

As we all can recall from our schoolyard days, bullies tend to pick on those who are least able to defend themselves. In this context, being a bully is inevitably tied to the idea of being a coward because bullies choose to pick on those who are weakest. This definition of a coward is not that of someone who lacks the courage to face danger (police do willingly put themselves in harm's way), but of someone who lacks the courage to face the reality of their own shameful behavior, and in fact, even celebrates their brutality against those who cannot defend themselves.

An example of this occurred in a raid on a legal marijuana dispensary in Santa Ana, California. Narcotics officers were caught in a "candid camera" situation.[48] They broke down the door of the dispensary, though the door was not locked, and came in with guns drawn, screaming at customers and employees to "get the fuck down on the ground," though medical marijuana dispensaries in California generally have metal detectors and post security guards at the door, making them among the *safest* public places in the state.

After they removed and/or arrested the patients and employees, they took down all the video surveillance equipment, but unknown to them, one camera remained up and running, recording them. This is certainly a rare piece of footage insofar as the officers are talking candidly, not attempting to present an official façade by justifying or defending their actions, or creating a false impression of themselves or their work. What follows is a sample of their conversation.

Male officer to a female officer: Did you punch that one-legged old Benita (referring to an older female patient in a wheelchair with one leg amputated)?

Female officer (laughing): I was about to kick her in her fucking knob.

(Officers all laugh.)

The officers, who were presumably still on duty, then got high (eating the marijuana edibles – the evidence), and then one of them played darts.

On a more general level, this type of bullying as a means of enforcement seems to also occur in the way police target and apprehend suspects. Radley Balko reports that when it comes to SWAT teams, they are now overwhelming used to serve warrants for non-violent crimes.[49] As you may know from your TV viewing, SWAT teams - Special Weapons and Tactics Units - were specifically formed to deal with highly dangerous crime scenes such as active hostage situations, shooters, and terrorist threats – not to conducts raids on small-time marijuana growers, low-stakes poker games, and local bars.[50]

He then points out, in contrast, how police SWAT teams during the Columbine High School shootings stood outside the school *even when they knew exactly where the killers were inside* while the killings were occurring. The police declined to enter the school "because they deemed the situation too dangerous."[51]

At the other end of the spectrum is the case of Whitey Bulger, the notorious Boston crime boss suspected of more than twenty murders. Balko describes how instead of sending a SWAT team to raid the house where he lived - after all, he was on the FBI's "most wanted" list and was most likely armed and dangerous - the FBI did enough investigating to learn that Bulger had rented a storage locker. Rather than storm his residence, they tricked Bulger into coming to his storage locker under the pretense that someone may have broken into it. He was arrested without incident.

The example of Whitey Bulger does more than illustrate how police are much more careful in their use of force when confronted with situations that would actually put them in harm's way. It also calls into question the entire operating procedure of the way in which police enforce our laws in the first place.

If they managed to lure a lifelong violent criminal who had been on the run for sixteen years with a simple ruse, how hard would it be to conduct similar investigations into the lives of other nonviolent suspects—engaged in the consensual nonviolent crime of selling marijuana, for example - and find a way to arrest them without storming into their homes in full military gear, guns drawn, and screaming for everyone (often young children) to get down on the ground?

Neil Franklin, a former Maryland narcotics officer speaking to Balko, describes such raids as "Oh, it's a huge rush."[52] Another former federal law enforcement officer, Jamie Hasse, confirms that a more nuanced approach is better all around (but much less "fun," if terrorizing people is your idea of a good time): "It's so much safer to wait the suspect out. ...So you wait until the guy leaves, and you do a routine traffic stop and you arrest him."[53]

Sonoma, California, defense attorney Omar Figueroa

notes: "Most marijuana offenders are low-hanging fruit. It's easier to go after them than after dangerous meth-heads. The cops like these easy marijuana busts. It's a form of sport, and statistics, to them. But they are blind to how they are ripping families apart."[54]

Police *could* use less violent, aggressive means to enforce our laws, but they *choose* not to. They could *choose* to focus their resources on more violent crimes. Instead, they *choose* to use the most intimidating tools they have against those least likely, willing, or able to put up any real resistance. This is the definition of a bully.

If we consider bullying as a more accurate description of police culture, then the idea of this continuum of bullying behavior allows us to see its worst manifestations in a larger cultural context. We can then hold individual officers responsible as well as their superiors, and the system, instead of just punishing a few individuals who end up as scapegoats.

When it comes to respecting our constitutional rights as citizens, we are too often confronted by a police culture that places government (police) powers above citizen rights, which is the exact opposite of what our Constitution intended. As Lincoln declaimed at Gettysburg, "...that government of the people, by the people, for the people, shall not perish from the earth."[55] Our police officers, sworn to serve and protect us, cannot act as bullies unless we continue to permit them to do so. Too often they are not acting of us or for us, but for themselves. How can we act to bring about a change in the culture and policies of our local police?

Examples and Solutions

In the recent deluge of bad publicity suffered by police throughout the country over the past several years, some police departments have hunkered down, defending their current policies and practices, while others have done and continue to do some serious soul searching about how to make policing safer and more effective for both citizens and the police.

The police force in Dallas, Texas, has become one of the models for police reform in the United States. For years, it had the highest rate of police shootings in the country. But in 2010, with a new police chief in charge, Dallas began the slow and difficult process of turning things around. In 2014 it had its lowest murder rate since 1930, while police use-of-force incidents declined, along with citizen complaints, arrests, and crime in general.[56]

You may have no idea about what your local police department's approach is to use of force, community policing, stop-and-frisk policies, and the like. They may not be well publicized and they vary widely among the more than 18,000 police departments nationwide. But whether they are entrenched in outmoded strategies or seeking to embrace new approaches, your direct involvement with your local police can have a significant impact on the way they see the "community," and ultimately impact how they police.

Each one of us, in our own particular neighborhood, is "the community" when it comes to police relations. If the only time the police interact with the community they serve is in criminal and emergency situations, that colors their view of "the community."

To have some input and influence on your local police, get to know them! Many departments host regular community outreach meetings, often sponsored by local churches or neighborhood groups. Start getting to know your police by attending some of these meetings. There you will get an idea of how the police view you, "the community," and how at least some of the community view the police. Nobody likes to be criticized about job performance, especially by those they consider "outsiders" who are "ignorant" about the "reality" of police work, and many police officers already feel alienated and under attack from the people they are attempting to serve. With that in mind, consider taking a strategically gentle approach and support change rather than demanding it. Start by engaging with your local police, listening and learning. Ask questions about not just their mission, goals, and policies, but about the officers themselves: Why did they choose to become police officers? What do they like about the job? What is hard about the job? What changes would they like to see in their relationship with the community? Take the time to understand their views before you start demanding changes.

Alternatively, you may want to talk to and join a local community action group that is already involved in building neighborhood/police relations. Do an internet search using the name of your town or city plus "community action groups" and you will find out who is doing what. And if none of them meet your needs, start a group of your own.

Culture Clash

*There is a dualism inherent in democracy — opposing
forces pushing against each other, always. Culture clashes.
Different belief systems. All coming together to create this
country.*

—Libba Bray, writer

*When people are frightened, intelligent parts of the brain
cease to dominate.*

—Dr. Bruce Perry, psychiatrist
and researcher

Police Culture and a Normal Distribution of Traits

If many police departments have a bully culture, then the abiding ethos of the larger American culture outside policing could not be more opposed. That ethos is, in short, "I have the right to Life, Liberty, and the pursuit of Happiness" in whatever form I choose (be it religious, sexual, economic, artistic, take your pick!).

This clash of cultures can be more or less pronounced in any given encounter, depending on where each party falls compared to the norms of each cultural trait. This has huge implications when it comes to the expectations and experiences that each party brings to any particular interaction. Having an understanding of those vastly different norms sheds light on how police/citizen interactions can go so wrong, so quickly. Then there is the question of whose cultural norms should prevail in these interactions?

Consider that in the social and psychological sciences, the most common distribution of any trait or attribute, whether it be a personality trait, a measure of intelligence, or a social attitude, is a bell curve. The bell curve distribution shows the largest cluster as the "average." The tendency of most people is to fall into a fairly narrow range of whatever is being measured. On either side of the curve will be some exceptional individuals who may exhibit either far more of a particular trait or far less. Just think of your math class – most of us fell somewhere in the middle in our ability to do basic math. A few of us were truly horrendous. Then there were always a couple of kids who found math ridiculously easy.

Applied to a police culture in which bullying is the norm, we can expect to find most officers grouped in the middle when it comes to bullying behavior. Some officers will fall below the norm and will find it uncomfortable to engage in bullying behaviors they find morally wrong. Those who fall on the other side of "normal" bullying are the "bad apples" who will often generate numerous complaints of excessive use of force. Yet they will usually remain on the force because they still fit into the overall culture of bullying, albeit a little too enthusiastically.

Those who fall below the norm will need to either quit, pretend to fit in, or find some other way to survive in a culture in which they refuse to be co-opted to the degree that most of us "average" people are. These rare people are those who the state of Israel calls the "righteous few": those few irrationally brave souls who risked their lives to save Jews from the Holocaust while everyone around them were just trying to save themselves. If we are honest with ourselves, most of us, when faced with what Zimbardo calls "powerful systemic forces," would neither heroically resist nor gleefully join in the mayhem. We would most likely conform to the norm and try to survive.

Former LAPD narcotics detective Dave Dodderidge describes the moment it all changed for him – when he could no longer just "go along." He was with his team, conducting a raid on a young woman that he realized would "ruin her life."

"There was one girl named Lisa who we arrested down there with the field enforcement team. And it was a marijuana charge. She was actually selling marijuana. She was a pretty black lady. And she was going to college and trying to make her way through so she could raise her two kids. And we went through her house and tore it up and took her kids away and put them in a home and put her in jail. I felt sick afterwards. That was one of the major turning points. We had just destroyed this lady's future and her family. And that's when it hit me pretty hard and I thought, 'This is crazy.'"

After that, he said, he "couldn't do it anymore," and he transferred to a desk job. His new job was to decide which drug cases to send over for prosecution and which to drop. Dropping a case was called an 849b1, the code it was assigned. Dodderidge describes how he kept his integrity: "When I retired from the police department, I was there [in that department] for a couple of years. They gave me a little award with a crown on it, that I was the 849b1 king. It was a semi-compliment. I released a lot of people through that."[1]

We might consider him an example of "below average" when compared to "average" police officers. Although he was in the culture of bullying, he found ways to subvert the culture to ensure his own sense of justice remained intact.

In another example,[2] Betty Taylor recalls a drug raid she joined as a SWAT team member in Lincoln, Missouri. They stormed the house, guns drawn, in full armor, screaming for everyone to get down. Taylor then describes how she entered the room where the suspects had put two children, brother and sister, ages 8 and 6. When she opened the door, in full SWAT gear, armed, the little girl stood between her and her little brother, ready to defend him, asking Officer Taylor, "What are you going to do to us?"[3] That was it for Taylor. Enforcing the law in this way – breaking down doors and terrorizing people who posed no real threat to the public or the police – made no sense. Later, she became a police chief herself and swore she would never assemble a SWAT team in her town.

On the other side of the scale are the so-called "bad apples." Jason Van Dyke, the officer accused of murdering Laquan McDonald in Chicago, is illustrative. According to records released to the public,[4] Officer Van Dyke had at least 20 previous complaints filed against him, mostly for excessive force and racial slurs. The average officer receives no complaints at all, statistically speaking. So, on our bullying continuum, officer Van Dyke falls far to the other side of average, but within a culture where bullying is the norm, it is not surprising there was a small but stable subgroup of officers who exhibited far more extreme bullying behavior than average. Punishing them as bad apples - if they get punished at all, and most never do - while leaving the bad barrel of police culture intact, makes it inevitable that more Jason Van Dykes will appear in due course, and that in the meantime, bullying in lesser forms will continue, unabated.

Mismatching Social Norms

Interviews with police officers who have held their fire in situations in which they could have used lethal force are particularly revealing about the distance between the social norms of an average citizen and police social norms.

The concept of social norms comes from social psychology and is described as informal understandings of what is acceptable behavior by individuals within a particular group. The group can encompass an entire society or be any subset in which separate behavioral expectations apply. Social norms are like the air we breathe. They are all around us all the time, but we don't notice social norms unless we find ourselves confronted with situations in which what is "socially normal" doesn't seem to apply.

Generally, we all move seamlessly between various groups and subgroups when it comes to social norms, and we are all fairly expert at identifying different social norms given the opportunity to interact with and observe a particular group. Police social norms, however, are so far from almost any other social norms we regularly encounter that when we do find ourselves in police interactions, the mismatch can lead to deadly and unfortunate consequences at worst, or at least mutual mistrust and loathing.

One officer describes pulling over some teenagers in a car and spotting a gun on the dashboard. He immediately told everyone to get out of the vehicle. The driver, realizing that the officer had seen the gun, said, "But officer, this isn't a real gun."

The officer described his reaction: "...he reached down for it I guess to show me it wasn't real. But I wasn't going to let him grab it because it looked real to me." He then grabbed the kid by the neck, and pulled him out of the car before he could reach the gun, and then berated him for his "stupid" behavior.[5]

What is so noteworthy about this scene is how both participants interacted based on their expectations of "normal behavior" – which were based on two very different sets of norms. For most of us, the normal response to someone who might view our behavior as threatening when it is not is to show that we mean no harm. In the case of having a toy gun, most people's first reaction is to say and *illustrate* that - "Hey, this is just a toy, see?" - and to show the officer the gun.

We are under the incorrect assumption that a police officer is giving us the benefit of the doubt because we have shown no overt signs of being threatening or aggressive.

The police officer's social norm, however, is entirely the opposite. He is viewing us and everyone who is not a cop as a bona fide threat until proven otherwise. So, reaching for a toy gun, or even reaching for your wallet, is seen as potentially life-threatening to an officer and, according to the law, can give him legal grounds for shooting you based on what is reasonable *to him*.

The mismatch of social norms continues even after the cop realizes the gun is a toy. He gets angry at the kid for doing "something stupid." However, it is only "stupid" if you understand the social norms of the police, which even the police do not admit or acknowledge.

If we were to educate our children about the social norms of the police, we wouldn't describe them as friendly protectors who want to help keep us safe (seeing them in this light is a good way to get shot), but as a group of armed and dangerous individuals, highly fearful and trained to respond aggressively to any perceived threat (even where no threat exists).

That description itself evinces a paranoid gunman more than a protector of the community. But the cop's anger is telling. He is angry because this kid doesn't understand his set of social norms and what he perceives as threatening. This kid, and most of us for that matter, rarely interact with the police. But police officers interact with the general public all the time. Isn't it more reasonable for the police to understand and accommodate our social norm rather than the other way around? In the situation above, the police officer is being "stupid" by not appreciating the norms this kid was presuming. The officer doesn't appreciate that it is *his* social reality that is so divergent from the social reality in which the rest of us conduct our day-to-day lives.

In the case of Tamir Rice, a twelve-year-old Cleveland boy, the results of this mismatch of social norms led to his tragic death. Rice was carrying a toy gun, with the orange tip marking it as a toy removed. The police were called and within *two seconds* of arriving on the scene, they shot Rice dead. A grand jury later concluded that Rice was mostly likely intending to show the police that he did not have a real gun. The police in this case were not charged because they "reasonably" could have concluded that the gun was real and that their lives were threatened.

What is lost in both of these cases is the larger context in which what is considered legally "reasonable" for police is often the exact opposite of what is considered "reasonable" for the rest of the culture in any other context: to explain and illustrate that you are not a threat. In our prevailing social norm, we assume people are not threatening until they show threatening intent. Assuming everyone is a threat until proven otherwise is not the social norm for most of us, and building a subculture around such norms inevitably leads to tragedy. The question is, is it "reasonable" for police to assume that everyone is a threat and treat all of us as "the enemy" until proven otherwise? Is this acceptable to us, the people whom the police are sworn to protect?

Culture Plus Training: How to Take a Bad Situation and Make it Worse

In June 2014, Jason Harrison was shot to death by police on his front porch.[6] He had a long history of mental illness and his mother had called police to have them take Jason to the hospital. When the police knocked on the door, Jason's mother walked out, casually telling police, "He's just off the chain."

Jason then comes out behind her, twiddling a screwdriver. He is not aggressive or threatening. He is not approaching the officers. He is just standing in the doorway. One officer immediately orders him to "drop that." Before he has any chance to respond, both officers yell at him simultaneously. His mother, quickly realizing that he is in grave danger, screams at him, "Jay, Jay, Jay!!" But within five seconds of their first request to "drop it," they shoot him five times, killing him.

It is hard to describe what happened to Jason Harrison as a "confrontation" in the way most of us understand that word. But police have a completely different definition of "confrontation" peculiar to their culture. In policing, having control of a person and getting him to comply in whatever way that gives an officer "control" is first on their list of priorities. Even in the most harmless encounter, an officer presumes danger to himself, which must be eliminated by establishing control. An officer will often begin an interaction with a question to which your answer will indicate to them, by both your content and tone, if you are compliant: "Do you know why I stopped you?" Almost any response that is noncompliant in either tone or content will result in a more aggressive attempt by the officer to assert control, either verbally or physically.

The rationale, as explained to me by police defense attorney Brien Farrell, is as simple as it is dangerously overbroad: "The police know from experience, if you or I are driving on the freeway and we suddenly see behind us a CHP [California Highway Patrol] car traveling in the same direction, that our foot immediately comes off the accelerator. That's the effect of a uniformed peace officer on you and me. We immediately go into our cautious 'yes sir, no sir" behavior. The police know through their experience that ninety-five percent obey and comply pretty darn promptly. The five percent who don't are the ones who end up in these videos. ...So, the police in general find that when they press forward and seek to get immediate control, the other people don't get involved and create a greater danger. And most of the time - the vast majority of the time - that is the effective strategy."[7]

The problem with this generalization is that while it might apply quite well to an "average" citizen, police are more often interacting with people who are mentally ill, impaired by drugs or alcohol, homeless, fearful, depressed, and/or distraught - and *then* confronted by a threatening, heavily armed officer screaming at them to "Drop it!"

If you are mentally ill, drunk, on drugs, or experiencing an anxiety attack, you might not understand what an officer is telling you when he yells "Drop it!" or "Show me your hands!" or some other request. Or if you do understand, it still might take you more than five seconds to process the order and react. When you are already impaired in one or more of the ways that a person can be impaired, the communication problem is magnified and compounded when you are confronted by an unfamiliar, threatening, and heavily armed police officer, in a situation that makes no sense to you.

For seven years, I worked as a counselor in a halfway house for mentally ill young adults between the ages of 18 and 35. They were diagnosed schizophrenic, manic-depressive, borderline personality, and the like. They heard voices, became catatonic, were sometimes threatening, occasionally suicidal. During the day, I was there with another counselor. At night, I was there alone with fifteen mentally ill people.

During those seven years, we never had a single episode of violence. We had many potential episodes, but in all of these we were able to de-escalate the threat, not by aggressively gaining control of the person, but by doing what is common sense to most people when faced with a potentially dangerous situation: talk calmly and softly to the distraught person. Make them feel less threatened rather than more afraid. Give them nonviolent options to choose from. Connect with them where they are, not where you want them to be.

Testifying for the President's Task Force on 21st Century Policing, Chuck Wexler, executive director of the Police Executive Research Forum, noted: "In traditional police culture, officers are taught to never back down from a confrontation, but instead to run *toward* the dangerous situation that everyone else is running away from. However, sometimes the best tactic for dealing with a minor confrontation is to step back, call for assistance, de-escalate, and perhaps plan a different enforcement action that can be taken more safely later."[8]

Jason Harrison didn't have to die, but in a police culture

that sees danger where there is none, which demands absolute control in the larger context of a society that celebrates individual freedom as its highest good, is it any wonder that an unarmed innocent citizen can be gunned down on his front porch?

Deconstructing Law Enforcement Cultural Myths

When confronted with almost any level of what might be considered police misconduct, we are reminded by the media and public officials that "Police are out there every day putting their lives on the line to keep us safe."[9]

This standard defense of the police, and justification for police misconduct, simply doesn't hold up under scrutiny. Being a police officer doesn't even rank in the top ten deadliest jobs in America.[10] Law enforcement officers have a greater likelihood of being killed driving to work[11] than dying on the job.[12] Less than 12 percent of police officers will ever draw and fire their weapons at another person in the entire course of their career.[13]

So why do we continue to hear (and believe) how police work is so dangerous?

In part, because we - and the police themselves - have confused the potential of danger with actual present danger. The potential danger of any one of us dying in a car accident, while much higher than almost any activity, is still less than one percent over a lifetime. If we considered that at any moment we might be killed while driving, we probably wouldn't drive at all. And in addition to the danger itself - unlike police officers - we are held fully accountable by both our insurance company and the law if we cause an accident. Under such circumstances, we might be willing to cut those who do drive (for the rest of us) all kinds of leeway in terms of getting into accidents, speeding, even killing people, since driving is so inherently dangerous! But we drive anyway with some idea that, though the relative risk may be high, the actual risk of us dying in a car accident is very low and we are personally responsible for driving safely, even if others do not. In short, most of us accept the risks of driving, and the responsibilities, and do not enter a state of intense fear and anxiety every time we get behind the wheel.

By contrast, we (and law enforcement officers) have convinced ourselves that because policing is *potentially* dangerous, police should be less accountable for inappropriate use of the very behaviors we are trying to limit – violence, dishonesty, and theft. One would think, when it comes to social responsibility, that such powers would come with *more* accountability (such as those that come with driving), not *less* accountability, since these powers are so tempting to abuse. It is the equivalent of a kid in the candy store with no one at the register. There are few limits and even fewer consequences to engaging in as much bad behavior as you want, all under the cover of law.

Assaulting a young man because he *might* be in possession of some stolen tools? Okay. Eat the marijuana edibles from the medical dispensary you just busted? Why not? Throw a guy in a wheelchair face down on the pavement, splitting open his head? Sure. If you believe your life is constantly under grave threat, these actions can seem reasonable and even appropriate.

With so little accountability built into policing, it can be hard to resist for some officers. But the justification for this doesn't hold up. The reality is that being a police officer is a relatively safe occupation and has never been safer.

They Just Want a Hug

Looked at another way, the difference between a real and potential threat returns us to the fight-or-flight response, both as an artifact of bullying and as a serious and detrimental health impact. The medical establishment has detailed the physiological response to a fight/flight situation (in which you perceive some threat, real or imagined), which it describes as an "acute stress response."

Over time, repeated stress responses contribute to high blood pressure, heart disease, anxiety, depression, addiction, even obesity.[14] Statistically, police have higher rates of every single one of these health problems,[15] not because of real threats, but because of self-inflicted psychological stress.

If police work itself is not nearly as dangerous as it is presented, and police are overreacting to stressors that are not life threatening, then perhaps it is the way the job is perceived that can cause police officers to behave in ways that are so aggressive and often violent. They perceive danger where there is none. They act as if their lives are being threatened when there is no threat. They have a "fight" response to situations that are neither fight nor flight, but are often benign – or, if at all threatening, could be dealt with in a variety of other ways, such as de-escalation.

Police officers have higher rates of alcoholism, depression, suicide, and heart disease than the general public.[16] If even a fraction of these diseases are caused by stress responses to nonexistent threats, then prior to stress management classes, police should receive some basic cognitive therapy to connect them with the realty of their work environment: largely safe, secure, and non-threatening.

When it comes to interacting with the community you are sworn to protect, if you constantly imagine yourself under attack and you are trained to respond to perceived attacks aggressively, the inevitable outcome for all of those you respond to aggressively is going to be that same fight-or-flight response: fear or anger. It becomes a self-reinforcing feedback loop of mutual fear, anger, and mistrust between cops and the people they are serving. As Tom Canard remarked: "I lost all respect for police."

This is not to say that police work is not stressful. It is, but for reasons other than "putting your life on the line every day."

Brien Farrell, the attorney for the city of Santa Rosa who spent twenty years representing police officers accused of excessive use of force, described his experience in Sonoma County this way: "There hasn't been a policeman killed in Sonoma County in the last hundred years, I think. What is more fundamental about their work is their repeated exposure to human tragedy. ...Police respond to lethal automobile accidents where a mother has been killed or a child catastrophically injured. They respond to suicides in progress and see someone put the gun in their mouth and blow their brains out. ...We as a community depend on them to respond to those incidents and responsibly investigate them and, if they can, de-escalate the situation and prevent any harm from occurring. That takes a heavy toll. They would like to be hugged by us. They want to be told 'thank you. I'm so glad that you do this for us. I don't know how you do it.' But when it all gets framed as 'I put my life on the line every day for you and if you're going to intensely question anything about what I do, I don't want to talk to you,' we're going to just have more conflict."

That pretense belies a basic human vulnerability.

"They won't say that [they are hurting]," Farrell continued. "They are too tough. ...but nobody is that tough. ...The only way I could defend them was in the beginning to tell them, 'You're not going to be an officer if I'm going to effectively defend you. You're going to be Joe, you're going to be Dennis, you're going to be Lisa. And you're going to tell me why you wanted to be an officer and why you still choose to be one. And you're going to need to tell me what scares you and what you feel proudest about, because if we can't explain those things they are going to view you as a badge and you'll go down.'"

Of course, on the other side, someone needs to be telling officers on a daily basis that they need to view the citizens they interact with as individual human beings worthy of *their* respect, rather than nameless potential enemies they need to subdue by whatever means necessary. They are "Joe or Dennis or Lisa" too, who have joys and sorrows, good days and bad, friends and loved ones, just like the officers.

As Bryan Stevenson put it in his moving book, *Just Mercy,* about seeking justice for wrongly accused death row inmates and child criminals given life sentences, when we feel we are victims, we easily and instinctually turn on those who are weaker still and make them victims of our fear and anger, and feel justified in doing so.[17]

Self-Inflicted Wounds

It is estimated that as many as 17 percent of police officers are suffering from Post-Traumatic Stress Disorder (PTSD). Many studies[18] have also shown that police feel ashamed and embarrassed about seeking psychological counseling for any difficulties they may be experiencing. To show weakness might make them vulnerable to the same sort of treatment they mete out on the street daily: bullying by their fellow officers.

I asked Dave Dodderidge if he ever discussed his doubts with other officers about the moral implications of ruining someone's life over a few ounces of marijuana. His reply was emphatic: "No, that is not something you would ever talk about."

In his book, *Into The Kill Zone,* author David Klinger describes how police officers who have shot and killed people in the line of duty are required to see a psychologist who must clear them before they can return to active duty. He writes that officers have a general distrust of their supervisors whom they fear are "out to get them"[19] and so many officers lied to the police psychologist for fear of retribution from their supervisors.

It's not the stress of "putting your life on the line every day" that is turning police into bullies. It is the culture of bullying, along with the exaggerated threat, coupled with the real and constant exposure to scenes of violence and mayhem that have helped create a law enforcement nightmare. As *New York Times* columnist David Brooks so eloquently put it, for many cops "the world is divided into two sorts of people—cops and assholes."[20]

We—all of us—are the assholes.

Even those who are critical of the police are loathe to condemn police "culture" as being fundamentally flawed, but that is exactly where the problem lies. Protesting the murders of unarmed Americans and seeking justice against those individual officers misses the fundamental causes that led to these tragedies in the first place.

Norm Stamper sums it up succinctly: Both the media and the public focus on the incident and completely lose sight of the system that created the culture which ultimately caused the incident.[21]

There is a line that runs directly from the police leaving Jill stranded on the side of the highway with her car in pieces to Tom Canard being face down in the mud with his tools strewn in a field, to the choking death of Eric Garner and the shooting death of Diaz Zeferino. They are simply degrees of bullying, of the "systematic abuse of power."

Shooting down an unarmed, non-threatening person is a logical extension and end point of a system that grants extraordinary powers to individuals, promotes the abuse of those powers, and aligns that abuse with policies that support it. It's a deadly and incendiary mix. The cultural norms of many police departments are not just dangerously out of sync with citizen cultural norms, they are toxic to the health and well-being of the police themselves.

How can we assist the police in dealing with the traumatic events they are regularly exposed to while reminding them that, generally speaking, the real threat to their health is the inaccurate perception that they are in constant danger, and the impact of that on their bodies and minds?

Examples and Solutions

If you have gone to some police/community meetings and you are getting to know your local police, you might want to learn about the type and amount of in-service training officers are required to take annually. "In-service" refers to on-the-job training that is designed to refresh current skills (such as firearms training) and update police with newer skills such as de-escalation techniques.

Currently, there is no national requirement for in-service training by police, and of the fifty states, only twenty-four mandate a set amount of yearly in-service training. Your local department may have no in-service training requirement at all! Or, as is the case in cadet police training in which they receive an average of fifty-eight hours of firearms training and only eight hours of de-escalation training,[22] you may want to advocate for more de-escalation training – which by its very nature reduces the use of force, and deadly force in particular.

Looming large in our discussion of police bullying is the constant sense of threat that police feel they are under. The degree to which this threat is real or imagined is certainly debatable, but in any case, the impact on an officer's emotional and mental health is real. Police officers live in a macho culture in which showing emotional wounds and mental anguish are signs of weakness. If the police can't easily admit to these vulnerabilities themselves, then certainly we can help provide "cover" for them by advocating for mental health services to the in-service requirements of every officer.

Emeryville, California Chief of Police Jennifer Tejada and Richard Goerling of the Hillsboro, Oregon Police Department commented in *Police Chief* magazine: "In all of the dialogue, in all of the mainstream trainings, and in all of the debates and town hall meetings, little consideration is given to what officers are experiencing physiologically or psychologically. Little consideration is given to what neurobiology and other science disciplines tell us about the impact of stress and trauma on the people behind the badge. It is generally understood that most law enforcement officers enter the profession to do good, to help their communities, and to fulfill a sense of service above self. It is also known that the law enforcement profession is stressful and often involves trauma, and that chronic stress and acute trauma cause psychological, physiological and social harm."[23]

As most of us can attest, we react much more quickly and often badly when we are stressed out, anxious, and otherwise psychologically impaired by events that may have happened in previous days, weeks, or even months, impacting our ability to deal with the situation at hand thoughtfully and calmly. Certainly, the police are no different, except that they are constantly exposed to traumatic events. Yet the police themselves tend not to acknowledge the impact of these stressors and, as the officers above point out, the general public, in their calls for change and reform, has even less appreciation or awareness of the toll police work takes on the psyche. More than just a hug, police need their local communities to advocate for regular and even required mental health counseling and, as Tejada and Goerling suggest, preventative mental health education and training, such as mindfulness work and other tools to enhance police performance and allow them to respond appropriately to the present situation rather than to imagined danger or past trauma.

Consider advocating for more mental health services for your local police department. As a former mental health professional, I would even go so far as to make mental health counseling mandatory for all police officers to help them deal with the tragedies and stress they regularly encounter.

Down The Slippery Slope

There is no greater tyranny than that which is perpetrated under the shield of the law and in the name of justice.

—Charles de Montesquieu (1689-1755)

Is a democracy which democratically cedes ever-more power to its government and/or those who control/own its resources still a democracy?

—Koan for Democracy

Rights and Reality Part Ways

It seems evident that the bully culture of policing in concert with policies that encourage and support that culture play a large role in our current policing crisis. What I found baffling, though, especially after watching video after video of police shooting, beating, choking, or otherwise assaulting unarmed Americans, was how what appeared to be gratuitous and uncalled-for police violence was entirely legal. *How is that even possible?* I wondered. The entirety of America's founding story is based on the rejection of overreaching government power and the rights of the people. What could be more important than preserving and safeguarding the rights of the people to be free of direct physical assault from the first line of government power: the police? What could be more overreaching than armed and trained cops assaulting unarmed and unthreatening citizens?

No matter how cynical we may be, these words still resonate in our hearts and minds when we consider what is best about our country:

We hold these truths to be self-evident, that all men are created equal, that they are endowed by their Creator with certain unalienable Rights, that among these are Life, Liberty and the pursuit of Happiness. / That to secure these rights, Governments are instituted among Men, deriving their just powers from the consent of the governed, / That whenever any Form of Government becomes destructive of these ends, it is the Right of the People to alter or to abolish it, and to institute new Government, laying its foundation on such principles and organizing its powers in such form, as to them shall seem most likely to effect their Safety and Happiness.[1]

Where and when, I wondered, did "we the people" consent to having cops assault us with legal impunity?

Clearly, I missed that class in American history. More specifically, the constitutional right that protects us against physical assault from government agents is the Fourth Amendment, which reads:

"The right of the people to be secure in their persons, houses, papers, and effects, against unreasonable searches and seizures, shall not be violated..."[2]

How, when, and why did it become "reasonable" to "seize" (in the language of the amendment) –that is, assault – unarmed and non-threatening citizens with both lethal and non-lethal force?

As I read about the disposition of these various cases, the same legal conclusions kept repeating themselves, as in the case of Officer Darren Wilson shooting Michael Brown in Ferguson, Missouri.

"After weighing the evidence, the grand jury decided that Wilson acted within the limits of the lethal-force law."[3] Followed by: "In a rare move and in an attempt to allay concerns about bias, McCulloch [the district attorney] made public the mountain of evidence presented to the grand jury."[4]

In view of our supposed rights, these are stunning statements. If Officer Wilson shot Brown without any bias and his shooting of unarmed Brown was "within the limits of lethal-force law," then apparently the police can kill people, black or white, in circumstances that most of us would describe as clear violations of our civil rights. What we never imagine is that we all are now subject to the same loss of rights that are often denied select groups. Most of us just don't know it – yet. But therein lies the great equalizing power of the Constitution.

The deep irony of our efforts to enforce equal rights under the Constitution, and make racial profiling in law enforcement a thing of the past, is that our success will be measured by the equal application of law enforcement humiliation and violence against all of us, for that is what we have sanctioned our police to do. Not exactly a laudable democratic goal. Equal justice in law enforcement is nothing more and nothing less than equal opportunity to inflict humiliation, abuse, injury, and death on us all. And it is we who have allowed this to come to pass. As cartoonist Walt Kelly said in his immortal Pogo comic strip: "We have met the enemy and he is us." But what is the Constitution and why do our eyes start to glaze over the moment someone starts to discuss it, while at the same time continuing to revere it as the holiest of holies when it comes to being an "American?"

As I recall from my kids' high school civics classes, the eye-glazing effect comes from two misconceptions. First, that the Constitution and its amendments are all ancient history, unchanging and inviolable. Second, that they have no visible impact on the daily life of anyone they know or care about. When was the last time you had a good dinner-table discussion about the impact of the Constitution on your vacation plans, mortgage payment, job prospects, or your child's latest report card?

But the reason we don't discuss the Constitution over dinner is not because it is immaterial to our daily lives, but because it is so fundamental that we simply take it for granted. The rights described in our Constitution are so ingrained in our sense of being "American" that they are invisible to us. We only discuss such things when they affect us negatively. To most of us white, middle-class Americans, that possibility seems far-fetched. But it is much more likely than we would like to think. The constitutional rights you think you have, and the constitutional rights you have, are – in fact – worlds apart. To understand this more fully, let's examine a simple traffic stop, which most of us have experienced, and which is much less incendiary than a lethal-force shooting.

Sandra Bland

Sandra Bland was pulled over by police on July 10, 2015.[5]
She had just moved to Texas from Illinois to start a new job
at Texas A&M University, of which she was a graduate. She
was 28 years old. It was 10 a.m. and sunny when she was
stopped. A state trooper, Brian Encina, pulled her over
because she failed to signal a lane change when she had
moved over to give him the right of way after spotting him
behind her.

The stop began the way many stops do. The officer
approached the passenger side of the car, asked for Bland's
driver's license and insurance, and told her why he pulled
her over. She was upset and he asked her what was wrong.
On the video, we can't hear her response. He takes her
license and insurance and walks back to his patrol car.

Several minutes later, he returns to Bland's car, this time
on the driver's side of the vehicle. Apparently, she is still
visibly upset because again Encina asks her if she is okay.
Bland explains that she is waiting for him to do his job. He
responds that she seems very irritated. Bland says that she
is irritated to be getting a ticket because she was only
changing lanes to get out of the officer's way. At that point
the officer's entire demeanor changes and he asks, "Are you
done?" Both the question and the tone clearly indicates that
whatever answer she might give is not what he wanted to
hear, and that he has no interest or concern for her being
upset anymore. She responds: "You asked me what was
wrong, and I told you."

He then asks Bland to please put out her cigarette. Bland
refuses, saying she is in her car and didn't have to. The
officer responds by telling her to step out of her car. Bland
says, "I don't have to."

The officer orders her: "Step out of the car." He opens her
door and keeps repeating, "Step out of the car." Bland keeps

saying, "You don't have the right to do this." He then says several times over her objections, "Step out or I will remove you." He then says, "I am giving you a lawful order." He starts to physically pull her out of the car and she asks him, "Are we going to do this?"

"Yes, we are," he responds. "Okay," she says, sounding as if she was going to get out of her own free will, but then she says to Encina, "Don't touch me! I'm not under arrest. You don't have the right to touch me."

Encina: "You are under arrest." (He gets on his radio, calling for assistance.)

Bland: "For what?"

Encina: "Get out of the car. I am giving you a lawful order."

Bland: "Why am I being apprehended?"

Encina: "I am gonna drag you out of here."

Bland: "So you're gonna drag me out of here?"

Encina: (Pulls out his taser and points it at her, screaming.) "GET OUT OF THE CAR! I AM GONNA LIGHT YOU UP! GET OUT! NOW!"

Bland: (Gets out of the car of her own free will.) "Wow, you're doing all this for a failure to signal."

Encina: "Get over there." (Points to the side of the road.)

The video footage continues, with Bland being arrested, alternately objecting, questioning her arrest, and threatening to sue the officer. Three days later, she was found hanged in her jail cell. The coroner ruled her death a suicide.

Privileges, not Rights

As CNN legal analyst and defense attorney Danny Cevallos commented: "Like most citizens, Bland was shocked at the notion that we can be ordered from our cars during a routine stop. It just feels wrong, doesn't it?"[6]

Everyday encounters with the police that never rise to the

level of an official complaint so often leave us feeling violated, and more specifically, that our rights have been violated. (The only reason the Sandra Bland case came to light was because she ended up dead in her jail cell.) We have an intuitive – if not legally formed – opinion that, as Americans, we have rights that protect us from mistreatment by both our government (including police) and other private citizens.

But in many far more egregious cases of apparent police misconduct, the police are never criminally charged and often never disciplined at all. How is it that we believe we have rights against such treatment, yet upon closer scrutiny, we find we have few or no rights at all?

In a very real way, understanding our rights with respect to the police is essential to understanding our rights as American citizens. Police are the first, most obvious, and most direct line of control that the government exerts over our freedoms as citizens. They are the sharp end of the spear when it comes to government power.

You may imagine that because you have had no negative encounters with the police that this is nothing that concerns you. But even if you have never been sick, do you forgo health insurance? Even if you've never had a house fire, do you not bother with home insurance? The risks and dangers of not protecting our rights are real. Just because we have not yet been subject to the heavy hand of law enforcement bullying does not mean we are somehow immune.

If we are ignorant and misinformed about our rights with respect to the police and the actual authority they legally wield, then our cherished freedoms and rights are illusory. They exist only insofar as those in power choose to allow them and they may be withdrawn at any time for any reason. In this world, we no longer have rights, we only have privileges. Those privileges are granted to us by the police at their discretion. Our freedoms, our rights, are no longer guaranteed by law and enshrined in the Constitution. They are subject to the whim of those in power. This is, in many respects, the America we now live in. Did you know this? I certainly didn't. I had no idea. In fact, I thought the exact opposite. Discovering this was truly stunning.

This is not the America most of us signed up for. Nor is it the America we hold up to the rest of the world as the exceptional example of liberty, justice, and freedom. How did we get here?

To understand our rights, we must turn to the Supreme Court, which has taken the lead in determining how our Fourth Amendment Rights shall be interpreted and applied. Before you decide that arcane and obscure points of jurisprudence are not worth your effort to comprehend, consider this: Every Fourth Amendment case involves mundane everyday circumstances that are easily understood by anyone who has ever driven a car, lived in a home, or walked down a sidewalk. In every case, the question is the same: What sort of power does the government, i.e. the police, have over me in this particular instance? Make your own judgment and then compare it to those of the Court. Do you think your rights as an American are being violated?

Pennsylvania v. Mimms

That Sandra Bland was legally required to get out of her car when ordered by Officer Encina dates back to 1977 in the Supreme Court case of Pennsylvannia v. Mimms. In that case, Harry Mimms was stopped by the police for having an expired tag on his license plate. The police had no reason to believe that Mimms had committed any other criminal act. Nonetheless, they ordered him out of his vehicle. As he exited, they noticed a bulge under his jacket. Frisking him, the bulge turned out to be a handgun that was unlicensed. The police charged Mimms with carrying a concealed and unregistered weapon.

Mimms's attorney argued that the gun charges against his client should be thrown out because when the police required Mimms to get out of his car, his Fourth Amendment rights against unreasonable search and seizure were violated. Simply put, while the police had reasonable cause to pull Mimms over for his expired license tag, insisting that he exit the vehicle was an unreasonable intrusion (a violation of his right to be free of being "seized" in this manner) because they had no reason to suspect him of any other crime.

The case went all the way to the Supreme Court and the court decided in favor of the police, stating that "the officer's safety is both legitimate and weighty, and the intrusion into respondent's personal liberty occasioned by the order, being, at most, a mere inconvenience, cannot prevail when balanced against legitimate concerns for the officer's safety."[7]

This decision was not unanimous. Among the three justices who dissented was Thurgood Marshall, the first African-American appointed to the Supreme Court. He wrote: *"Until today, the law applicable to seizures of a person has required individualized inquiry into the reason for each intrusion, or some comparable guarantee against arbitrary harassment. A factual demonstration of probable cause is required to justify an arrest; an articulable reason to suspect criminal activity and possible violence is needed to justify a stop and frisk. But to eliminate any requirement that an officer be able to explain the reasons for his actions signals an abandonment of effective judicial supervision of this kind of seizure and leaves police discretion utterly without limits. Some citizens will be subjected to this minor indignity while others –perhaps those with more expensive cars, or different bumper stickers, or different-colored skin – may escape it entirely."*[8]

He then concluded: *"...this kind of disposition...[creates] the unfortunate impression that the Court is more interested in upholding the power of the State than in vindicating individual rights."*

What is most noteworthy in his dissent as well as in the decision itself is that at no time did the officers believe that Mimms was, in fact, a danger to them. Justice Marshall pointed out that the whole purpose of the Fourth Amendment requires that law enforcement have "an articulable reason" for physically seizing and searching someone to "guarantee" citizens' rights against "arbitrary harassment." In this case, the reason, officer safety, was retroactively manufactured. During this traffic stop, the officers had no reason to fear for their safety.

We don't live in a police state in which law enforcement can stop and search people "just because." But this case gave officers the power to do just that. That they don't order every one of us out of our cars today is at their discretion. They are granting you a privilege, not acknowledging your rights. After the Mimms case, police could now order you out of your car for any reason, or no reason at all, and then subject you to a physical search even when they have no reason to believe you have committed a crime or are any danger to them whatsoever.

Or, as in the case of Sandra Bland, the only articulable reason they have is a desire to demean and humiliate you, in the guise of "officer safety." Welcome to the brave new world of police powers.

Why the Constitution Still Matters (more than ever)

As you can see, the United States Constitution is alive (if not well), and is impacting the lives of every one of us, all the time, in the most mundane yet intimate ways. If you are stopped for a routine traffic ticket, you can be ordered out of your car and searched because the officer wishes to search you, not necessarily because he believes you have committed any crime or present a threat to his safety. In this particular scenario you no longer have a right against unreasonable "seizure," but the police may grant you the *privilege* of not being ordered from your vehicle.

While you might be under the misapprehension that your rights, as codified in the various constitutional amendments some two hundred years ago, are safe and secure, nothing could be further from the truth. As Thurgood Marshall's dissent bluntly puts it, there is an ongoing battle between the power we accord the State, specifically law enforcement, and our rights as Americans. This case is just one of many in which the *"... right of the people to be secure in their persons...against unreasonable searches and seizures"* was substantially reduced and the power of the police significantly increased. This is what it looks like to have our "unalienable rights" taken from us.

What rights do you *think* you have when, in fact, they have been so parsed as to be almost nonexistent? The answer is quite shocking. But to understand how far down this slippery slope we have gone requires some understanding of the document which we have imbued with so much power - the Constitution - and how its greatness is only as great as those who uphold its spirit and intent. For, like any contract, its value is entirely dependent upon honoring the intentions which underlie it.

Where do Our Rights Come From?

Whatever you think the Constitution is, it is first and foremost just a document. That is, it is some pieces of paper with writing on them. This is obvious, but it points to something which is all too easy to lose sight of. The pieces of paper and the writing on them have no inherent value themselves. All the power these words have is that with which we have imbued them. The power they represent are the informal understandings about how we agree to treat each other – the understandings we have about ourselves and our fellow human beings, put into words. The Constitution is the formal expression of informal understandings between Americans. It is our social contract with each other and our government.

The first formal expression of those understandings we have as Americans is the Declaration of Independence, specifically that stirring preamble: *"We hold these truths to be self-evident, that all men are created equal, that they are endowed by their Creator with certain unalienable Rights, that among these are Life, Liberty and the pursuit of Happiness. That to secure these rights, Governments are instituted among Men, deriving their just powers from the consent of the governed."*[9]

Even now, these are radical ideas, especially that each of us has unalienable rights which are neither enhanced nor reduced or denied by the circumstances of our birth, our class, our caste, our religion, our race, or our sex.

Of course, at the time of the Declaration, "men" referred only to white men, not black men, and obviously not women. Yet, within the historical context of the times, this statement was a formal recognition of an informal but growing awareness that all people were deserving of basic respect and dignity by virtue of their humanity alone. Thus, the intent of the declaration is unmistakable: that all men (regardless of how the definition of "all men" might change in time to include all black men, all women, all LGBT people, etc.) had certain unalienable rights.

Any other narrower interpretation of those words, "all men," while certainly plausible, has been rejected time and again by the American people - directly in the form of constitutional amendments (outlawing slavery, giving women the right to vote) and indirectly by their constitutional interlocutors, the Supreme Court, in cases such Brown v. Board of Education on school segregation and the recent Obergefell v. Hodges on gay marriage, as well as legislatively with the Voting Rights Act of 1965.

Yet at various other times, the Supreme Court has upheld as constitutional laws that seem to directly contradict that fundamental truth that all men have "unalienable" rights. Slaves had no rights until the Emancipation Proclamation was ratified as the Thirteenth Amendment. Prior to that was the Dred Scott case in which the Court decided that no person of African ancestry could be an American citizen, free or slave. Then there was the Lochner v. New York case in which the Court held that New York's law putting a daily maximum on the hours that bakers could work was unconstitutional, declaring that unequal bargaining power and health concerns should not be of interest to the state. There are many more such cases, some of which we will examine. Suffice it to say that the Constitution has been subject to and continues to be a basis for whatever biases we bring to bear on the construction of our social relations. It is far from a static document. The intentions with which we, the people, apply our Constitution determine our rights or their absence.

The Fourth Amendment

To appreciate and understand the degree to which our rights in relation to the police have been eroded to the point where the police can arbitrarily stop us, search us, take our private property, and send us to jail virtually at will, it is critical to understand the larger context of our constitutional rights and more particularly our Fourth Amendment rights.

Let's look once more at the Fourth Amendment:

"The right of the people to be secure in their persons, houses, papers, and effects, against unreasonable searches and seizures, shall not be violated, and no warrants shall issue, but upon probable cause, supported by oath or affirmation, and particularly describing the place to be searched, and the persons or things to be seized."

This amendment is brilliantly compact and seemingly unambiguous. To the States that passed it in 1791, its intent probably seemed quite self-explanatory. The context in which it passed was in direct response to what the colonists had just experienced at the hands of British authorities, essentially the local law enforcement of the day.

The British, in their efforts to quell the growing resistance of the colonists to unfair taxation, started issuing "general writs of assistance." These writs were essentially search warrants that had several unique features: a) they never expired, b) they didn't have to show any specific cause for searching a particular person or his property, nor even an exact location; c) they didn't have to list any particular evidence of a suspected crime; d) they could be could be transferred; and e) officials were not responsible for any damage they caused in the process of executing such orders.

In short, the British, assisted by local law enforcement (hence the name "writ of assistance"), could enter any home for which they had such a writ, at any time, for any reason, searching for any unspecified evidence, and then depart after damaging the property in their search, leaving the owner to clean up and pay for damages caused by their search. These powers most closely resemble what, today, we would describe as a "police state."

The Fourth Amendment was a direct response to such arbitrary and sweeping police powers. It states quite directly that law enforcement a) must have a reason for any search or seizure, b) the reason must be specific to both the person and the items being sought, c) it must be based on probable cause – that is, law enforcement must show they have substantial cause (i.e. some preliminary evidence) to believe a crime has been committed, and d) all of this must be approved (i.e. a warrant issued) by a neutral party - a judge - standing between the police and the citizens, to ensure it meets all these requirements.

It is also worth noting that the amendment begins with the basic assertion that Americans have a fundamental right to be secure in their homes, persons, and possessions, and that this can only be violated under the most compelling circumstances. Thus, the *intent* of the amendment seems unmistakable: When it comes to police powers, protecting a citizen's rights comes first and can only be abrogated when a whole series of strict tests are met.

There is nothing particularly mysterious or complex about this amendment. (Although constitutional lawyers will disagree with me, I'll stand by my layman's understanding, which I suspect is how most other citizens would understand these words.) It addresses very basic rights that we all now take for granted: that the police cannot come into our homes or businesses without a very good reason. That the police cannot just stop us and search us outside our homes for no reason. That the police cannot humiliate and demean us arbitrarily, whether they believe we have committed a crime or not. That we are innocent until proven guilty. That we have rights that are unalienable – that is, we are due respect by our government, no matter what.

But like any contract, the Fourth Amendment is open to multiple interpretations. The most obvious points of ambiguity are: a) What exactly defines a "reasonable" versus an "unreasonable" search and seizure? b) What exactly constitutes a "search" and a "seizure?" c) What qualifies as "probable cause" to search someone and their property?

When it comes to police powers, these definitions make

all the difference between a Fourth Amendment that protects citizens against exactly the abuses that the new Americans were intent on preventing or subverting the intent of the Amendment and allowing police to stop, search, and arrest anyone at any time, and for any reason.

You might think that such critical issues of government powers would be something that would be left up to the American people to decide. After all, the rest of the sentence in the Declaration of Independence citing our unalienable rights concludes with the affirmation that the government derives its "just powers from the consent of the governed." The powers of our government are only "just" when they come by way of our consent. So, the degree to which the police have power over us would seem to be something over which we would want to exercise such consent. But the determination of these definitions that ultimately determine the powers of the police has been entirely decided by nine unelected government officials: The Supreme Court of the United States.

Whether this structure for deciding such fundamental issues is appropriate is beyond the scope of our discussion. For our purposes, though, it is important to know that the Court has been determining the relationship between us and American law enforcement for the past two hundred and forty years. Understanding their decisions and how they impact our lives right now and how they might impact them in the future is not immaterial.

If there is even the *potential* for you and your family to be abused, humiliated, assaulted, or even killed by the State, wouldn't you want to know this and do whatever you could to guard against it? If you understood that law enforcement had the power to take everything you own – your home, your bank accounts, and your business – without cause, wouldn't you want to know this, too, and guard against it?

It may come as a surprise to learn that this is all within the power of law enforcement, courtesy of the Supreme Court.

Stop and Frisk—It's Not Just for Black People

When can the police stop and search ("seize" in the language of the Fourth Amendment) you in a public place? Until 1968, only if they had "probable cause" to believe you had committed or were about to commit a crime. After all, this is what the Fourth Amendment clearly states. This all changed in 1968 in the case of Terry v. Ohio.

Detective Martin McFadden was on his regular beat in downtown Cleveland when he observed two men, John Terry and Richard Chilton, pacing back and forth in front of a store. It appeared to him that they were casing the store in preparation for a possible robbery. Another man joined them in a brief discussion and then left. Then Terry and Chilton walked away, and McFadden followed. Several blocks away they met up with the third man, at which point McFadden identified himself as a police officer and seized Terry and frisked him. He found a revolver in Terry's overcoat. He then searched Chilton and found another gun. The third suspect was unarmed. But there was no evidence that the men were, in fact, going to rob the store. And walking back and forth in front of it was not a criminal act.

Terry was charged and convicted of carrying a concealed weapon. His attorney appealed all the way to the Supreme Court, contending that Detective McFadden's search and his subsequent discovery of the gun were the result of an illegal search that violated John Terry's Fourth Amendment right against search and seizure without probable cause. That is, however suspicious Terry's behavior might have been, it did not rise to the level of "probable cause" of a criminal act, and McFadden certainly had no knowledge of the fact that

Terry was carrying a concealed weapon.

The Supreme Court acknowledged that McFadden's suspicions did not rise to the level of probable cause. So they created, out of whole cloth, an entirely new standard for invading a citizen's person and privacy, which is nowhere to be found in the Constitution - that of "reasonable suspicion," which is a lesser standard than the already vaguely defined "probable cause."

The Court wrote: *"A person can be stopped and briefly detained by a police officer based on a reasonable suspicion of involvement in a punishable crime. If the officer has reasonable suspicion the detainee is armed, the officer may perform a "pat-down" of the person's outer garments for weapons. Such a detention does not violate the Fourth Amendment's prohibition on unreasonable searches and seizure, though it must be brief."*[10]

Of course, this may sound pretty innocuous and reasonable. Police can only stop citizens if they think they have committed a crime, and they can only frisk citizens if they believe them to be armed. But the dissenting justices looked into the future and saw this as the beginning of the end of our Fourth Amendment protections against police powers. They stated so in no uncertain terms:

Dissenting opinion by Justice Abraham Fortas: *"There have been powerful hydraulic pressures throughout our history that bear heavily on the Court to water down constitutional guarantees and give the police the upper hand. That hydraulic pressure has probably never been greater than it is today. Yet if the individual is no longer to be sovereign, if the police can pick him up whenever they do not like the cut of his jib, if they can 'seize' and 'search' him in their discretion, we enter a new regime. The decision to enter it should be made only after a full debate by the people of this country."*[11]

Dissenting opinion by Justice William O. Douglas: *"To give the police greater power than a magistrate is to take a long step down the totalitarian path. Perhaps such a step is desirable to cope with modern forms of lawlessness. But if it is taken, it should be the deliberate choice of the people through a constitutional amendment."*[12]

Twenty-five years later, New York City Police Chief William Bratton introduced "stop and frisk" as a major component of his policing strategy. This now infamous policy, based on the Terry ruling, resulted in entire communities of young black and Latino men, having done nothing wrong other than "acting suspiciously," were stopped and searched, essentially treated as if they were criminals. But in almost 90 percent of the stops, those suspects were found to have no drugs or guns on their person and had (other than looking "suspicious") committed no crime.[13] So much for Terry stops requiring "reasonable suspicion" of an actual crime being committed or the "reasonable suspicion" that they were armed. Terry had become exactly what Justices Fortas and Douglas feared: a long step down the path towards a police state, in which law enforcement can stop anyone with no cause and subject them to search and seizure, or target a particular group as "suspected criminals."

You may think, as I once did (especially if you are white and have not had much contact with the police) that if you have nothing to hide, who cares if you are stopped by the police?

But if you have ever been wrongly accused of something by your partner, your parent, your friend, your boss, you know immediately what the problem is: You are being seen as a dishonorable person, as "less than." It feels terrible, and when it happens enough times you will begin to feel angry, resentful, disrespected, and devalued. You feel criminalized.

Even if you've never done anything wrong, you start to look over your shoulder. This is the opposite of freedom. This is the instilling of fear and intimidation by our government, and it is against all that we hold dear.

It is also worth noting that both justices felt that this was such a dramatic expansion of police powers that it should not be left to the Supreme Court, but should instead be - as the Declaration of Independence requires - "derived from the consent of the governed." But we never had that debate nor gave our consent.

Even the act of deciding which constitutional cases should be heard by the Court versus which are of such importance that they need to be subject to a full national debate are political decisions in which the justices often disagree. But when one faction of the Court can outvote the other, the decision to have Americans control their own government is denied.

Of course, to date, our police forces have only selectively applied the Terry ruling, primarily against people of color. But there is nothing in the ruling that stops law enforcement from using it against the rest of us and, ironically, that would solve the whole legal problem of racial profiling that surrounds stop-and-frisk policies. The use of this expanded police power is simply a wake-up call for the rest of us to protect our rights - or else lose them without even knowing what we have lost until it is too late. Walking around without fear of being accosted by the police should be a right, not a privilege.

No 'Reasonable Suspicion?' Just Get Citizens to 'Voluntarily' Waive Their Rights

You might imagine that creating an entirely new and lesser standard of "cause" for circumventing a person's right to be free from law enforcement search-and-seizure powers might have been sufficient for the Supreme Court. But this was not the case.

What if, for instance, the police are doing traffic stops of all drivers on a highway searching for drunk drivers or doing a drug sweep in a bus of *all* passengers. Or they simply approach you on the street and start asking you questions for no apparent reason. They don't even have reasonable suspicion, let alone probable cause, to stop and question you. Can you simply refuse to stop and answer the officer's questions, which are, in and of themselves, an invasion of privacy because you did not initiate the encounter? Can you just walk away?

Yes, you could – if you were able to figure out if you were being "briefly detained," a la Terry, or not. But how would you even know you had this right? How would you know whether the police officer has stopped you for "reasonable suspicion?" He certainly isn't going to tell you!

In the case of Schneckloth v. Bustamonte, the Court decided that the police could get you to waive your Fourth Amendment right even if you had no idea you had the right to refuse their intrusion in the first place.

This case, as described by the court, unfolded as follows:

"While on routine patrol in Sunnyvale, California, at approximately 2:40 in the morning, Police Officer James Rand stopped an automobile when he observed that one headlight and its license plate light were burned out. Six men were in the vehicle. Joe Alcala and the respondent, Robert Bustamonte, were in the front seat with Joe Gonzales, the driver. Three older men were seated in the rear. When, in response to the policeman's question, Gonzales could not produce a driver's license, Officer Rand asked if any of the other five had any evidence of identification. Only Alcala produced a license, and he explained that the car was his brother's. After the six occupants had stepped out of the car at the officer's request, and after two additional policemen had arrived, Officer Rand asked Alcala if he could search the car. Alcala replied, "Sure, go ahead." Prior to the search, no one was threatened with arrest, and, according to Officer Rand's uncontradicted testimony, it 'was all very congenial at this time.' Gonzales testified that Alcala actually helped in the search of the car by opening the trunk and glove compartment. In Gonzales's words:

[T]he police officer asked Joe [Alcala], he goes, 'Does the trunk open?' And Joe said, 'Yes.' He went to the car and got the keys and opened up the trunk.

Wadded up under the left rear seat, the police officers found three checks that had previously been stolen from a car wash."[14]

Bustamonte was subsequently charged and convicted with possession of the stolen checks. The search of the car was deemed legal not because the police had either probable cause or reasonable suspicion to search, but because Bustamonte had "voluntarily" waived his right against the unreasonable search. However, his attorney appealed all the way up to the Supreme Court, arguing that it was impossible for Bustamonte to give his "voluntary" consent to waive his right against unreasonable search and seizure if he was unaware he had such a right to waive in the first place.

In dissent, Justice Thurgood Marshall opined: "*Several years ago, Mr. Justice Stewart reminded us that '[t]he Constitution guarantees…a society of free choice. Such a society presupposes the capacity of its members to choose.' I would have thought that the capacity to choose necessarily depends upon knowledge that there is a choice to be made. But today the Court reaches the curious result that one can choose to relinquish a constitutional right – the right to be free of unreasonable searches – without knowing that he has the alternative of refusing to accede to a police request to search. I cannot agree, and therefore dissent.*"

Dissent by Justice John Brennan: *"The Court holds today that an individual can effectively waive this right even though he is totally ignorant of the fact that, in the absence of his consent, such invasions of his privacy would be constitutionally prohibited. It wholly escapes me how our citizens can meaningfully be said to have waived something as precious as a constitutional guarantee without ever being aware of its existence. In my view, the Court's conclusion is supported neither by 'linguistics,' nor by 'epistemology,' nor, indeed, by 'common sense.' I respectfully dissent."*

Dissent by Justice Thurgood Marshall: *"I must conclude, with some reluctance, that, when the Court speaks of practicality, what it really is talking of is the continued ability of the police to capitalize on the ignorance of citizens so as to accomplish by subterfuge what they could not achieve by relying only on the knowing relinquishment of constitutional rights. But such a practical advantage is achieved only at the cost of permitting the police to disregard the limitations that the Constitution places on their behavior, a cost that a constitutional democracy cannot long absorb."*[15]

Marshall continued: *"[The] Court now sanctions a game of blind man's bluff, in which the police always have the upper hand, for the sake of nothing more than the convenience of the police. But the guarantees of the Fourth Amendment were never intended to shrink before such an ephemeral and changeable interest. The Framers of the Fourth Amendment struck the balance against this sort of convenience and in favor of certain basic civil rights. It is not for this Court to restrike that balance because of its own views of the needs of law enforcement officers. I fear that that is the effect of the Court's decision today."*

This "game of Blind Man's Bluff" is exactly what I experienced during my arrest. It was clear that the police were following some set of rules which they knew and I didn't, and, most significantly, they were not about to share those rules with me. The goal of this subterfuge was not to uphold the law or police constitutionally, but to see if I would, at minimum, give up my constitutional rights through ignorance (not remaining silent, allowing searches which could be refused), or actively violating my rights (searching without a warrant, using excessive force), again assuming I would not know my rights. It seems beyond question that our Constitutional rights were never intended to be used as a means to trap citizens, but as a check on police powers. Yet the police, with the help of the Supreme Court, have found a way to dishonor the intent of the Fourth Amendment and use it abrogate our rights.

As Michelle Alexander described it in *The New Jim Crow*, It is easy enough for police officers to make a question – "Can I talk to you?" - sound like an order to which most of us will comply, never realizing we have the right to refuse. "Because almost no one refuses, drug sweeps on the sidewalk (and on buses and trains) are easy. People are easily intimidated when a police officer confronts them..."[16]

Therefore, it is no surprise that nearly everyone submits to officers' interrogations, assuming that they have no right to refuse, or if they do refuse, the situation will get even worse, so they comply – even to the point of consenting to searches of their person, vehicle, or home, all under the false claim of "voluntary" consent.

Contrast this with the laws that require all persons participating as subjects in medical research to provide "informed consent" before taking part—specifically, "any individual who may be exposed to the possibility of injury, including physical, psychological, or social injury, as a consequence of participation as a subject."[17]

The assumption is that we have a human right to choose to have our bodies used in medical research or not, and no government or private business has the right to use us for research without our knowledge and voluntary consent. How is it that we require medical researchers to get informed consent before subjecting citizens to potentially harmful experiments, but we don't require the police to get informed consent before violating citizens' civil rights? In both cases a person is "exposed to the possibility of injury." In the case of your Fourth Amendment Rights, whether you have incriminating evidence on your person or not, your right to be free of unreasonable search and seizure has been injured, and you were never informed that you had the option to protect that freedom.

The Exclusionary Rule – The Ends *Do Not* Justify the Means

As you read each of these cases, you may be thinking to yourself, "The only reason these guys are appealing these convictions is because they were guilty in the first place. If they were innocent, like me, the cops would have done their stop, frisk, and search and then let them go. No harm, no foul." Yes, that's true, just like the New York City citizens – ninety percent of them black or Hispanic - who were stopped, frisked, and then let go because they had not committed any crime. But they were "criminalized" nonetheless.

To those of us who have never been stopped, questioned, and frisked by the police, this may seem a trivial and inconsequential price to pay for our safety and security, since we are, after all, "innocent" of any wrongdoing. But the experience of being presumptively "criminalized," even when you know you have nothing to hide, is the difference between a police state in which you are presumed guilty and a democracy in which each citizen's rights are a sacred trust. There is nothing trivial or inconsequential about preserving that trust. Tom and Jill were innocent of any crime. Yet the way in which they were treated - as criminals - left them with indelible and lifelong distrust, if not outright disrespect, for law enforcement.

The essence of these cases, too frequently overlooked, is not that these "guilty" criminals should be let off because of a legal technicality, but whether the police be allowed to violate their rights (and all the rights of those who are *not* guilty of any crime) to secure an arrest and conviction. In each case, the Court made what was heretofore illegal police conduct legal. Thus, as Justice Brennan noted in the 1963 case of Ker v. California, the case which launched the dismantling of the Fourth Amendment, *"The recognition of exceptions to great principals always creates...the hazard that the exceptions will devour the rule."*[18] These cases illustrate how our basic Fourth Amendment protection against unreasonable search and seizure has suffered death by a thousand cuts. Each cut is seemingly minor on its own, but taken as a whole, the result is lethal.

Even if you are not an attorney, you are no doubt familiar with the Exclusionary Rule if you have seen even a couple of television crime dramas. The Exclusionary Rule is applied when some psychopathic career criminal who is indisputably guilty walks away scot-free because the police seized evidence of his crime without a search warrant or without probable cause, thus the case is "thrown out" because the police violated the criminal's rights.

The criminal smirks with the knowledge that he has just literally gotten away with murder, and you, the viewer, are convinced that there must be something wrong with our Constitution if guilty murderers receive "Get-Out-Of-Jail-Free" cards based on such legal "technicalities."

While this does occur on rare occasions, what is missing from this picture is the requirement of the Constitution that both limits government powers and seeks to hold government, in this case law enforcement, to a higher standard than the criminals they are seeking to apprehend.

As Thurgood Marshall wrote in his dissent in the aforementioned case of Bustamonte: *"Of course, it would be "practical" for the police to ignore the commands of the Fourth Amendment if, by practicality, we mean that more criminals will be apprehended, even though the consti- tutional rights of innocent people also go by the board."*[19]

The Exclusionary Rule is not there to protect the criminals, though on occasion it will do just that. It is there to protect the rights of all the rest of us against arbitrary search and seizure. While you may be innocent, do you really want to live in a country where the police can stop and search you, your home, and your car for any reason (or no reason at all), even if you have done nothing wrong? Each of the rulings discussed above lessens the protections against unreasonable search and seizures for *every citizen,* guilty or innocent. There is no caveat that says, "Only violate the constitutional rights of the bad guys." All of us - white, black, innocent, and guilty – are subject to these far- reaching and intrusive police powers. Of course, you might object and wonder if illegal police searches are really a significant problem or a rare occurrence? According to a Department of Justice (DOJ) investigation into the Baltimore Police Department following the death of Freddie Gray, the answer is yes. Illegal searches by police are very common in Baltimore,[20] and similar widespread violations have shown up in other DOJ investigations, though the investigations themselves were not even launched to look at illegal police searches. But the more important point, to my mind, is this: Do you want a country in which you have rights against warrantless searches and seizures, or would you rather hope that the police, in their "discretionary capacity," won't come to your door (and enter your home) because of the color of your skin, or the thickness of your wallet, or whatever other privilege might make you immune? I most definitely prefer rights over privileges.

Thus far, the Fourth Amendment cases we have examined all revolved around our rights in public spaces - driving in public, walking in public. But there is an entire Supreme Court jurisprudence regarding our Fourth Amendment rights as they apply to the ultimate sanctuary of protection against the law enforcement intrusion: the home. And, no surprise, the Court has extended its assault on our Fourth Amendment rights in this arena as well.

Your Home is No Longer Your Castle

Though you probably don't know it, your home holds a special place in constitutional law. The commonly used phrase "A man's home is his castle" is not just a poetic way of describing the exalted status people accord their dwellings, however humble. It also refers to an actual legal doctrine: The Castle Doctrine, which dates back to seventeenth-century English law.

In its essence, the Doctrine recognizes the home as a sacred space in terms of the privacy and security it provides its owners (or renters). Thus, while the relatively recent invention of the automobile may have made it easier for the Supreme Court to justify exceptions to the probable cause and warrant requirements of the Fourth Amendment, the fact is that homes haven't changed much in the last few thousand years. They have a physical location that is not mobile (mobile homes excepted, and yes, the Court has dealt with these, as well). And they have barriers to entry and window coverings to prevent the public from seeing inside. In short, a private home is about the most private place, outside of our physical bodies, that any of us can hope to have. British and American law recognized and honored that by creating a high bar for law enforcement to enter a private home.

In addition – though not specified in the Fourth Amendment, but recognized by the Court as a related Right with a long history in English and American law – is the requirement that even with a warrant, law enforcement must knock first, announce themselves, and give the occupants time and opportunity to voluntarily open the door. Just because you had a warrant didn't give you, the government, permission to bust down someone's door unannounced.

You may think, "What's the big deal? These are criminals we are talking about. Why should the police bother to knock?"

The answer is looking at you in the mirror. *You* are not a criminal. How would you feel if the police, wrongly, of course, came to your house with guns drawn, didn't announce themselves, broke down your door, and then shot you, your wife, or your children because you, not knowing they were the police, tried to defend yourself? Would that be okay with you because the *next time* they might actually shoot someone who *might* be guilty of a crime? The Castle Doctrine recognized that these restrictions on government intrusion protected all of us against an abuse of power.

Our rights sometimes protect the guilty, but they are there to protect us all. The question that continually must be asked is how many of *our* freedoms are we willing to sacrifice to catch one more criminal. Is one more criminal even worth the sacrifice of any of our freedoms and protections against government-authorized uses of force? Is there some balance of innocent people's rights being violated that justifies the benefit of one more criminal being arrested? What is that number? I don't know, but I would err on the side of protecting my rights. Where do you come down on this fundamental question? For any of us to impact policing in our communities, each of us must answer this for ourselves.

Again, these rights may seem so basic as to not be worthy of discussion. But these laws were born into a world where might made right, and no assumptions of safety and security against the power of governments were presumed. So, to have the government pass laws that protected the people's rights from the power of government itself was nothing short of revolutionary. But the rub is that these protections are not at all guaranteed except by our vigilance. And, as of late, we have not been vigilant.

This is true because the government is a living, breathing organism. It is just like us. It is made up of people. And just like us, it can be self-serving and driven not to serve us, as is its stated purpose, but to perpetuate its own power at our expense. Unfortunately, we have become complacent and oblivious to the significance of the slow, steady erosion of our rights over the past fifty years. Even those who have dedicated themselves to preserving our rights, such as the American Civil Liberties Union, cannot prevail without the support of a large proportion of the American public. But most of us are just too busy trying to get through each day to concern ourselves with the public good. Or worse yet, there are many of us who willingly cede our rights to government if we believe that it will only use those expanded powers against those "other" people. But inevitably, those "other" people end up being us.

The beginning of the end of the special status of the home in the Fourth Amendment began with Ker v. California (1963). As is often the case, these larger questions are grounded in the most mundane of circumstances.

The police were watching a known drug dealer. It was night and a car pulled up to the suspected drug dealer's vehicle, but the police were too far away to see if an actual drug purchase had taken place. They followed this vehicle as it left and got the license plate number but lost the car in traffic. Checking the license plate with the DMV, they learned it belonged to George Ker. The police went to his address and then got a passkey to his apartment from the building manager. Then, with no arrest warrant for Ker or search warrant for the apartment, they let themselves in. Inside were Ker and his wife with two pounds of marijuana. The police arrested them both, and they were convicted of possession. Wasn't their arrest (and the evidence that led to it) illegally obtained due to the Fourth Amendment requirement of a warrant (based on probable cause) for entering their home, granted by an independent judge?

In a five to four decision, the Court created a host of exceptions to the Fourth Amendment and the long-standing requirement for officers to announce themselves before entering. Police could now enter a home unannounced, and under certain circumstances (described as "exigencies"), didn't need to bother with a warrant at all. Just like that, the citizen's right to a judge-approved warrant was drastically reduced. The police could now make their own judgments about whose home to respect and whose home to ransack. The so-called "exigencies," in the majority opinion, were as follows:

"(1) where the persons within already know of the officers' authority and purpose [this is called the 'hot pursuit' exigency – obviously if a suspect flees into a building, the pursuing officer has no need to knock and announce himself], or (2) where the officers are justified in the belief that persons within are in imminent peril of bodily harm, or (3) where those within, made aware of the presence of someone outside (because, for example, there has been a knock at the door) are then engaged in activity which

justifies the officers in the belief that an escape or the destruction of evidence is being attempted."[21] Additionally, *"compliance is not required if the officer's peril would have been increased or the arrest frustrated had he demanded entrance and stated his purpose."*

As you can see, the last three exigencies leave plenty of room for the individual police officer to make a judgment in favor of more violent and aggressive entry into a home based on very subjective judgments and gives precedence to police powers over citizen rights.

In dissent, Justice Brennan laid out that this was setting a dangerous precedent. First, he outlines why not requiring police to announce their presence is so dangerous, both in terms of citizen rights and the physical safety of everyone involved:

"...Two reasons rooted in the Constitution clearly compel the courts to refuse to recognize exceptions [to the Fourth Amendment] *in other situations when there is no showing that those within were or had been made aware of the officers' presence* [by knocking and announcing].

The first is that any exception not requiring a showing of such awareness necessarily implies a rejection of the inviolable presumption of innocence. The excuse for failing to knock or announce the officer's mission where the occupants are oblivious to his presence can only be an almost automatic assumption that the suspect within will resist the officer's attempt to enter peacefully, or will frustrate the arrest by an attempt to escape, or will attempt to destroy whatever possibly incriminating evidence he may have. Such assumptions do obvious violence to the presumption of innocence. Indeed, the violence is compounded by another assumption, also necessarily involved, that a suspect to whom the officer first makes known his presence will further violate the law. It need hardly be said that not every suspect is, in fact, guilty of the offense of which he is suspected, and that not everyone who is in fact guilty will forcibly resist arrest or attempt to escape or destroy evidence.

"The second reason is that, in the absence of a showing of awareness by the occupants of the officers' presence and purpose, "loud noises" or "running" within would amount, ordinarily, at least, only to ambiguous conduct. Our decisions in related contexts have held that ambiguous conduct cannot form the basis for a belief of the officers that an escape or the destruction of evidence is being attempted.

"Beyond these constitutional considerations, practical hazards of law enforcement militate strongly against any relaxation of the requirement of awareness. First, cases of mistaken identity are surely not novel in the investigation of crime. The possibility is very real that the police may be misinformed as to the name or address of a suspect, or as to other material information. That possibility is itself a good reason for holding a tight rein against judicial approval of unannounced police entries into private homes. Innocent citizens should not suffer the shock, fright, or embarrassment attendant upon an unannounced police intrusion. Second, the requirement of awareness also serves to minimize the hazards of the officers' dangerous calling. We expressly recognized in Miller v. United States that compliance with the federal notice statute 'is also a safeguard for the police themselves, who might be mistaken for prowlers and be shot down by a fearful householder.' Indeed, one of the principal objectives of the English requirement of announcement of authority and purpose was to protect the arresting officers from being shot as trespassers...for, if no previous demand is made, how is it possible for a party to know what the object of the person breaking open the door may be? He has a right to consider

it as an aggression on his private property, which he will be justified in resisting to the utmost."[22]*

While the police did not have to break down Ker's door, because they had a passkey, the exigencies the court approved did not distinguish between the police letting themselves into a home unannounced or simply breaking down the door, with or without announcing their presence. Justice Brennan notes that this ruling gives police carte blanche to forcibly enter a home any time they *suspect* evidence *might* be destroyed. With all these suppositions justifying police use of unannounced forced entry, what is left of the Fourth Amendment?

Justice Brennan: *"The command of the Fourth Amendment reflects the lesson of history that 'the breaking an outer door is, in general, so violent, obnoxious and dangerous a proceeding, that it should be adopted only in extreme cases, where an immediate arrest is requisite."*

"The recognition of exceptions to great principles always creates, of course, the hazard that the exceptions will devour the rule. If mere police experience that some offenders have attempted to destroy contraband justifies unannounced entry in any case, and cures the total absence of evidence not only of awareness of the officers' presence but even of such an attempt in the particular case, I perceive no logical basis for distinguishing unannounced police entries into homes to make arrests for any crime involving evidence of a kind which police experience indicates might be quickly destroyed or jettisoned. Moreover, if such experience, without more, completely excuses the failure of arresting officers before entry, at any hour of the day or night, either to announce their purpose at the threshold or to ascertain

---

* Police errors in which they enter the wrong home – or have the right home but the occupants are completely innocent – has occurred many hundreds (perhaps thousands) of times over the past forty-five years, resulting in both injury and even death of entirely innocent citizens and police officers as well. Many of these disastrous errors are detailed in Balko's book, *Rise of the Warrior Cop.*

that the occupant already knows of their presence, then there is likewise no logical ground for distinguishing between the stealthy manner in which the entry in this case was effected and the more violent manner usually associated with totalitarian police of breaking down the door or smashing the lock."[23]

What is stated here regarding the violation of the rights of the innocent holds true for each and every one of these cases. Law enforcement cannot pick only the guilty when it makes exceptions to the Fourth Amendment. These exceptions are indiscriminate and impact every citizen's Rights.

Twenty-one years later, nearing the end of his thirty-four years on the Court, Brennan was beyond despair at the most recent blow to our Fourth Amendment rights. In U.S. v. Leon (1984), police executed what was a presumably valid search warrant only to have that warrant deemed invalid by the court insofar as it did not establish the probable cause. Basically, the judge had simply rubber-stamped the warrant without doing the job the Constitution required: make sure there was probable cause to issue the warrant in the first place.

The Supreme Court overruled the lower court in a six-to-three split. The court justified this "good faith" exception as follows:

"The question whether the exclusionary sanction is appropriately imposed in a particular case as a judicially created remedy to safeguard Fourth Amendment rights through its deterrent effect must be resolved by weighing the costs and benefits of preventing the use in the prosecution's case in chief of inherently trustworthy tangible evidence. Indiscriminate application of the exclusionary rule – impeding the criminal justice system's truth-finding function and allowing some guilty defendants to go free – may well generate disrespect for the law and the administration of justice."[24]

Somehow, the six justices missed the potential for "disrespect for the law" that might result if law enforcement can invade your privacy with no probable cause, so long as they "believe" they are acting legally. As Radley Balko describes it: "The ruling was essentially an instruction manual for police to use to get around the Fourth Amendment."[25]

Here is some of Justice Brennan's dissent, a lament for our Fourth Amendment rights: *"Ten years ago, in United States v. Calandra, I expressed the fear that the Court's decision "may signal that a majority of my colleagues have positioned themselves to reopen the door [to evidence secured by official lawlessness] still further and abandon altogether the exclusionary rule in search and seizure cases.*

"Since then, in case after case, I have witnessed the Court's gradual but determined strangulation of the rule. It now appears that the Court's victory over the Fourth Amendment is complete. That today's decisions represent the piece de resistance of the Court's past efforts cannot be doubted, for today the Court sanctions the use in the prosecution's case in chief of illegally obtained evidence against the individual whose rights have been violated – a result that had previously been thought to be foreclosed.

"The Court seeks to justify this result on the ground that the 'costs' of adhering to the exclusionary rule in cases like those before us exceed the 'benefits.' But the language of deterrence and of cost/benefit analysis, if used indiscriminately, can have a narcotic effect. It creates an illusion of technical precision and ineluctability. It suggests that not only constitutional principal but also empirical data support the majority's result. When the Court's analysis is examined carefully, however, it is clear that we have not been treated to an honest assessment of the merits of the exclusionary rule, but have instead been drawn into a curious world where the "costs" of excluding illegally

obtained evidence loom to exaggerated heights, and where the "benefits" of such exclusion are made to disappear with a mere wave of the hand.

"The majority ignores the fundamental constitutional importance of what is at stake here. While the machinery of law enforcement, and indeed the nature of crime itself, have changed dramatically since the Fourth Amendment became part of the Nation's fundamental law in 1791, what the Framers understood then remains true today – that the task of combating crime and convicting the guilty will in every era seem of such critical and pressing concern that we may be lured by the temptations of expediency into forsaking our commitment to protecting individual liberty and privacy. It was for that very reason that the Framers of the Bill of Rights insisted that law enforcement efforts be permanently and unambiguously restricted in order to preserve personal freedoms. In the constitutional scheme they ordained, the sometimes unpopular task of ensuring that the government's enforcement efforts remain within the strict boundaries fixed by the Fourth Amendment was entrusted to the courts.[26]

Absent the Exclusionary Rule, which requires that law enforcement have either probable cause or a search or arrest warrant before they go entering, searching, and arresting people in their homes, offices, cars, boats, et al., law enforcement could subject any innocent person and their home, etc., to search, seizure, and arrest with virtually no restraint or consequence, except perhaps to say, "Oops, sorry about that!"

As the Court stated in *United States v. Di Re*, (1948), "a search is not to be made legal by what it turns up. In law it is good or bad when it starts and does not change character from" what is subsequently found.[27]

So, while a few guilty folks might escape justice, the

Exclusionary Rule protects all the rest of us and our most basic Fourth Amendment right to be free of unreasonable search and seizure. The essence of the Exclusionary Rule is that the ends do not justify the means, if the means result in the abrogation of the rights of all the rest of us (innocent) folks. The flip side is that not catching a few criminals because the police have failed to obey the law is a small price to pay for having police obey the law the other 99 percent of the time. How else could we tell the difference between the "good" guys and the "bad" guys?

Solutions

The most obvious solution to the problem of Supreme Court decisions that are deleterious to citizen rights and freedom would be to elect presidents and senators who would then nominate and confirm justices who value the Fourth Amendment over and above police powers. But because Supreme Court justices have lifetime appointments, that is a very slow road to reclaiming our rights.

Fortunately, there are many other ways to effect change when it comes to overreaching police powers in your community. The fact that there are roughly 18,000 police agencies in the United States, all which have varying degrees of independence, is cause for despair among some police reformers because no change in one department - even if it produces outstanding results - is then required as a national policy by the other 17,999. But the bright side of this is that with so many small local police departments, often with locally elected sheriffs or locally elected politicians who select their police chiefs, local political pressure both in the voting booth and in policymaking is a very impactful way to advocate for change.

The other critical point is that even though the Supreme Court may have granted police excessive powers, the police are not required or obligated to exercise those powers. That is, individual departments can hold themselves to a higher standard when it comes to protecting the rights of citizens. This is the discretionary aspect of policing, which cuts both ways. Departmental policy *and* culture can promote policing that is focused on community relations and respect for citizens' rights instead of abusing their power "just because we can."

Specific policy changes that you can advocate for locally include:

- Stop "broken widows" policing, which criminalizes minor offenses and has resulted in communities (particularly minority communities) feel they are under siege by the police rather than protected by them. For example, decriminalize and/or de-prioritize marijuana possession (where it's still illegal), loitering, jaywalking, bicycling on the sidewalk, public consumption of alcohol, and disturbing the peace. This does not mean the police need to ignore these types of complaints, but that they are handled as a social and public health issue rather than as a criminal act.

- Restrict or ban stop-and-frisk policies that are based on race, on being in a high-crime area, on looking "nervous," or on matching a generalized vague description of a suspect (i.e. black male, age 15 to 25), all of which do not amount to either "reasonable suspicion" or "probable cause."

- Advocate for a restriction on no-knock warrants and promote the requirement for police to secure a warrant before entering a suspect's home. This prioritizes citizen's rights to be safe and secure in their homes and requires police to engage in reasonable due diligence and caution before putting themselves and citizens in harm's way.

As previously mentioned, all of your efforts will be exponentially more impactful if you are part of a group. Those in power often find it easy to write off individuals on issues because they represent, presumably, only themselves. A group potentially signifies a broader, community-based concern with all the implications that has for voting, publicity, organized opposition, and the like. Talk to your neighbors about issues that concern you. Form alliances, take action. Waiting for others to act on your behalf is not a strategy; it's conceding your rights.

For more information on current policy initiatives and research in these areas, I recommend the website campaignzero.org. It has a comprehensive list of policies, initiatives, research, and examples of successful policy changes around the country.

CHAPTER FOUR

Through the Looking Glass

*If I had a world of my own, everything would be
nonsense. Nothing would be what it is, because
everything would be what it isn't. And contrary wise,
what is, it wouldn't be. And what it wouldn't be, it would.
You see?*
　　　—**Lewis Carroll,** *Alice's Adventures in Wonderland*

*Liberty lies in the hearts of men and women; when it dies
there, no constitution, no law, no court can save it; no
constitution, no law, no court can even do much to help
it. The spirt of liberty is the spirit which is not too sure
that it is right; the spirit of liberty is the spirit which seeks
to understand the minds of other men and women; the
spirit of liberty which weighs their interests alongside its
own without bias.*
　　　—**Supreme Court Justice Learned Hand**

How Did We Get Here?

By now, you might be wondering about the Supreme
Court justices intent on dismantling our Fourth Amendment
rights and expanding the powers of law enforcement to an
unprecedented degree. As Butch Cassidy kept asking the
Sundance Kid, "Who are those guys?"

And, perhaps more importantly, *"Why are they taking
away my rights?"*

If I didn't try to understand who was undertaking this
fifty-year-long assault on my rights and why they were doing
it, how was I going to be able to defend my freedom?

The value in understanding the roots of law enforcement's
current excess of powers is that without such knowledge we
have no firm footing on which to oppose this assault against
our fundamental rights. It also places the erosion of our
Fourth Amendment rights within the larger context of
America's political evolution. The powers we accord police
are just one part of what sort of country we want to leave
for future generations.

It may come as a surprise to some that it is the so-called
conservatives on the court who continually vote in favor of
increased government powers at the expense of the
individual freedoms of Americans. This may seem odd given
the popular view of conservatives as being staunchly against
government regulations, government programs, government
debt, and government restrictions on our freedoms. Liberals,
in contrast, are portrayed as wanting more and bigger
government, more taxes, more spending, and more
regulation. So you would think that, philosophically-
speaking, conservatives would be fierce defenders of Fourth
Amendment rights against an overreaching liberal desire to
expand governmental powers.

Not when it comes to law enforcement powers.

Even the most cursory examination of the clichés describing both liberals and conservatives reveal that these are very far from the political reality that exists today in these United States. Conservatives are more than willing to support both "big government" and big deficits when it comes to military spending and military action (and most recently, tax cuts for the wealthy), but not social welfare programs or education. On the other hand, liberals generally want less military spending and, arguably, less use of force to resolve our international conflicts, but are more than willing to spend on education and social welfare programs. Socially, conservatives argue for fewer individual freedoms for select groups of Americans (gays, women, African-Americans, non-Christians, criminals, and even "suspected" criminals), but for more freedoms for other groups (gun owners, the wealthy, and corporations). Liberals desire more rights for the former group of "minorities" (though women are actually a majority) so that they are on par with heterosexual white men, while wanting more restrictions on gun owners, the rich, and the corporations. And, of course, in the area of law enforcement, conservatives are self-described as "tough on crime" while liberals are deemed "soft on crime," as conservatives eviscerate our Fourth Amendment protections against the powers of government and spend billions increasing the size and scope of our police force - as if that is somehow entirely disconnected to all of our rights to be free of government intrusion into our lives. So much for conservatives wanting less government power and more individual freedoms, or liberals bent on restricting individual freedoms in favor of more government restrictions. Each group wants more government or less government depending on their very different priorities.

Nothing is as it seems.

On the Supreme Court, the Conservatives are described as "originalists" or "textualists" and claim that they do not "interpret" the Constitution, they simply apply the law as it is written, relying on the text and "original intent" of the Constitution. Who could be against that? After all, the Constitution is the acknowledged "law of the land." Do we really want those activist "liberal" judges exacting their own interpretations of our sacred founding document?

But it was very conservative justices who created out of whole cloth the entirely new and lesser standard of "reasonable suspicion," allowing police to stop and frisk anyone, for virtually any reason. It was the same conservatives on the Court who authorized a whole set of exceptions to the Fourth Amendment warrant requirements for entering our homes, found nowhere in the original text of the Constitution. And it was the conservatives who in 2016, in Utah v. Strieff, voted to allow police to stop a citizen on the street without any suspicion of committing any crime, demand his identification, and then, if he has a completely unrelated arrest warrant (for a minor traffic ticket, in this case), search and arrest him, all based on the initial illegal seizure of the person who was stopped arbitrarily. In short, it encourages police to randomly stop and question anyone, knowing that if they "get lucky" and stop someone with a warrant, they can arrest them, and if the person they stop and question has no warrant, which of those entirely innocent people will take their case to the Supreme Court to stop these constitutional violations?

If Justice Brennan announced the death of the Fourth Amendment in 1984, then Justice Sonia Sotomayor delivered the eulogy in 2016. Her entire dissent is worth reading, but here is the conclusion, which goes to the heart of the loss of our rights for *all* of us:

"*...this case tells everyone, white and black, guilty and innocent, that an officer can verify your legal status at any* *time. It says that your body is subject to invasion while the courts excuse the violation of your rights. It implies that you are not a citizen of a democracy but the subject of a carceral state, just waiting to be cataloged.*

"We must not pretend that the countless people who are routinely targeted by the police are 'isolated.' They are the canaries in the coal mine, whose deaths, civil and literal, warn us that no one can breathe in this atmosphere. They are the ones who recognize that unlawful police stops corrode all [emphasis added] our civil liberties and threaten all [emphasis added] our lives. Until their voices matter too, our justice system will continue to be anything but."[1]

Unless those conservatives were holding séances to communicate with the Founding Fathers about their original "intent" - and not inviting their liberal colleagues - there isn't any reason to think that they have any more insight, knowledge, or wisdom when it comes to applying this two-hundred-forty-year-old document to our current situation than the liberal side of the Court.

The other camp, the so-called liberal "activists," supposedly apply the law while considering changes in everything from new technology, social movements, and changing citizen practices and sentiment to current research in any number of fields to cases they review. They are portrayed as wildly out of control. Or perhaps they are simply doing exactly the same thing as the so-called "orginalists." They are applying the *intent* of the Con-stitutional Amendments *as they understand them*, unless they have possession of the secret, one-and-only copy of the *Here's What We Really Intended Instruction Manual for these Amendments* by James Madison and friends.

Even if the generalizations about these political/ ideological differences are patently false, there is still a coherence of ideology that separates the conservatives and liberals on the Court and in the rest of our political lives.

Understanding these differences has a profound effect on our lives because they determine whether the Court protects the democratic rights of historically disenfranchised Americans (women, minorities, suspected criminals, etc.) or hands over additional rights to already entitled Americans (corporations, the government, military contractors, the wealthy). Whose rights get preference? When it comes to rights, there is no free lunch. One person's rights are another person's harm. We must decide how to balance these competing interests. The Constitution has a *preference,* but it does not have a *requirement,* which means we get to choose right now, each and every day, how we balance these competing interests. That's why the Constitution still matters.

The differences among these priorities in rights predate even the American Revolution and, in fact, go back much further than that.[2] The differences seem to be inherent in human personality and even human biology. The reality is that Supreme Court justices reflect the same differences we see in America at large. They are people like us. And like us, they have biases. And they interpret the Constitution in a way that conforms to those biases, whether they acknowledge them or not.

Justice William O. Douglas, the longest serving justice on the Supreme Court (1939–1975), wrote in his auto-biography that upon joining the Court in 1939, he received news from longtime Chief Justice Charles Hughes that stunned him. Hughes told him: "...you must remember one thing. At the constitutional level where we work, ninety percent of any decision is emotional. The rational part of us supplies the reasons for supporting our predilections."[3]

Even Douglas, an experienced attorney and newly minted Supreme Court justice, was shocked. "I had thought of the law in the terms of Moses—principles chiseled in granite. ...I had never been willing to admit to myself that the 'gut' reaction of a judge at the level of constitutional adjudications, dealing with the vagaries of due process, freedom of speech, and the like, was the main ingredient of his decision."[4]

Yet here we are, seventy-five years after Douglas's disillusionment (or revelation, depending on your perspective), still watching the same political theater when it comes to selecting Supreme Court justices. Legal scholar Adam Benforado notes that many studies have confirmed that in terms of judicial activism from the bench, the conservative justices rank higher than the liberals on the Supreme Court, though the conservatives keep insisting they are just "following the Constitution as it is written."[5]

Justice Douglas, forty years earlier, wrote: "...they [the justices] represent ideological schools of thought that are highly competitive. No judge at the level I speak of was neutral. The Constitution is not neutral. It was designed to take government off the backs of the people..."[6]

Here is Chief Justice Roberts in his confirmation hearing in 2005, wearing the conservative mantle of the "textualist" judge: "Judges are like umpires. Umpires don't make the rules; they apply them."[7]

Benforado describes judges appointed by Democrats as more likely to favor minority rights, workers, women, and the undocumented, while Republican appointees tend to favor business interests and the government."[8]

Legal scholar Barry Friedman goes to great lengths to illustrate how judicial originalists such as the late Justice Antonin Scalia cherry-picked facts from the historical record, while conveniently ignoring contradictory (to Scalia's legal vision) history, to eviscerate our Fourth Amendment rights. Scalia and his colleagues seem to believe that the Fourth Amendment does not, in fact, require the police to secure warrants at all, but simply to conform to a standard of "reasonableness" as defined in 1789.

But as Friedman points out, originalists are mistaken on

two counts. First, the idea that originalists only apply the law, but do not interpret it, is patently false. If they did not interpret it to apply to all the novel legal questions of modern life (searches of cell phones, cars, computers, etc.), then the law would have "withered on the vine long ago."[9] Thus, the idea that originalists somehow "apply" the law to situations and technologies that the founders could never have imagined, yet manage to not "interpret" the law, doesn't pass a test of common sense. The very laws that originalists claim to base their decisions on evolved (and continue to evolve) over time, and they are some of the featured actors in that legal evolution.

Second, even if they are using the mistaken standard of the law being frozen in time, they are ignoring critical historical facts of the period they claim as justification for their decisions. Friedman comments that Justice Scalia seemed to have missed the fact of the American Revolution in many of his decisions and dissents, continually relying on British common law precedents, many of which the revolutionaries had explicitly rejected.[10] Based on the historical record, Friedman notes, Americans most certainly preferred warrants that were quite specific in their scope, and "to the extent Justice Scalia and his colleagues believed otherwise, they simply were wrong."[11]

It is quite evident that there are two radically different views of the intent of the Constitution and how the principles which embody that intent should be applied. No one is "unbiased" here. We can choose, by our actions, opinions, votes, and political activities which view we would like to prevail, even if that view is contrary to the Constitution itself.

Regarding President Nixon's "law and order" policies in the early 1970s, which began this shift in the culture of law enforcement, Justice Douglas wrote: "The Nixon program, if honestly embraced, should have included a national debate on constitutional amendments. If government was to be all-powerful, if the individual was to be further submerged, the Bill of Rights should be revised."[12]

"...Do we want torture used in prisons? Do we prefer holding men and women incommunicado, as in Russia, for nine months? Do we want the privacy of homes and offices broken down by electronic surveillance? Whose homes? Despised minorities or the affluent people as well?"[13]

The truthful answer to these questions is: Yes, some of us do!

And the Constitution allows us to act in direct contradiction to its stated aspirations, if we so choose.

The question that arises in this ongoing historic shift in our Fourth Amendment rights is, what is the original intent of the Constitution, as far as we can tell from the clues we have available?

In the public's mind, if we take our cues from much of the media, the conservatives are always cast as the "true" patriots, upholding "traditional" American values (and by, implication, the Constitution), while those liberals keep trying to change the Constitution, take away our freedoms, and encourage anti-Christian, anti-free-market policies. Being a liberal in America always makes you slightly suspect, as if you're not a "real" American. You always feel slightly on the defensive. At least I always did. Until now.

Conservatism and the American Revolution

Published back in 1948, long before the culture wars engulfed us, Yale Professor Leonard Woods Labaree wrote a book entitled Conservatism in Early Colonial America.[14] Surveying newspapers, speeches, letters, and diaries from that time, Labaree found a cluster of political views coupled with personality characteristics that informed the conservative colonialists of the period. The primary conservative characteristics were:

- Resistance to change, most pronounced among the economically and socially privileged.
- Religious beliefs which held that resistance to established authority was morally wrong.
- Self-interest among the ruling class, who had the most to lose in a political revolution.
- A belief in a natural hierarchy among men in which those with wealth and power were called upon to rule the "lower classes" who should "not trespass on the position reserved for their betters."[15]

As you might guess from these qualities, these early American conservatives were not the patriots who fought in the War for American Independence. Nor were they the drafters of the Constitution. They were the so-called "loyalists" who joined with the British to fight against the Americans or, in the case of roughly 200,000 of these conservatives, fled to Canada, which was still under British rule. Do these descriptions sound familiar?

If patriotism means embracing the intent of the Constitution to guarantee "all men their unalienable rights," it is clear that colonial conservatives were wholly against such radical notions. Today's conservatives are not all that different. But because conservative arguments must be couched in the language of the Constitution, they take the concepts of "rights" and "freedoms" and rationalize them to fit, as Justice Douglas wrote, "their gut instincts," to get the result they want. So "freedom" becomes the freedom of law enforcement to protect themselves rather than protecting the rights of citizens; rights becomes the right of industry to pollute public natural resources at the cost of citizens' freedom to enjoy clean air and clean water. Freedom becomes the right for anyone to possess a gun, but not for communities to be protected from gun violence. These are freedoms, certainly, but they are freedoms conferred upon a few at the expense of the many, the very opposite of a government "of the people, by the people, for the people."

The Constitution as a Liberal Document in Spirit and Intent

The Constitution itself was written in reaction to a decidedly conservative colonial aristocracy, and so it's spirit and intent are decidedly liberal. In America, the feeling that we have certain rights is based on the embodiment of that spirit. Some of the ideas are grounded in our hazy notion of our constitutional rights, specifically, in the case of Sandra Bland – pulled from her car for no other reason than that she refused to put out her cigarette – our Fourth Amendment right against unreasonable search and seizure, also popularly known as our "right to privacy."

Other rights are grounded in what Yale Law Professor and constitutional scholar Akhil Reed Amar calls the "Symbolic Constitution." His list includes the Declaration of Independence, Lincoln's Gettysburg Address, the Brown v. Board of Education decision, and Martin Luther King's "I Have a Dream" speech.[16] I would add the Pledge of Allegiance to this list.

What all these documents have in common is that they are aspirational. They demand that we be our better selves, our compassionate selves, our generous selves. These ideals are what we communicate to our children in school, at home, and we hope, in deed and action in our daily lives. We celebrate them in our movies, songs, and books. We, as a people, seem to very much agree on what it means to be our best selves. These aspirational ideals and the Constitution itself are melded together in the social and cultural fabric of what we think of as the best qualities of America and Americans.

While Amar concludes that the American Constitution contains these "great themes of equality and inclusion," it is also true that it has deemed equally valid cruel and despicable cases that have also been "themes" in America's history: the constitutional support of slavery, denying blacks their rights as citizens of this country, the constitutionality of separate but equal, denying women the vote, the right of working men and women to form unions, and so on. While the Constitution has often brought out the best in us, it has also brought out the worst in us because it is only as honorable as we make it. The Constitution allows us to override its liberal intent if we so choose. So, while we may walk around in our daily lives assuming the liberal intent and spirit of the Constitution, conservative Supreme Court justices have turned that intent on its head, giving law enforcement powers that are directly contrary to both our formally recognized Fourth Amendment rights and our unenumerated, but no less real, "lived" rights.

We are naive if we assume that just because the spirit and intent of our Constitution is liberal that conservative changes to the letter of the law will not undermine and negate those founding principles. But if we do not understand the liberal basis of our Constitution, we will fail to see how it is endangered and how to best defend it.

The Constitution—Liberal in Form and Content

Beyond the dry, dense, and parsed minutiae of the Supreme Court's application of the Fourth Amendment, there are "lived" rights that we have come to believe we have. As constitutional scholar Akil Reed Amar colorfully writes: "Nothing in the written Constitution explicitly guarantees the right to have a pet dog, to play the fiddle...or to wear a hat."[17] Yet we have all these rights without even considering them as "rights." As Amar notes: they are "simply facts of life."[18]

These "lived rights" are not illusory, made up, or wishful thinking on our part. They inform the Constitution itself and are both recognized (at times) and denied and disregarded (at times) by the Supreme Court and law enforcement. They are exalted in the other foundational documents noted above and we consider them to be part of our birthright as Americans. The fact that they are not explicitly written down does not make them any less real. Sandra Bland's objections to being asked to put out her cigarette (and refusing), being ordered to step out of her car (and refusing), and to being arrested (for refusing to get out of her car) all reflect a sense of lived rights - *This is not how I should be treated as an American.*

A bird's eye view of the Constitution reveals a radical and fundamental bias in the way in which laws and rights must interact. The pre-Amendment Constitution concerns itself with the ways in which America's government should arrange itself: the branches of government and the relationships among them, and how we, the people, will elect them. It says virtually nothing about either laws (other than that Congress will pass them and the President will - or will not - sign them), or the rights of citizens or their relation to government. Then come the amendments, specifically the first ten amendments, collectively known as The Bill of Rights, and after the Civil War, the Thirteenth and Fourteenth Amendments.

What is fundamental to the constitutional amendments is that they explicitly identify both specific and unenumerated rights instead of laws. Thus, it is our rights and not our laws that form the basis of the social contract among Americans. Simply put, before we, as Americans, make any law, which by its nature restricts our freedom, we must first measure it against our rights. And because rights have primacy, we can then understand that Amar's "lived" rights are not fanciful, or "granted" to us by the government, but rightfully "assumed" by us. They are our birthright, as the Declaration of Independence states: "all men are created equal...endowed by their Creator with certain unalienable rights..."

The default setting of the Constitution is that we, as citizens, have whatever rights we can conceive of until denied by law. A law, if it does not infringe on those rights, can then be called "constitutional." It is our rights that have primacy, and laws, insofar as they protect our mutual rights by restricting some other freedoms, are grudgingly legitimized, only after careful consideration.

One way to appreciate both the subtly and the importance of this structure is to consider its opposite: an "Un-Constitution." What would that look like? An Un-Constitution would replace rights with laws. So instead of a right of freedom of speech, we would have a constitutional law against all political speech. If you spoke about something that might be considered "political," you could be charged with a crime. If there was some question about the charge against you, your case might be brought before the Supreme Court, who would decide if you had violated the law against free speech.

Likewise, instead of a right against unreasonable search and seizure, all searches and seizures would be deemed lawful unless proved otherwise. Basically, you would have no rights except those granted in the shadow of the laws restricting all freedoms. This is, in fact, how the Chinese system works. There is a right to free speech except when it contravenes any of a slew of government laws and regulations that effectively allow the government to control all the views that get expressed.[19] Freedom of speech is, in China, not a right but a privilege, controlled and granted by the government.

Our social contract presumes we are accorded rights first and then laws second, insofar as they do not transgress those rights. The great importance of this is that it places laws in their proper place in our social contract. The contract itself, by the very way it is formulated, demands that we remain vigilant about laws which grant our government, and law enforcement in particular, more power, more discretion, and more leeway to restrict our rights, whatever we believe those rights to be. This is why the Constitution specifically speaks of other retained rights in the Ninth Amendment[20] and "privileges and immunities" in the Fourteenth Amendment, none of which are specified. They are not specified because they are rights in general, not specific rights, and are our birthright. It is laws, which restrict our freedoms, that must be specified and not assumed.

That is why we (myself - having my bank account emptied before I was even charged with a crime; Tom - shoved face down in the mud, falsely accused of stealing tools that were his; Jill - pulled over as a suspected drug runner only to have her car stripped and left in pieces on the highway; and Sandra Bland - ordered out of her car for refusing to put out her cigarette and then arrested for resisting that order) had this feeling of incredulity coupled with outrage. We have been rocked in a cradle of rights since we were born. Taught by our parents, our teachers, our peers, the books we read, and the movies we watch - even by strangers on the street - that a priori, as Americans - we are deserving of respect. Respect is a lived right, as real as any other right in a country founded on rights.

If basic respect is a fundamental lived right, how is it that this government servant has the power to humiliate and abuse me with no cause? It is like being in another country. You don't speak the language; the rules are different, and nothing makes any sense.

The Ninth Amendment reads as follows: *"The enumeration in the Constitution, of certain rights, shall not be construed to deny or disparage others retained by the people."*[21]

None of these other rights is specified. What do we make of this? Constitutional scholar Amar concludes that these "other unspecified rights" are quite fluid and are "what the people believe their rights to be at any given moment."[22]

So how is it that our "lived rights" with respect to law enforcement's authority seem to be completely out of touch and at odds with the legal right of the police to inflict all manner of harm, insult, disrespect, and even death upon so many of the citizens they purport to serve?

To gain some measure of understanding here, we have to, once again, turn to the Supreme Court.

Time and again, the Court has struck the "balance" between police powers and individual rights in favor of the police – until "balance" is nothing more than an illusion. Our lived rights no longer exist except as arbitrary and at-the-discretion-of decisions by individual police officers, which of course means they are no longer rights. They are privileges selectively granted by the government.

The Constitution reflects the intensity of the founders' desire to protect the underdog, the minority, the weaker party against the power of overreaching governmental (and, by implication, non-governmental) authority. Thus, it is hard for conservatives to wrap themselves in the flag when they fundamentally don't believe that rights and freedoms should be available to all. Conservatives overcome this bias by a providing a continual drumbeat of threats for those who can be swayed by a social context in which they feel especially fearful and threatened. Under such threats, conservativism seems a safer, more prudent, and logical choice. You willingly cede your rights to the government because you assume that the government's additional powers will only be used against those other "bad" Americans.

Until they aren't. Until you find yourself on the other end of the safety-and-security equation, stripped of your rights, your freedoms, and your privacy.

Sandra Bland's treatment by Officer Encina is an example of how constitutional law (his order to have her exit her vehicle) can be twisted to serve the arbitrary and unjust actions of a single government agent (or the entire government). When police forces proudly state that they obey the Constitution, that is small comfort when we understand that the Constitution can just as easily justify the abuse of power as it can protect us from that abuse. The devil is always in the details. How is the law applied, and does it encourage or discourage the better angels of our nature?

Social Norms, Laws, and Abuse of Discretionary Powers (The Road to Hell is Paved with Good Intentions)

If one of our unenumerated rights ("This is the way we do things here in America") is to be accorded a minimum level of respect by our government, and the Supreme Court continually decides that law enforcement should possess increasing powers to invade our privacy and search our persons in the name of "officer safety" or "stopping crime," then these seemingly laudable goals open the door to the legally sanctioned abuse of these powers.

In each of these Supreme Court cases – and there are well over a hundred of them at this point – that continue to expand police powers, a gap is opened between the intent of the increased power and the potential for it to be an abuse of power. This gap is called "discretionary" power.

Most if not all of us who drive have experienced the discretionary power of law enforcement. If you have ever been pulled over for a driving infraction, you may have had the officer let you off with a warning (at his discretion), or knock your speeding ticket down a few miles per hour to save you some money (at his discretion), or written a ticket for only one infraction when he could have written you up for several (at his discretion). Alternatively, you may have received no break whatsoever, also at the officer's "discretion."

Discretion is the human factor in the application of any law. It is the spirit and intent behind the law as expressed by the individual applying it. The potential to abuse power falls under the concept of "discretionary power" and is sort of the corollary of our rights. Just as we can choose to be our best selves as we exercise our rights, the police can "choose" to exercise their powers (rights) with discretion, either to use them respectfully in the spirit they were intended or to demean, humiliate, injure, or even kill.

The Supreme Court, which legitimizes or denies police powers when held up against our rights as citizens, helps to create a culture in which the abuse of power can flourish. Even if these police powers are granted with the best of intentions – to stop crime, to keep officers safe, to protect the public - they have the corrosive effect of sanctioning the misuse of power, however unintentionally. It just makes it too easy for officers, who have all the same human flaws we all have, to behave badly. The authors of the Constitution knew this, which is why they placed citizen rights above those of the government. Power too easily brings out the worst in any of us.

The Court could just as easily limit police powers in a way that points police in the direction of respect for citizens instead of bullying. The balance lies in either honoring the Constitution's clear intention of favoring the individual's Fourth Amendment rights and freedoms over the officer's powers or not. As Justice William Douglas wrote: "The

Constitution is not neutral."[23]

Sandra Bland did not break the law by telling Officer Encina that she was upset about him giving her a ticket. But at that moment, Encina *chose* to abuse his discretionary power. First, he "asked" Bland to put out her cigarette. Bland, registering the complete change in his tone and his request (phrased as a question, but having the tone of an order), refused. She asserted her right to smoke in her car. Encina then abused his power (his ability to order Bland out of her vehicle) to demean and humiliate her. She was no more of a threat to him after she refused to put out her cigarette than she was before. The law didn't *require* him to order her out of her car, but it did *allow* him to.

Notice that laws in general restrict us from harming others (in this case, the law was supposedly protecting Officer Encina from a potential assault by Bland); they do not promote our aspirations or our better selves.

The law against murder serves to preserve our lives, but it says nothing about treating others with respect, compassion, or kindness. Likewise, laws prohibiting theft preserve our personal property, but say nothing about treating others fairly in consensual business dealings. Even seat belt laws, which have been challenged in court as infringing on our right to privacy – to choose whether we want to wear a seat belt - have been upheld because non-seat-belted drivers are more likely to cause injury to others than seat-belted drivers. Again, harm to others generally trumps your right (freedom) to "do whatever I want" or even to harm yourself. The general principle of our social contract is that the balance between freedom and security rests on whether your freedom infringes on someone else's life, liberty, and pursuit of happiness.*

---

* With some notable hypocritical exceptions, this is clearly not true in the case of drug laws which involve consensual "harm," which can easily be construed as an individual "freedom." No one forces anyone else to ingest drugs. The war on drugs has been an unqualified failure as a means of restricting their use. And legal drugs such as alcohol and tobacco cause far more direct harm both to the actual users and non-users than do illicit drugs.

It quickly becomes clear that, in general, laws function as a deterrent and prohibition against our worst tendencies, but do not require that we behave in ways that provide "liberty and justice for all,"[25] or "the riches of freedom and the security of justice."[26]

At best, our laws infer what we aspire to be by telling us what we cannot be: a murderer, a thief, a trespasser. A law may protect a right, as the law against murder protects our right to life. But we have many more rights than there are laws to protect them. At best, laws point to their opposite, but they cannot require us - by any force, direct or indirect - to be kind, just, compassionate, or fair. To rise to those heights, we must be taught by example, learn from experience, and demand it from ourselves and others, including law enforcement. But even if we cannot legislate "doing what is right," our laws, based on principles of justice, can either encourage or discourage those aspirations. They can either extend the opportunity for those with power to abuse their power or they can limit that potential.

When the Supreme Court sanctions such discretion (and we allow them to do so), we permit wide latitude for law enforcement to act with cruelty, prejudice, and arbitrariness, even as it claims to be acting fairly "under the law." Officer Encina's treatment of Bland shows how discretionary power can work to encourage a culture of abuse and bullying.

It should also give us pause when we hear our politicians speak of our country following "the rule of law,"[27] (as opposed to the "rule of men" based on arbitrary and personal whim) in a tone that suggests some fair and impartial process. What we too easily forget, because it is often hidden from view, is that the law is ultimately applied by human beings who will at times apply it with all the pettiness, cruelty, and unfairness that all human beings are capable of - given, yes, discretionary power.[28] Besides willful abuse of that power, there is much recent research that shows that bias and prejudice often operate unconsciously even when we are trying to be impartial.[29]

We are not compelled to treat people kindly any more than Officer Brian Encina was "compelled" to give Sandra Bland a lawful order to get out of her vehicle. But the law gave him the authority to do so. He could also grant her the "privilege" of remaining in her car, smoking her cigarette. But she no longer had that right. He was legally empowered to be a bully, to treat her with disrespect, and to ignore her right to smoke in her vehicle and not be touched by the officer or exit the vehicle. His rights as a law enforcement officer trumped her rights as a citizen. That is not the intent of our Constitution. Undoubtedly, it was not the intent of the conservatives on the Supreme Court when they decided Pennsylvannia v. Mimms. But instead of heeding the Constitution's instruction to place citizens' rights before government power, they placed ill-founded faith in the police. The road to hell is paved with good intentions.

If Bland had complied with Encina's lawful order to exit her car, she probably would have been searched, ticketed, and let go. She would have been demeaned and humiliated, but she would have remained free. Most of us would have taken the humiliation and, as Tom Canard said, "lost all respect for the police." But if we are to live up to the ideals we hold dear, it is incumbent upon us to defend our rights - maybe not the way Sandra Bland did, but through organized, public, and overtly political action.

There is no "right" here when it comes to rights. To a large extent, we each get to choose which rights we believe we have and then to exercise our ability to persuade, convince, and cajole our spouse, neighbors, colleagues, and friends of the value of equality, justice, and freedom – rather than inequality and servitude - as we understand them, and to entwine our lived rights with our legal rights. There is no guarantee that liberty and justice will prevail. Indeed, if the American people decide that giving up some or all of their rights is worth some promise of safety and security, then we will have no rights. That is entirely possible as the Constitution is written, and it is an open question as to how far down that road we have already gone.

The Constitution is very clear in its form as well as its spirit and intent that restricting the abuse of discretionary power by government and government-like actors is of the highest good. If mistakes are to be made, they should err on the side of protecting the individual against the abuse of power by the government and those with the means and power to control the government. This is why the vote was initially accorded to every white man (as opposed to only men who owned property - i.e. the wealthy), and then extended to all men and eventually all women - though not without ongoing attempts to disenfranchise voters through literacy tests, poll taxes, and now voter identification requirements. The intent of the latter efforts is to deny a group or class of people their democratic rights. The intent of the Constitution is equally clear: to reduce the potential for those with wealth and power to control the levers of governmental power to achieve their own selfish ends.

Yet when the Court continues to extend ever more power to law enforcement at the expense of citizen rights, it sends an unmistakable message to those in power: *Your powers take precedence over citizens' rights. If there is any question on which side of that equation you should be, asserting your authority is paramount. The rights of the American citizen are secondary.* This was never the intent of our Constitution.

While there are many other factors contributing to a police culture of bullying, the legal sanction for the abuse of discretionary power is unequivocal. *Officer Encina, you can order someone out of their car for your own safety, but you also have the discretion to order someone out of their car to humiliate and demean them, just to show them who is boss. They may think they have rights, but you have power and the legal authority.* That is the message we are sending our police departments. And power - and abuse of power - in law enforcement, thanks to the Supreme Court, now trumps our rights. Even our right to life.

Solutions and Examples

Richmond, California, where I have lived for the past three years, provides one of the most dramatic and inspiring examples of a transformation in law enforcement in a city that had been plagued by violence, poverty, unemployment, and an antagonistic relationship between its police and the majority/minority community that calls Richmond home.

For most of its existence, Richmond has been a company town, dominated by a huge Chevron refinery and the adjoining offices that employ more than 1,200 people in a city of 103,000. During World War II, Richmond boomed, with a Kaiser shipbuilding plant and other war efforts (home of the original "Rosie the Riveter"), along with an influx of African-Americans from all over the South to provide much-needed labor for these production facilities.

In postwar years, Richmond underwent a gradual, corrosive deindustrialization that many Midwest cities experienced. Factories shut down as manufacturing moved overseas; well-paying middle-class jobs disappeared; gangs and drug dealers took their place among the empty lots and abandoned buildings. By 2004, Richmond ranked eleventh on the list of the most dangerous cities in America.[30] The city was run as a patronage system in which local companies (Chevron, most significantly), unions, and developers made both campaign and charitable contributions to various organizations and politicians in exchange for sweetheart deals that left the community without jobs, public services or protections from the environmental degradation that Chevron imposed and previous businesses had left behind.

But in 2005, the citizens of Richmond elected a mayor and a slate of candidates who, though branded as "radicals," did nothing more or less than advocate for the local citizenry - making jobs, housing, and environmental concerns the leading priorities, along with reforming Richmond's corrupt, "good old boys" police department.

The city hired Chris Magnus, as unlikely a candidate as you could imagine, as the new police chief. Magnus was white, gay, and most recently the Chief or Police in lily-white Fargo, North Dakota. Nonetheless, Magnus quickly reorganized the department, placing reform-minded officers in charge while leaving other officers with more seniority serving under them. This caused significant resentment and lawsuits against the department by its own officers, but in the end, Magnus was vindicated both on the street and in court. From 2007 to 2015, Richmond recorded only one fatal shooting by police. Violent crime was down. Property crime was down.

Part of that success was due to the creation of the Office of Neighborhood Safety (ONS), which received city funding to employ six full-time youth mentors to work with the city's worst gang members by offering them job training, counseling, life skills classes, and even financial incentives to change the path they were on. On the street, Magnus had officers connecting with the community, reaching out, getting to know people, and working with groups to solve problems as opposed to just "fighting crime." Another community group, Richmond Ceasefire, brought together church leaders, community groups, and the police for nighttime walks to reclaim violence-plagued neighborhoods, and actively sought out known shooters to offer them a choice: Change your behavior with community support or expect to go to prison.

In the case of every initiative that helped move the city of Richmond in a better direction, there were no laws *requiring* these efforts. Chief Magnus, his officers, and the community chose to do the *right* thing, rather than just the *legal* thing. Many police departments claim with pride that they police "constitutionally," but that is cold comfort to anyone who understands the Constitution as it is now interpreted and applied. Constitutional policing represents the bare minimum of a standard that police should meet. To truly serve and protect the community, the police need to go far beyond what is legal and do what is right. What is right is something that each community can and should define for itself, working with their local police department. To find out more about what efforts are underway to foster better policing in your community, do an internet search for "police community programs."

CHAPTER FIVE

Use of Force

You're a chickenshit motherfucker.
— Officer Scott Tobler (Sidney, Nebraska, June 27, 2013) to a couple asserting their right to record him on video

I don't care what the Supreme Court [says].
— Trooper Donald Fougere (New York City, September 25, 2015) to a videographer outside trooper headquarters

Police Power and Your Body

The lurid and tragic videos of unarmed citizens being gunned down by the police take on deeper and more complex meanings when placed in a larger context. The use of excessive force and the unjustified use of lethal force by law enforcement are the logical and inevitable worst-case manifestations of a police culture founded on the systemic abuse of power.

But if that context explains why such killings occur, it does not explain how it is that officers are almost never held accountable, either criminally or civilly, for these types of deaths. The specific legal exceptions accorded law enforcement when it comes to use of force shed light on how this bully culture is enabled by our legal system. It is worth taking a closer look at the ways in which police are empowered to use force because not just your rights, but your life, may depend on some understanding of what the police can and cannot do to you when it comes to force and what you can do to protect yourself and change use-of-force policy in your police department.

When it comes to force, instead of doing "what's right," police can claim they are doing "what's legal" and leave it at that. Or as the videos described below illustrate, some officers dispense with what is legal altogether and act out their worst impulses because they live in a culture and a system that tacitly condones such behavior. When it comes to the use of force, what is right and what is legal would seem to reside in entirely different countries. And even doing what is legal is sometimes viewed by the police as an annoying inconvenience of policing in America. The idea of upholding the law in the process of enforcing it seems positively anathema to some in law enforcement.

However, as you view video after video of police hitting,

beating, and shooting citizens in what seem to be entirely unjustifiable circumstances, there are just as many defenders of the police who claim that these videos do not show the whole story, or the officer's perspective, in terms of a *perceived* threat to his life or other factors that they believe explain and - legally if not morally - justify these behaviors.

This defense of virtually any use of force by the police, no matter the circumstance, is based on a fundamentally flawed view of the relationship between law enforcement and the community. It holds that because the police are there to protect us, any violation of our rights by the police, including all manner of assaults and even killings, must be excused because law enforcement is the only thing standing between us and those "others," i.e. the criminals.

The problem with this argument is that it supports and fosters a police culture that makes all of us, criminals or not, criminally suspect first and citizens with rights second, if at all. These videos are testament to that reality. This is exactly what Justice Sonia Sotomayor meant when she wrote in her dissent in Utah v. Strieff: "*...your body is subject to invasion while the courts excuse the violation of your rights. It implies that you are not a citizen of a democracy but the subject of a carceral state, just waiting to be cataloged.*"[1] Yet many Americans seem quite willing to live in a carceral state – provided, of course, that it is only those "other people" who are subject to its excesses.

The legal basis on which this unconstitutional "invasion of your body" rests is found in two Supreme Court cases. In the parlance of the Constitution, the use of force by police is a form of "seizure," the ultimate "seizure" being the use of lethal force. As such, it is once again the Fourth Amendment, which protects us against unreasonable search and seizure, that must be interpreted to find the balance between government use of force against its citizens and the citizens' right to be free of being "seized" to the point of injury or death. The Court laid out its challenge quite succinctly in Tennessee v. Garner (1985), the first of two cases that have formed the basis of all police use of force since.

"Apprehension by the use of deadly force is a seizure subject to the Fourth Amendment's reasonableness requirement. To determine whether such a seizure is reasonable, the extent of the intrusion on the suspect's rights under that Amendment must be balanced against the governmental interests in effective law enforcement. This balancing process demonstrates that, notwithstanding probable cause to seize a suspect, an officer may not always do so by killing him. The use of deadly force to prevent the escape of all felony suspects, whatever the circumstances, is constitutionally unreasonable."[2]

The Court saying to law enforcement in so many words that "even if someone has committed a crime and is trying to escape, you can't just shoot them!" is disconcerting, at least to my mind. It reveals a degree of violence and power inherent in policing that many of us would prefer to consign to episodes of our favorite – fictional – TV drama. But no, it's all too real.

This ruling would appear to be a victory for citizens' Fourth Amendment rights. After all, the Court held that even when police had probable cause to believe a suspect had committed a crime, specifically a felony, they could not simply kill him in the process of trying to make an arrest, but could only do so under certain circumstances, specified as follows:

"...such force may not be used unless necessary to prevent the escape and the officer has probable cause to believe that the suspect poses a significant threat of death or serious physical injury to the officer or others."[3]

The example in this case was the 1974 shooting (and subsequent death) of Edward Garner (no relation to Eric

Garner), an eighteen-year-old black man, in Memphis, Tennessee, by Officer Elton Hymon. Garner had apparently burglarized a home and was making his escape when Officer Hymon arrived on the scene. It was dark out, and Hymon heard a back door slam and saw a figure running across the backyard of the house. Here is how the Court described what happened next:

"With the aid of a flashlight, Hymon was able to see Garner's face and hands. He saw no sign of a weapon, and, though not certain, was "reasonably sure" and "figured" that Garner was unarmed. He thought Garner was 17 or 18 years old and about 5' 5" or 5' 7" tall. While Garner was crouched at the base of the fence, Hymon called out "police, halt" and took a few steps toward him. Garner then began to climb over the fence. Convinced that if Garner made it over the fence he would elude capture, Hymon shot him. The bullet hit Garner in the back of the head. Garner was taken by ambulance to a hospital, where he died on the operating table. Ten dollars and a purse taken from the house were found on his body."[4]

What the Court left undecided was what constituted a danger to the officer and the public. A suspect with a gun, or a knife? With more than 300 million guns in the hands of Americans, how do you determine which legally armed citizen is a threat? What constitutes a "threat?" What if the suspect is not threatening the use of the weapon? Could he still be shot? Does a verbal threat constitute a danger that warrants shooting a suspect? What if the suspect might be armed, or might not be? Does just the possibility of an armed suspect justify an officer killing a potentially unarmed person? The possibilities seem endless.

In 1989, the Court took up these very questions in the case of Graham v. Connor.

DeThorne Graham was a diabetic experiencing an insulin reaction. He asked a friend, William Berry, to drive him to a convenience store to purchase a sugar drink. But there was a long line inside, so he entered the store and exited it immediately. This was observed by Officer Connor, who thought he might have just witnessed a robbery. He stopped Graham and Berry in the car Berry was driving (on their way to a nearby friend's house). Unconvinced of Graham's claim that he was diabetic, Connor called for backup while trying to determine if a robbery had taken place. By this time, Graham had lost consciousness. The Court describes what happened next:

"In the ensuing confusion, a number of other Charlotte police officers arrived on the scene in response to Officer Connor's request for backup. One of the officers rolled Graham over on the sidewalk and cuffed his hands tightly behind his back, ignoring Berry's pleas to get him some sugar. Another officer said:

"'I've seen a lot of people with sugar diabetes that never acted like this. Ain't nothing wrong with the M.F. but drunk. Lock the S.B. up.'

"Several officers then lifted Graham up from behind, carried him over to Berry's car, and placed him face down on its hood. Regaining consciousness, Graham asked the officers to check in his wallet for a diabetic decal that he carried. In response, one of the officers told him to 'shut up' and shoved his face down against the hood of the car. Four officers grabbed Graham and threw him headfirst into the police car. A friend of Graham's brought some orange juice to the car, but the officers refused to let him have it. Finally, Officer Connor received a report that Graham had done nothing wrong at the convenience store, and the officers drove him home and released him."[5]

Graham ended up with a broken foot, cuts on his wrists, a bruised forehead, an injured shoulder, and a permanent ringing in his ears. Graham sued Officer Conner for excessive use of force in violation of his Fourth Amendment right against unreasonable search and seizure. The Court then clarified very specifically, but broadly, what use of force was reasonable and how it was to be determined and by whom.

Justice Rehnquist, for the majority: *"The 'reasonableness' of a particular use of force must be judged from the perspective of a reasonable officer on the scene, rather than with the 20/20 vision of hindsight. ...The calculus of reasonableness must embody allowance for the fact that police officers are often forced to make split-second judgments – in circumstances that are tense, uncertain, and rapidly evolving – about the amount of force that is necessary in a particular situation."*[6]

The impact of this ruling on law enforcement's ability to use force without fear of legal consequences cannot be overestimated. In this case, the standard for determining acceptable use of force by the police was now based on "the [subjective] perspective of a reasonable officer on the scene." Furthermore, what might be considered the more objective perspective of 20/20 hindsight was specifically disallowed. In addition, no matter how bad the officer's judgment might appear to be after the fact (shooting an unarmed suspect who was simply reaching for his wallet, as has happened numerous times in previous years), "an allowance for the fact that police officers are often forced to make split-second decision" must be given priority. These entirely subjective judgments that now determine if force is justified were called "objective reasonableness" by the Court.

From the perspective of law enforcement, all of these exceptions seem perfectly sensible and justifiable. After all, if police officers are so paralyzed by the fear of making a wrong decision in a life-threatening situation, they and the citizens they are sworn to protect might end up dead at the hands of a criminal. What purpose would that serve? This formulation allows the police to go out and do their best to stop the bad guys while acknowledging and excusing them from making the occasional "mistake," even if that mistake costs some innocent person his life.

What this calculus fails to account for, however, is a context in which police constantly feel their lives are threatened – that they are under attack, if not physically, then certainly emotionally and psychologically. The police are so primed and ready to believe their lives are in danger that they now confuse and conflate citizens *standing up for their rights* as an imminent danger to an officer's life. They see life-threatening danger where there is no danger. They treat a citizen attempting to assert her rights as an indicator of mortal threat. And that threat must be dealt with in the most aggressive and assertive fashion - i.e. with force, citizen rights be damned. So, Dethorne Graham, whom the police only *suspected* of robbery and who was posing no threat, reasonably had his foot broken, his wrists cut, his shoulder injured, and his hearing permanently damaged in the process of being detained.

To understand how police can react violently when a citizen is simply affirming his or her constitutional rights, consider two videos I came across during my research. They do not end in violence, but they clearly illustrate how even citizens posing no threat except the threat of asserting their rights throw police officers into paroxysms of rage and complete disregard for the law they are supposed to uphold.

In the first video, officer Scott Tobler objects to being videotaped by a citizen as he investigates a broken window complaint. The courts have generally ruled that filming public officials carrying out their duties in public is protected by the First Amendment right to free speech, provided there is not direct physical interference of the officer carrying out his duties. In this case, the officer was being filmed from a vehicle some distance away.

The officer approaches the vehicle and demands to see the

driver's license, registration, and insurance. The driver, Steven Bell, asks if he has committed a crime or if he is being detained on "reasonable suspicion." Tobler, having no cause to detain him, says nothing, but continues to demand the driver's identification, a violation of Bell's Fourth Amendment right against unreasonable search and seizure. Nonetheless, Bell complies with this illegal demand, and then when Tobler confirms he is not being detained, Bell requests his ID back "since I am free to go."

Again, Tobler ignores Bell's rights and starts questioning him about why he is following him around. Bell, asserting his right not to answer any of Tobler's questions because Tobler has just acknowledged he is not being detained, refuses to respond. Tobler then threatens Bell with arrest for obstructing him in his duties by distracting him with his presence. When Bell insists that he is well within his legal rights to drive by a crime scene as many times as he wishes, Tobler goes ballistic, screaming at Bell inches from his face, culminating in his denouement: "You're a chickenshit motherfucker!" at which point his fellow officer physically restrains him from what seems to be potential violence.

While one can argue the degree to which Bell was or was not distracting Tobler from his duties, the reality this video reveals is the legal double standard under which the police so often operate. They invoke their full legal rights against any criminal liability for shooting unarmed citizens, but cannot contain their rage when a citizen actually insists on his right to videotape the officer, a public official, in the execution of his duties in a public space. It illustrates an irreducible truth: You can't gain the trust and respect of the citizens you serve when you selectively apply the law to serve your personal definition of justice.

In the second video we will consider, New York Trooper Donald Fougere confronts Adam Rupeka for videotaping trooper headquarters from a public sidewalk. Fougere demands to see some identification, and Rupeka explains that unless he has committed a crime, or the trooper suspects he is about to commit a crime, he doesn't have to identify himself. Fougere continues to insist, so Rupeka calmly explains that the Supreme Court has determined that it is perfectly legal for him to film whatever he wishes in a public place, and since he is not committing a crime, he doesn't have to provide any identification. At which point Fougere responds: "I don't care what the Supreme Court [says]. ...You can cite whatever you want."

It goes without saying that should Fougere shoot an unarmed person under questionable circumstances in the future, he will care very much what the Supreme Court has said.

What is particularly interesting about these citizen/police interactions is that they are sometimes partially "staged" by citizens in much the same way that secret shoppers are sent into retail stores or undercover diners are placed in restaurants: to find out if employees are adhering to the policies and standards of the establishment. In this case, the question is: Are police officers upholding the law as they enforce it?

Because these citizens are prepared for a confrontation, they take all necessary precautions to avoid the risks that an unsuspecting citizen might inadvertently take that would justify an officer's use of force. They remain calm, they are not physically aggressive in any way, they are not committing any crime, and they inform the officers of their purpose and their legal rights. Yet even in such benign and unthreatening circumstances, the officers take umbrage at their authority being questioned to the point where - in the first video - Officer Tobler starts to attack the citizen and must be restrained by a fellow officer. In the second video, Officer Fougere remains relatively calm, but informs the citizen that when it comes to his rights, he "[doesn't] care what the Supreme Court [says.]"

Such rage might be somewhat amusing in any other context in which a calm, thoughtful person easily gets the better of a mean-spirited bully. But these are heavily armed officers used to having things their way, no matter what. The threat of violence on the part of the officers in these confrontations is palpable. Only the calm demeanor of the videographers and the intervention of other officers prevent them from escalating the conflict into a use-of-force situation with potentially lethal results.

In such a police culture, the Court's use-of-force decision provides virtually any officer who feels his life is threatened for any reason, or no reason at all, the option to use violence - even lethal force - with impunity. In the case of Eric Garner, choked to death by officer Daniel Pantaleo for allegedly selling cigarettes on the street, a grand jury declined to charge Pantaleo with any crime.

Many people were outraged at this apparent injustice. But consider the story Pantaleo told the grand jury. According to his attorney,[7][*] Pantaleo explained that when he jumped on Garner's back and put his arm around Garner's neck, he was attempting to use an approved police use-of-force hold designed to throw a person off balance and bring them to the ground. But Garner didn't go down, and Pantaleo feared that he would be shoved through the plate-glass window that was just behind him as he tried to bring Garner down. At that point, he began choking Garner to death.

Once Pantaleo had invoked the "life-threatening danger" he felt he was under, his use of lethal force was legally justified, according to Graham v. Connor. No one could say he hadn't felt threatened because no second guessing of

[*] The grand jury testimony was sealed so this account was reported by Pantaleo's attorney in the Washington Post, Dec 4, 2014, www.washingtonpost.com/news/morning-mix/wp/2014/12/04/report-what-the-lawyer-for-the-nypd-officer-told-the-grand-jury-about-the-death-of-eric-garneric-garner/?tid=a_inl

police officers is permitted under the ruling. Nor could there be any consideration of the larger context of why Pantaleo chose to use physical force in the first place on a suspect who was not armed, not threatening, and was not resisting arrest except verbally, asking politely that the officers not touch him.

The only reason Pantaleo was in danger was the result of his own actions. Yet the entire context in which Pantaleo chose to use force in the first place, which put him in a situation that caused him to feel his life was in danger, was immaterial. And the standard for determining the reasonableness of his actions was, as the Court had instructed, based on those of a "reasonable officer on the scene." The court has handed over the determination of "objective reasonableness" to the subjective judgment of the police themselves. The police are now arbiters of what is and what is not "reasonable" under the circumstances. Given that any officer who uses force must, perforce, consider it reasonable or else he shouldn't be using it almost requires that his fellow officers find whatever force that's used to be reasonable – by definition of having used it at all. The circularity of this logic is impenetrable. The grand jury came to the inevitable and forgone conclusion that Graham requires: Pantaleo had acted "reasonably" in his use of force based on the legal standards under which he was operating. He felt his life was in danger. Never mind that he had put his own life in danger by choosing to jump on Eric Garner and wrestle him to the ground rather than de-escalating the confrontation and trying to resolve it without force.

As the law currently stands, an officer can escalate a conflict until he feels his life is threatened, shoot that person, and then justify his shooting by citing the very threat that he created by his own aggressive actions.

Taken individually, all of these legal protections afforded police as they go about their duties seem eminently reasonable *if* one assumes that the first priority of the police is to protect and serve its citizens – even its criminal citizens, even when it puts the police themselves at risk. But when the police view citizens as the enemy – when they are fearful, paranoid, and have as their top priority "making it home at night" - these reasonable legal protections become license to assault, injure, and even kill "so I can make it home." These laws do protect police officers in cases in which their lives are truly endangered, but also protect officers and their departments from any accountability in cases where the very culture of policing results in the unnecessary, unjustified use of force, even lethal force.

The problem with these rulings is that they provide no mechanism for the community, with whom the police directly interact, to develop, create, and change the ways in which they interact. These rulings deprive citizens of the most basic constitutional intent - that the government derive its powers from the consent of the governed. How do we, as a community, want to be policed?

In these rulings, the government - specifically the police - cannot be second guessed, except by other police. They do not derive their power from our consent. They have derived it from the Supreme Court. And the Court has decided that any decisions regarding use of force are only subject to the standards of the police themselves. The equation requiring citizen consent is replaced with no balance between the citizens' rights and the police officers' power. The use of that power is entirely justified by the police themselves. Nor is there any means or method by which to address the larger context in which such decisions (to use force or not, to shoot or not, to tase or not) are made. The police control the context (I felt I was being threatened) and thus the result (so I shot/choked/tased, beat him), no matter how unjustified.

What many outside observers find disturbing is that these officers are almost never held accountable for their actions.

What is more problematic is that the system and culture in which they work is never held accountable. Police immunity from criminal prosecution does not suggest that police officers get up in the morning and think: "I'm looking forward to shooting someone today because I know that I'll never be held either criminally or civilly liable for it." Rather, the law encourages and supports a culture of abuse and disrespect in which occasional excesses in use of force are just the "cost of doing business" in most departments. While they may be regrettable, they don't require that the agency in question examine, let alone change, the fundamental way in which it approaches policing, which ultimately leads to what the rest of the community finds to be outrageously unjust.

While these officers may have been negligent, showed poor judgment, and used excessive force, they did so with the tacit approval of their superiors and colleagues. Their actions, that time, just happened to result in a particularly bad, and public, outcome. If Eric Garner had not died from Detective Pantaleo's choke hold, would we have ever heard of Eric Garner? Almost certainly not. Garner's death begs the question of how police are allowed to abuse their powers in ways great and small in the first place, regardless of the outcome.

In so many other cases that never make the national news, but which are equally unjust, the local prosecutor declines to even present the case to a grand jury or a judge, having already concluded that no crime was committed. And why would they bring such charges? Most criminal offenses are prosecuted by local or county prosecutors. It is these same local prosecutors who work day in and day out with the police sending criminals to jail. The prosecutors are often in elected positions and they depend on the support of powerful police unions to get elected. Regardless of any claims of prosecutorial independence, filing criminal charges against a local police officer is highly political. Except in the most outrageous and egregious cases of inappropriate use of force, no prosecutor wants to criminally charge the very police she has to work with on a daily basis to protect the rest of the community. It's a clear conflict of interest that makes applying the law to potential police misconduct doubly difficult.

Civil Lawsuits

In many of the cases I've referenced, no criminal charges against the officers are ever brought. But the families of victims filed civil lawsuits that resulted in large cash settlements for the families. These civil lawsuits are only for monetary damages and do not require "guilt beyond a reasonable doubt," but a lower standard of proof known as "preponderance of evidence." It is easy to imagine that such cash settlements are tantamount to admissions of guilt by the officials whose agencies make these payments, and that these financial punishments would be significant deterrents from further use of excessive force. Sadly, such is not the case.

First, the officers sued are protected by qualified immunity, which allows government officials "to make reasonable but mistaken judgments"[8] in the execution of their duties. This is a seemingly reasonable approach to the problem of government officials being personally liable for executing their official duties in cases where there is some uncertainty about whether they are violating a citizen's rights. Or, as the Court described who immunity would not apply to: "The plainly incompetent or those who knowingly violate the law."[9]

As in all of these legal standards, however, the devil is in the details. What constitutes "plainly incompetent" and how do you prove someone "knowingly" violated the law if you can't get inside their heads? The Supreme Court continued to decide these questions in favor of law enforcement. In the case of Brosseau v. Haugen, they decided that the police deserved qualified immunity in the shooting of an unarmed man as he attempted to escape arrest.

"Qualified immunity shields an officer from suit when she makes a decision that, even if constitutionally deficient, reasonably misapprehends the law governing the circumstances she confronted. ...qualified immunity operates 'to protect officers from the sometimes hazy border between excessive and acceptable force.' Because the focus is on whether the officer had fair notice that her conduct was unlawful, reasonableness is judged against the backdrop of the law at the time of the conduct. If the law at that time did not clearly establish that the officer's conduct would violate the Constitution, the officer should not be subject to liability or, indeed, even the burdens of litigation."[10]

So, though the burden of proof is lower than in a criminal trial, a police officer is still given wide latitude to violate a person's civil rights, even to the point of "seizing" him by shooting him to death, even if those actions were violations of the Constitution, so long as they were "reasonable" violations under the circumstances. And the standard for "reasonableness" still remains the subjective judgment of the officer on the scene.

At this point, even when a civil lawsuit has been filed against the officer and it is not dismissed immediately by a judge using the "qualified immunity test," the officer is most often provided with legal defense by either the police union, or the city or county that employs him. And, if he should lose the case - or, more often, settle out of court, which is how most of these civil suits are resolved - neither the officer, the police department, or even the city admit any guilt, nor do they suffer any financial repercussions. In most cases, insurance companies and taxpayers pay the settlement. It's no wonder then, even when the city loses a civil lawsuit in the millions of dollars, that the officer involved is rarely, if ever disciplined at all, let alone fired. In the eyes of the department and the city, he was most likely acting in accordance with, if not the explicit departmental policies, certainly the unspoken cultural norms of the department - and simply had the rotten luck to get caught up in a "bad situation." In the larger context of law enforcement's culture of power, these "mistakes," no matter how outrageous, are just the cost of doing business.

Examples and Solutions

In an eighteen-month period in 2010/2011, Las Vegas police shot and killed fifteen citizens and were party to twenty-five officer-involved shootings.[11] A DOJ investigation soon followed that resulted in more than eighty recommended changes, most of which the department implemented. Since that time, the Las Vegas police have reduced the number of officer shootings per year by almost half,[12] with an average of six fatalities per year compared to twenty-five in 2010 and eighteen in 2011.[13]

How did they do it?

Not surprisingly, it was a combination of changing both the culture and the training in the department. Chief among the changes:

- More training and emphasis on de-escalation in citizen/police interactions
- Reality-based training in potential use-of-force scenarios – specifically creating much more ambiguous exercises, which officers would more likely encounter.
- Citizen oversight, coupled with several new internal review boards (Office of Internal Oversight, Use of Force Review Board, and a new Tactical Review

Board) that analyze department policies, training methods, and shooting statistics – and make the results public.

The Use of Force Review Board has a citizen majority of board members (one of only nine such majorities among more than 18,000 police departments throughout the United States), and their power is substantial. Here is how member Jay Bloom describes their scope of authority:

"We can determine that an incident is 'administratively approved' which means everything was done by the book and there was simply no other option for the officer. In that moment, death or serious injury was imminent for either the suspect, officers and/or civilian bystanders. By using deadly force, the officer hopefully saves the life of the innocent. This is the finding for which we hope in every use of force investigation.

- *"Alternatively, we can determine that an incident was approved, but there was a 'tactical or decision-making' issue. This means the officer had no choice but to use deadly force at that critical moment, but his or her decisions leading up to that point of no return could have been better. Could the officer have done things differently to have avoided the deadly encounter in the first place?*
- *"We can find that there was a policy or training failure, meaning that the officer did everything according to policy or training, but the policy or training has shortcomings and needs to be reviewed and/or modified.*
- *"The last option is administrative disapproval, meaning the use of force was not within policy nor compliant with the training Metro provides*

its officers. Depending on the severity, it can result in additional training, suspension, termination or even criminal prosecution for the officer.[13]

Note how the review board can examine and pass judgment on "decisions leading up to that point of no return." This is a huge departure from the federally sanctioned legal standard that specifically disallows the consideration of the larger context to be considered when determining the appropriateness of an officer's use of force. Now the question of how that use of force might have been avoided in the first place is taken into account. The question is not "did the officer feel his life was in danger at that moment," but "could the officer have de-escalated the situation, so he would never have felt his life was in danger."

Las Vegas is now a model for reducing the use of (potentially deadly) force throughout the country, though by its own admission, the changes it has implemented are just the beginning of the changes it needs to make. For more information on use of force and how to advocate for better use-of-force policies and training, visit: useofforce project.org.

CHAPTER SIX

A Tragedy in One Act

We must recognize the full human equality of all of our people before God, before the law, and in the councils of government. We must do this, not because it is economically advantageous, although it is; not because the laws of God command it, although they do; not because people in other lands wish it so.
We must do it for the single and fundamental reason that it is the right thing to do.

—**Robert Kennedy**, June 6, 1966 (Speech at the University of Cape Town, South Africa)

February 28, 2015

Do you recall the semester in high school when you studied one of Shakespeare's tragedies? For me it was *Macbeth*. The first thing we learned was that the definition of a tragedy is that the hero dies. The second thing we learned was the idea of the tragic or fatal flaw: a particular personal quality of the hero that in moderation might be a positive trait, but in excess and with no countervailing force, leads inexorably and inevitably to the downfall of the hero with exactly the opposite outcome the hero intended.

Taking his cue from Greek tragedy, Shakespeare's tragic heroes suffered from the most common fatal flaw – hubris: too much ambition, too much confidence, too much superiority – causing them to act when they should have rested, rest when they should have acted, lied when they should have been truthful, and been truthful when they should have lied. Meaning well, they ended up bringing death and despair to themselves and those they loved.

This tragedy is that of Sergeant Jonathan Frost of the Eaton County (Michigan) Sheriff's Department and Deven Guilford, a seventeen-year-old high school junior from Mulliken, a village in Eaton County, with a population of about 550. This tragedy particularly struck home with me because, despite my social conscience, I still harbored some thought that my whiteness and my son's white skin offered a measure of immunity from police violence. And like Deven Guilford, I could see my son attempting to stand up for his rights and coming to the same tragic result. This terrified me.

Drive west along I-96 from Detroit and you quickly escape the urban blight and struggling recovery of a globalized rust-belt American city. First rolling hills, then farms, then scrubby forests. There is nowhere in Michigan where you are more than six miles away from a body of water – a small lake, a river flowing into one of those lakes, or even one of the Great Lakes - Michigan, Huron, Superior, Erie. If you are of a certain age, you might begin to recall Hemingway's Nick Adams coming-of-age stories, all set in Michigan.

Lansing, the capital of the state, comes next. An hour-and-a-half from Detroit, it feels much farther. Like many state capitals, it was never a hub of commerce, but was picked as the capital to lessen the influence of bustling Detroit, already a burgeoning city in the mid-1800s. Lansing is something of a bucolic bureaucratic oasis of government, universities, and insurance companies. Hours are regular, jobs are tenured, wages are good, and homes are cheap. You can live well in Lansing, if not with the buzz and hum that comes with an economically booming metropolis.

To get to Mulliken, you now leave Lansing and the interstate and enter an entirely different America. On M-43, the truck stops fall away and the road becomes a two-lane highway with fewer cars. Farms bump up against the road, and in about twenty minutes you reach Grand Ledge, a town of about eight thousand where all the kids from the surrounding villages, including Mulliken, attend high school.

The high school is almost one-hundred percent white. This is not surprising since Eaton County itself is ninety-seven percent white. The average income is higher there than in nearby Lansing. It is a happily middle-class white suburban community, offering the affordable luxury of a semi-rural lifestyle for mid- and upper-income employees in Lansing. Deven Guilford was white. Deven's family owned a small construction company that Deven's parents, Brian and Becky, ran out of their home.

Deven attended high school in Grand Ledge. The night he died, February 28, 2015, was a Saturday. It was cold, with snow on the ground, but the roads were clear. He was returning home to Mulliken from Grand Ledge. He was driving his girlfriend's car. He was on M-43. Coming the other way was a car that appeared to have its high beams on. If you've ever had this experience, you know that high beams in your eyes on a two-lane highway is blinding. If the road you are on curves at that moment, you might not see the curve at all. Deven flashed his high beams at the other driver, the best way to let a driver know that his high beams are on.

The driver was Sergeant Jonathan Frost, 38 years old, white, and an eight-year veteran of the Eaton County Sheriff's Department. He was on duty, driving a new, marked 2015 Ford Explorer. When Deven flashed the sergeant, he quickly did a U-turn, turned on his flashing lights, and pulled Deven over for flashing his high beams at him. Five minutes and fourteen seconds later, the white, unarmed, seventeen-year-old boy was dead. Here is transcript of that five-minute interaction, which you can also view online, as captured by Sergeant Frost's body camera and, in part, by Deven Guilford's cell-phone video camera.

Sgt. Frost [speaking to himself]: Stopping this car for flashing me with their brights. I did not have my brights on. [First contact with Deven Guilford] Hello.

Deven Guilford: How are you doing?

Sgt. Frost: Can I get your driver's license, registration, proof of insurance, please. Pulled you over today 'cause you flashed me; I didn't even have my brights on.

Deven Guilford: Yes, you did, sir.

Sgt. Frost: Nope, I didn't, partner.

Deven Guilford: Sir…

Sgt. Frost: I'm telling you because when I turned around…

Deven: I couldn't see, I could not see.

Sgt. Frost: I didn't have 'em on, all right?

Deven Guilford: Dude, trust me, I, I know...

Sgt. Frost: Trust me, okay, I did not have them on. When I turned around I flashed them on to show you that they weren't on.

Deven Guilford: No, you turned them off when you came around.

Sgt. Frost: No, I didn't. Driver's license, registration.

Deven Guilford: I watched you turn them off.

Sgt. Frost: Driver's license, registration, proof of insurance, please. I did not have them on.

Deven Guilford: I did nothing wrong.

Sgt. Frost: Driver's license, registration, proof of insurance, please.

Deven Guilford: I don't even know you're an officer, three forms of identific... [unintelligible]

Sgt. Frost: Driver's license, registration, proof of insurance, please, you've been pulled over, my name is Sergeant Frost.

Deven Guilford: [unintelligible]

Sgt. Frost: My name is Sergeant Frost of the Eaton County Sheriff's Office.

Deven Guilford: Can I see your badge number?

Sgt. Frost: You cannot see my badge number. [speaking to dispatch] 2372 start me another car, please.

Deven Guilford [Guilford cell-phone video clip 1 begins]: I am video and audio recording for my safety and your safety.

Deven Guilford recorded the police stop on his cell in two different parts. This is part one.]

Sgt. Frost: That is absolutely fine, so am I.

Deven Guilford: You just told me that I could not have your badge number; that's against the law, sir.

Sgt. Frost: My badge number, no, you asked me to show it to you.

Deven Guilford: Yes, and you said no.

Sgt. Frost: I cannot show it to you, my badge number.

Deven Guilford: You told me no, is that correct?

Sgt. Frost: No, it's not.

Deven Guilford: That is correct, sir. Am I being detained?

Sgt. Frost: You have two choices at this point, sir.

Deven Guilford: Am I being detained?

Sgt. Frost: I'm giving you the option...

Deven Guilford: Am I being detained?

Sgt. Frost: Yes, you are.

Deven Guilford: For what crime?

Sgt. Frost: You flashed me with your high beams.

Deven Guilford: You had your brights on sir, I swear to God, you had your brights on.

Sgt. Frost: This is your option right now; you, right now, are refusing to give me your ID.

Deven Guilford: I have not committed a crime.

Sgt. Frost: Refusing to give me your ID in a traffic stop is a misdemeanor. Right now you are committing a misdemeanor. You have two choices: you can get with the program and start complying with this traffic stop or you're going to be taken to jail; those are your two choices. Driver's license, registration, and proof of insurance, please.

Deven Guilford: I do not have my license, sir. I am going to get it.

Sgt. Frost: You don't have your driver's license?

Deven Guilford: I do not have it.

Sgt. Frost: Why is that?

Deven Guilford: Because I just drove my brother to the church.

Sgt. Frost: You do not have your driver's license on your person, correct?

Deven Guilford: Yes, I do.

Sgt. Frost: Where is it?

Deven Guilford: You do not have to see it.

Sgt. Frost: I do have to see it.

Deven Guilford: Why do you have to see it? Your, you had your brights, I could not see; I was going to crash, I did not, I, I cannot see; you had your brights on you sir; I'm not lying to you, I was just doing that to be polite; I didn't want you to flash someone and have someone go off the road and crash, you know.

Sgt. Frost: Do you realize that if you had complied with this traffic stop, it would have gone a whole different way for you?

Deven Guilford: Yes, I do, but, yes.

Sgt. Frost: Do you realize that I would have explained to you that I'm driving a brand new vehicle tonight?

Deven Guilford: Yes

Sgt. Frost: I have been flashed a couple times because these headlights are new. I've stopped a couple vehicles tonight and no people have gotten citations but those headlights are brand new, they're brighter on that vehicle than they are on normal cars.

Deven Guilford: They're super bright, you need to get new ones.

Sgt. Frost: But my high beams were not on, that's what I would have come and explained to you.

Deven Guilford: Oh I'm sorry, then, I'm sorry.

Sgt. Frost: Okay, but now I need your driver's license, registration, and proof of insurance, please.

[pause] [Guilford cell-phone video clip 1 ends.]

Sgt. Frost: Where is your driver's license, now.

Deven Guilford: I do not have to give you that.

Sgt. Frost [speaking to dispatch]: Central, 2372, start me another car, priority.

Sgt. Frost [speaking to Deven Guilford]: You do have to give me your driver's license.

Deven Guilford: I'm making a phone call.

[Sgt. Frost opens driver's side door]

Deven Guilford: No.

Sgt. Frost: Get out of the car, get out of the car, I'm telling you right now, [unintelligible].

Deven Guilford [unintelligible]: Hey.

Sgt. Frost: You're gonna get tased.

Deven Guilford; Do not touch me, officer, do not touch me, you cannot open my car.

Sgt. Frost: Get out of the car [unholsters taser], now, out of the car [points taser at Guilford], out

of the car or [Guilford cell-phone clip two begins] you're gonna get tased.

[Deven Guilford recorded the police stop on his cell in two different parts. This is part two of provided video.]

[Deven Guilford holding cell phone in right hand]

Deven Guilford [back turned toward passenger seat, handling cell phone. Turns head toward Sgt. Frost]: He says...

Sgt. Frost: Out of the car or you're gonna get tased; everything's being recorded son, I got no problem with that [Guilford begins stepping out of car], get out of the car.

Deven Guilford: Yes.

Sgt. Frost: Get down on the ground now. [Guilford stands beside driver's door] Down on the ground now. [Guilford kneels facing driver door as it closes]

Deven Guilford: Oh my gosh, stop yelling at me.

Sgt. Frost: Down on the ground, right here facing me, down on the ground now. [Sgt. Frost pointing with taser]

Deven Guilford: What do you mean?

Sgt. Frost: Get on your belly right now.

Deven Guilford: This is what American...

Sgt. Frost: Put your phone down and put your arms out to your side now, arms out to the side.

Deven Guilford: Are you, I don't have a weapon, [Sgt. Frost pulls cell phone from Deven Guilford's hands and tosses it onto the ground to the rear of the car] hey.

Sgt. Frost: Get your...

Deven Guilford: You can't do that.

Sgt. Frost: Son, get your hands behind your back, you're under arrest.

Deven Guilford: You can't do that.

Sgt. Frost: Get your hands behind your back.

Deven Guilford: Officer, what are you doing?

Sgt. Frost: Get your hands behind your back, you're under...

Deven Guilford: Officer, [Taser deployed] OW!

[sound of Taser]

[three gun shots]

[loud scream]

[two gun shots]

[two gun shots]

Deven was declared dead at the scene. Sergeant Frost claimed that after he tased Deven Guilford, Deven got up off the ground and attacked him, hitting him several times in the head. Frost felt he was losing consciousness and that Deven might then take his gun and shoot him, so he drew his gun and shot Deven seven times, the fatal shot being a bullet to Deven's head. There is no video of Deven attacking Frost because Frost's camera was dislodged at the moment the alleged attack commenced and Deven's phone had been tossed into the nearby snow by Frost.

Within this five-minute tragedy are layers upon layers of complexity, context, mistakes, and regrets.

Was the traffic stop itself legal? (It's not clear.)

Why didn't Deven Guilford simply cooperate with Sergeant Frost?

Why did Frost escalate the confrontation by opening Deven's car door and attempt to physically drag him from the car, instead of waiting for backup?

Why did Frost further escalate things by threatening to tase Deven instead of waiting for backup?

Why did Frost then tase Deven, provoking an alleged

violent reaction, when Deven had already left his vehicle and laid face down on the ground without the use of any physical force by Frost?

The Eaton County district attorney declined to prosecute Sergeant Frost for shooting Deven Guilford, stating: "Deven's actions placed Sgt. Frost in imminent danger of death or great bodily harm. From the perspective of the officer, Sgt. Frost honestly and reasonably believed that Deven posed a threat of serious bodily harm to himself, or even death, if Deven got control of his service weapon. As such, Sgt. Frost was legally justified in shooting Deven in self-defense."[1]

What the district attorney does not address is those moment-by-moment decisions made by Frost and Guilford that led to the tragic outcome in the first place. Nor can he. His job is to parse the criminal law as it applies to the moment when Frost decided to use deadly force. How Frost got to that point, no matter how much those intervening decisions may have contributed to the final outcome, has no legal bearing on his ultimate decision to pull out his gun and shoot Deven Guilford. For instance, Deven could have reasonably believed that his life was in danger from Sergeant Frost based on the sergeant's aggressive behavior, yet his right to self-defense is not a factor in determining Frost's criminal liability.

The Guilford family, in turn, sued Sergeant Frost for violating Deven's civil rights. In a civil lawsuit, there is an opportunity to look at the larger context of Frost's actions in contributing to Deven's death. In their suit, they contend: "The acts of FROST in stopping, demanding identification, ordering GUILFORD from the car, arresting him as if he were a felon, tasing him, and then killing him were all separate and distinct illegal and unreasonable seizures under the 4th Amendment."[2]

Did Sergeant Frost violate Deven Guilford's Fourth Amendment Rights? Rather than take its chances in court, Eaton County settled a federal lawsuit brought by the family against Officer Frost, paying out $2.4 million.

What lies between these two legal interpretations of the facts is something different and more fundamental. It is what Brien Ferrell, the attorney who spent twenty-four years defending police officers, told me in reference to Sandra Bland. But it applies equally well to Deven Guilford and so many others:

"To me the most important question isn't: Is it legal for the officer to order her out of her car as the situation was escalating? [The most important question is] What was the right thing to do? What was the right thing to do?"[3]

Knowing the right thing to do does not require a law degree. Knowing the right thing to do requires doing exactly what political philosopher John Rawls suggested in his essay, "Justice as Fairness:"[4] forming agreements that are based on fairness for everyone, not for only those who hold power and authority, and then doing our best to honor those agreements in practice, in our everyday interactions with one another. This requires great humility and honesty, mostly honesty, about oneself. In other contexts and other situations, such personal accountability may be less consequential, but in law enforcement, it can be a matter of life and death, as it was here.

If we consider Sergeant Frost the tragic hero of this situation, despite the fact that it was Deven, not Frost, who died, doing the right thing was not something Frost was able to do. Part of why he was not able to do the right thing is more understandable in the larger context of the traffic stops Frost was making in the first place.

In the investigation that followed and as Frost eventually acknowledged in his conversation with Deven, he was driving a new vehicle that, even without the high beams on, was blinding drivers he approached. He had, in fact, been flashed by at least two other drivers already, both of whom he had then pulled over for flashing him and let off with warnings.

You might think that a police officer who discovers that his new vehicle's lights are improperly adjusted and are causing drivers to be blinded, creating a potentially deadly traffic hazard, might do the right thing and return to the station and change cars. But Frost stayed out on the road, blinding drivers.

Not only did he continue subjecting drivers to his blinding headlights, he used their flashing him as a pretext to pull them over. The Michigan law regarding headlights does not specifically address the legality of flashing your lights at someone to warn them that their high beams are blinding you. All it says is that a vehicle within five hundred feet of an oncoming vehicle " "shall use a distribution of light or composite beam so aimed that the glaring rays are not projected into the eyes of the oncoming driver."

As the Guilfords' attorney points out in his lawsuit: "… on its face, the Michigan statute does not prohibit the momentary flashing of headlights, but only the glaring of beams sufficient to impair the vision of an approaching vehicle within 500 feet."[5]

Besides, what other means does a driver have to warn another driver that the lights of his oncoming car are blinding him? In this context, not only was Deven's flashing of the officer not illegal, but a practical warning about a dangerous situation. The only illegal activity being committed was by Sergeant Frost as he continued to drive around with his misaligned headlights blinding unsuspecting drivers, who were then pulled over for a crime they did not commit. If we go by Michigan law, which says nothing at all about high beams but only addresses "glaring beams" of any kind, then clearly Frost was committing the crime while Guilford's momentary flashing of his high beams was within the law.

But it is not the legality here that is at issue. Frost was aware that the lights of his vehicle were blinding oncoming drivers. He also knew they had no other means of alerting him to this fact. And yet he continued to pull them over for what was at most a questionable traffic infraction and quite possibly a perfectly legal - and required - safety precaution that might save other drivers' lives.

There is nothing right about any of those decisions. But there is a consistency to them. They show a consistent pattern of disregard for the safety of the citizens Frost is sworn to protect and a disregard for what Frost knows is common driving etiquette. He is, in short, being a bully - by using his authority and power to commit a crime (albeit, minor), and then using his own infraction to stop and intimidate citizens who have done nothing more than warn him (or any other driver) that they were blinded by his lights. They must not flash their lights at him while he continued to drive around with his misaligned lights blinding oncoming drivers? Really?

Watching the video of the traffic stop, it is quite obvious that Frost is both aggressive and defensive when Deven insists that his high beams were on. He is well aware that though they might not have been technically on, in terms of their effect, they might as well be. But rather than admit this at the outset, he basically withholds this critical piece of information, allowing him to insist that Deven is the one who is mistaken, if not actually lying.

Unfortunately, there is little information about Jonathan Frost as a police officer, or as son, father, husband, or friend. The privacy laws granted the police are second only to those granted doctors. It is almost impossible to find out if police officers have prior complaints against them or other disciplinary issues until it is too late. But there is no reason not to give Sergeant Frost the benefit of the doubt.

He was most likely a good police officer acting in a way that conforms to the norms of his department. There certainly was never any comment from the Eaton County Sheriff's Department that driving around in a vehicle with blinding headlights was in any way improper, nor his use of this pretext to stop drivers as inappropriate. But it is improper. It is inappropriate. It is not the right thing.

And Frost knows this, which is why he doesn't mention it until well into the traffic stop. And he does it in a way that still manages to put the blame on Deven for their conflict, saying: "Do you realize that if you had complied with this traffic stop it would have gone a whole different way for you? …I have been flashed a couple of times because these headlights are new. I've stopped a couple of vehicles tonight and no people have gotten citations, but those headlights are brand new, they're brighter than they are on normal cars."[6]

This is the elephant in the room of this five-minute tragedy. What Frost is saying, without quite saying it, is: "Yes, I'm at fault here for blinding you in the first place, but that doesn't matter. If you just submit to my bullying like everyone else, you can go on your way."

The entire interaction is based on Sergeant Frost knowingly blinding drivers and then stopping them and admonishing them for illegally flashing him, all the while not telling them that they are, in fact, correct regarding his lights blinding them.

Obviously. the other drivers, more seasoned in the ways of police officers, chose not to confront Frost with the just plain wrongness of the whole scenario. They probably thought: *You are blinding me with your lights and then I get a warning for flashing you?! You gotta be kidding!* But they just kept their mouths shut and took it.

Why does this matter when it comes to the entire ensuing and horrible dénouement of Deven Guilford's death? Because it is a pattern of behavior that led to Frost's inability to de-escalate a confrontation with an unarmed seventeen-year-old boy.

Frost was already on the defensive because he knew what he was doing was not right. That Deven confronted him about this, insisting he had his high beams on and then refusing to be cooperative, only increased his attempts to assert his authority over Guilford. He had already done this to at least two other drivers. He was already committed to what amounts to entrapping drivers into flashing him and then demeaning them by telling them that their experience of being blinded by his high beams was simply not the case. He was calling them liars.

Within 12 seconds of admitting this to Guilford, Frost escalated the entire confrontation by opening Guilford's car door and attempting to physically drag him out of the car. Up to this point, there had been no threat of physical violence by either party. Why did Frost decide to use force at that point?

According to Frost's written statement, as reported by the district attorney, Frost feared that Deven might be a member of a local anti-government militia group and was calling them for help. It was right after Frost acknowledged his misaligned headlights that Deven told him: "I'm making a phone call."[7]

But there was nothing in Guilford's appearance or actions that indicated he was a member of any such group. And even if this were the case, Deven never requested any "help," or gave out his location. Even if he had called for help, it would have taken some time to arrive, if that were even a realistic possibility. And Frost had already called for backup, which was roughly ninety seconds from arriving at his location, which Frost would have known had he taken a few seconds to check.

At this point, it was clear that Guilford and Frost were at a standoff. But rather than de-escalate the conflict or wait for backup to assist him, Frost used force. Why?

A more likely explanation in the context of the confrontation is what psychologists describe as the "Escalation of Commitment to a Failing Course of Action," otherwise known as doubling down on what has already shown itself to be a bad idea. This is such a common human behavior that there has been plenty of research done on it. It is done in every walk of life, from the personal to the political. It is all too often seen in financial dealings and is colloquially described as "throwing good money after bad."

There are two complementary schools of thought as to why we continue a course of action that is failing. The first is self-justification. Simply put, once you are committed to a specific course of action, you feel bound to continue it because doing otherwise would be to admit to yourself and others that your initial decision was wrong. It takes a lot of humility to admit when you are wrong. It's embarrassing. Most of us try to avoid such admissions. Even in Shakespearean tragedies, characters exhibit this behavior. Like Macbeth, we have too much pride, hubris, and arrogance to see the truth about ourselves when it is unflattering. We'd rather die trying than admit failure.

Self-Justification Theory emerged out of the idea of cognitive dissonance, which holds that when a person's behavior conflicts with their beliefs about themselves (e.g. I'm an honest person, I'm a successful person, I'm a smart person), they experience an uncomfortable psychological and emotional tension. To reduce that tension, they can either change their behavior (stop doing what is not working and admit their error) or, as is more often the case, start to rationalize their behavior so it continues to fit in with their idealized vision of themselves.

In the July 2011 issue of *Police Chief* magazine, Brian Fitch, a psychologist and lieutenant for the Los Angeles Sheriff's Department, describes how police officers seek to reduce the "cognitive dissonance" of doing wrong while still believing they are upholding the law, using any number of self-justifying thought processes. Here is a partial list:

- Denial of Victim - Because you're a "criminal" or a suspected criminal, you can't be a "victim" of any police abuse.
- Victim of Circumstance - Other officers engage in misconduct so I just went along with what they did.
- Advantageous Comparisons - Other officers (or suspected criminals) do much worse, so my misconduct doesn't amount to anything.
- Higher Cause - This is the classic "the end justifies the means," rationalizing that any abuse or harm I inflict is justified for the "greater good" of protecting society, punishing the bad guys, and the like.
- Blame the Victim - Because you did something wrong, you deserve whatever you get.
- Dehumanization - Criminals (or suspected criminals) are the "other" – not fully human which justifies any abuse they might suffer.[8]

Do any of these rationalizations sound familiar? They should. We all engage in them all the time.

In the context of the confrontation between Frost and Guilford, Frost explicitly used several of these justifications, and we can infer the use of several others. He explicitly blamed (denied) the victim for the confrontation, telling

Guilford this would have gone a whole different way if Guilford had only done what he was told. He dehumanized Guilford by insisting that because Deven refused to show him his license, Frost's own improper behavior of blinding Guilford with his lights didn't matter. And his "advantageous comparison" was to think that while he may have temporarily blinded Guilford with his headlights, Guilford refusing to show him his license made his (Frost's) behavior somehow less guilty.

There's more. In his written report, Frost claimed he was a "victim of circumstance" in that he escalated the confrontation because he feared for his life, even though until the moment of the actual shooting there was no threat of physical violence from Deven Guilford. And finally, Frost indirectly justified his blinding other drivers with a "higher cause" – they were breaking the law by flashing him – while he hid behind the technicality of not actually having his high beams on, though never acknowledging his own improper behavior of knowingly and repeatedly blinding drivers.

The other theory explaining commitment to a failing strategy is known as Prospect Theory, first developed by Nobel Prize-winning economist Daniel Kahneman and his colleague, Amos Tversky.[9] In a series of experiments, they presented subjects with the chance to either make a financial gain or suffer a loss, the chances of each being equal. If the chance of both outcomes is equal, you would think that half the subjects would have selected one option and the other half the other option. But by a large margin, most subjects were willing to accept more risk to avoid suffering a loss than to achieve a comparable gain. This tendency is described as "loss aversion." In the context of doubling down on a failing course of action, it suggests that most people have a stronger instinct to continue a failing course of action because losing seems so much worse emotionally than winning, all things being equal.

Simply put, we are much more likely to take high-risk actions to avoid what we perceive as a loss, even when we already have evidence that what we are doing just isn't working.

If we apply both the cognitive dissonance (self-justification) theory and the loss aversion bias to Frost, you can see why he might choose to continue down the path he was on, even though his efforts to get Deven to cooperate were failing. His inclination to take a large risk and physically escalate the confrontation was necessary to justify all of his previous improper behavior. Otherwise, he would have been forced to admit his own actions were wrong.

From a Prospect Theory perspective, the prospect of loss that Frost was faced with was not the loss of his life, but the loss of his presumed authority. The loss of his authority loomed much larger in his mind than the risk involved in escalating the conflict. He was naturally disposed to overestimating the loss he would suffer while underestimating the risk of escalating the conflict.

The moment that Frost acknowledged his own complicity in this stop-gone-wrong is exactly when he escalates the confrontation from verbal to physical. Nothing had changed in terms of the actual danger Guilford posed to Frost. He was no more threatening, aggressive, or defiant than he had been. In fact, Guilford never threatened Frost's physical safety, but he did threaten Frost's authority, and that was what Frost could not abide. At that moment, when Frost acknowledged his own improper behavior, he needed to have Guilford submit and acknowledge that he, Frost, still had the power and the authority even in the face of his own wrongdoing.

Deven Guilford died not for endangering Frost's life but for defying him. For attempting to assert his rights and to get Frost to acknowledge the truth behind his own improper behavior. Frost was not doing the right thing. What Deven

Guilford didn't understand was that his lived rights and his actual rights were completely disconnected, and that unlike the rest of us, Frost had virtually no constraints on what he could do to impose his will, no matter how wrong he was.

In the ensuing investigation, it came to light that Deven had been watching online videos of citizens being beaten and shot by police, and while he wasn't anti-police, he had expressed concerns to his family about citizens' rights. His refusal to provide Frost with his license as well as his questioning of Frost and recording the encounter on his cell phone were all, apparently, his attempt to assert what he thought were his rights as an American.

A year after Deven Guilford's death, an article published in the *Lansing State Journal* was headlined "Guilford Shooting Still Divides Eaton County." There are those who still argued that Deven was to blame for his death. If he had only complied with Frost, he would have gotten off with nothing more than a warning.

That is most likely true. Deven Guilford would be alive today if he had obeyed Frost. But it begs the question of why his non-compliance should have ever resulted in his death. Here in America we have a right to question, to object, to protest, to hold government accountable for its actions. We celebrate those rights. Do we forfeit our lives when we (nonviolently) object to official mistreatment if we don't object in just the right way? Frost had the gun, the authority, and the age and experience to resolve the conflict safely, with no one harmed. But his anger and frustration got the better of him and he acted on it with deadly results. Frost, not Deven Guilford, was responsible for that.

Deven's death goes beyond what our legal rights are to the question that precedes and grounds those rights: How do we want to live with each other? How do we want to treat each other? Our rights and laws are the formal statements that answer those questions. And if our laws are not reflective of how we want to live together, there is something wrong with our laws, not with the people who object to them.

The truth is, we all justify our unattractive behavior all the time in the same ways that Frost justified his behavior. And we all tend to want to avoid losses, either real or imagined, to our authority and self-esteem, if not our pocketbooks. The difference is that we don't end up killing people because of our emotional limitations. We don't have a gun, baton, taser, and handcuffs to use when we feel our authority is being questioned. We don't have the power or authority to act out when our basic human frailties get the best of us. Our tragedies are small and personal. We lie to our spouse and we fight and then apologize. Our boss treats us badly and we might object and get fired. Or we might get an apology. But we don't get stopped, humiliated, tased, and then shot by our boss. Our worst selves are played out on a small stage.

In a Shakespearean tragedy, however, it is always those with the power who are the tragic heroes. Our police are our tragic heroes. Yet, at the same time, they are victims. We have given them the power and authority to protect our highest ideals, but we have failed to give them the wisdom and knowledge of the risks that having such power entails. They are only human, but we give them superhuman responsibilities and are then surprised when they fail to fulfill our ideals. How can they when we make it so easy not to?

Gratuitous Humiliation

In March 1997, Gail Atwater, a white woman, was driving home from a soccer game with her two children, ages five and three. She and her daughter were not wearing their seat belts. A Lago Vista police officer, Bart Turek, observed this and pulled her over. But rather than giving her the usual ticket and having her buckle up, the officer started yelling at her. When she asked him to lower his voice because he was scaring her children, he told her she was going to jail. When she asked if she could take her children to a neighbor's house two doors down, he refused. At that point her children were "frightened, upset, and crying," according to Atwater. She was arrested, taken to jail, booked, searched, and held until she posted a $310 bond an hour later.

Atwater and her husband, an emergency room physician, sued the officer and the City of Lago Vista, claiming that Atwater's Fourth Amendment Rights against unreasonable search and seizure had been violated because not wearing a seat belt was punishable only by a fine, making her arrest both unnecessary and constitutionally unreasonable.

Her case went all the way to the Supreme Court, where she ultimately lost in a five-to-four split.

The majority, in its opinion, acknowledged that *"the physical incidents of arrest were merely gratuitous humiliations imposed by a police officer who was (at best) exercising extremely poor judgment. Atwater's claim to live free of pointless indignity and confinement clearly outweighs anything the City can raise against it specific to her case. "*

Yet in denying her claim, they concluded: "Atwater's arrest was surely "humiliating," as she says in her brief, but it was no more "harmful to...privacy or...physical interests" than the normal custodial arrest,"[10] and so was not "unreasonable" under the Fourth Amendment.

How can we expect law enforcement officers to do what is right when they are being told by no less than the Supreme Court of the United States that inflicting "gratuitous humiliations" and "pointless indignity" upon citizens they are sworn to serve and protect can be done with impunity? If your job allows you to gratuitously humiliate the people you serve, how would you react if one of them, seventeen years old, naïve, and idealistic, challenges and objects to your abuse of power?

You would, most likely, defend your authority by whatever means necessary, because by now, after eight years on the job, you are used to dishing out humiliation and indignity without anyone objecting. Perhaps, if you are having a particularly good day, you might not take it personally. You might be able to step back and defuse the situation, not because you had to, not because it was the right thing to do, but because you could. But maybe you're having a bad day. Or maybe you are just so used to everyone submitting to your authority, no matter how unjust it is, that it has become the norm, the status quo. And like any normal person, you will defend what you have, the status quo, as if your life depended on it, even against an unarmed seventeen-year-old boy.

Whatever moral sense an officer may start out with can be easily dispatched for all the self-serving reasons we all have for behaving badly. The difference is that the officer can get away with such behavior while the rest of us cannot. Our friends and family, our colleagues, clients, and customers won't put up with it. But as "customers" of law enforcement, who possess a monopoly of power, we have no choice but to put up with it because we have no other options we can exercise. Police officers know this. That is why in law enforcement the flaw is fatal. And we have made it so.

Deven was white. He thought he had rights. Perhaps he imagined he would have a story to tell his high school friends and a video to put up on YouTube. He never imagined he would end up dead.

Yet being white provides only the illusion that we are immune from the all-too-human flaws of law enforcement officers. As Deven Guilford and Jonathan Frost found out, no one is immune.

The fatal flaw of Sergeant Jonathan Frost is the same flaw that we all have: pride - that we are somehow exempt from the humbling experience of acting from the worst in ourselves, and perhaps most difficult - admitting it. The Greeks recognized this flaw three thousand years ago: pride, hubris, in the face of the gods. In Greek and Shakespearean tragedy, the hero is brought down by his flaw. Our legal system has protected Frost from the criminal consequences of his actions. But it's up to us to protect ourselves from law enforcement's fatal flaw. No gods are showing up to bring justice to our human failure. Only we can do that.

Examples and Solutions

Police and police unions are insular organizations, generally unwelcoming of outsiders and resistant to change. Police unions do not have the public's best interests in mind; they have their union members' best interests in mind (unfortunately that interest is often defined too narrowly). And often that means protecting a bad cop from any kind of disciplinary action at any cost. This adversarial relationship extends to the department itself, with police unions suing their departments (as in the case of Richmond, California) when they make reform-minded efforts that damage the careers of officers who are resistant to reform. This bunker mentality, coupled with the power and resources of police unions, can be a major impediment to police reform.

An egregious example is that of Hector Jimenez of the Oakland Police Department. In 2007, Jimenez shot and killed an unarmed man after he ran from his car after a traffic stop. This shooting was deemed justified by the department. Then in 2008, Jimenez shot and killed another man, also unarmed, who was running from his vehicle after a traffic stop. In this instance, the department fired Jimenez after determining that the man he shot was not a threat to Jimenez's life or anyone else's. Nonetheless, the police union contract allowed Jimenez to appeal his termination and have it decided by an arbitrator, who returned Jimenez to the force, over the objections of the Oakland P.D.

In 2008, an off-duty Pittsburgh, Pennsylvania, police officer had one too many drinks at his wife's birthday party and then proceeded to pistol whip and shoot (accidentally) a passerby he claimed had punched him. His victim was not the person who allegedly punched him (that person was never identified), so he beat and shot a total stranger. The officer was fired but got his job back after he appealed through his union. A police official commented: "Why would you employ a police officer that pistol-whipped and accidentally shot someone on his night off? The common person says, 'This is crazy.' And they're right: It is crazy. It's just never gotten enough attention."[11]

An analysis of more than 80 police union contracts by checkthepolice.org found the following four departments had substantially fewer impediments than the others to ensuring appropriate and transparent investigation and discipline of police misconduct:

Santa Ana, California
Riverside, California
New York, New York
Madison, Wisconsin

All the rest of the departments had two or more of the following contractual impediments to more accountable policing:

Disqualifying police complaints after a relatively short period of time.

Restrictions and/or delays in interrogating the officers involved in complaint action.

Giving officers unfair access to information (for example, providing officers with all the evidence of the complaint prior to being interviewed, allowing them to tailor their responses to the complaint).

Limits on oversight and discipline (see the examples above).

Requiring the city to pay for police officer misconduct.

Erasing an officer's misconduct records after a given period of time.

These problems are compounded by thirteen states passing police officers' bill of rights that make such impediments statewide law. You can read the contracts themselves (maybe your city is in their database) at checkthepolice.org.

While you may not be able to directly influence a police union, you do have the power to influence the negotiators on the other side of the table – namely, your elected representatives, who spend your tax dollars to fund the police. Make them accountable for making the police department accountable. Reach out to your local politicians and find out where they stand on police contract accountability and let them know what a fair police contract should and should not contain.

If you want to get more involved in police oversight, find out about the citizens' police oversight board in your community. For more information on such boards throughout the country, along with research on the best practices of such boards, visit the National Association For Civilian Oversight of Law Enforcement (nacole.org).

And know your rights and be sure your loved ones know their rights as well. Visit:
www.aclu.org/know-your-rights, www.nlg.org/know-your-rights, or iamerica.org/know-your-rights.

The War in the Shadows

*The thing I discovered that was most life-changing for me
[was] I heard stories [from the Latino and African-
American task force members] that were negative that
they had or a family member had with law enforcement,
that going to a Catholic boys' high school, and where our
sons went to school, none of those things happened, nor
were any of those stories ever shared. Nothing like them.*

—**Brien Ferrell,** white member of the Sonoma
County Task Force on Community Policing

Racism and the Invisible Hand

In 2015, a reporter for *Propublica.org,*, Paul Kiel, did an investigation into debt collection patterns across the United States. Not debt collection for folks who pay their bills on time, but debt collection for those folks who have fallen behind on their payments.

Kiel collected the records for every person who had been sued for non-payment of a debt in three cities: Chicago, Newark, and St. Louis. He then analyzed that data, and what he found was surprising, though not in the way you might expect.

In every single case, the highest rates of defaults were in black neighborhoods. Even when you compared these neighborhoods to white neighborhoods with similar income levels, the folks in the black neighborhoods had much higher levels of loan defaults, lawsuits, and wage garnishments.

The obvious conclusion you might jump to was that this was a classic case of the old practice of "redlining," in which banks would deny African-Americans home loans because they were black. They were "redlined," that is, treated in a discriminatory manner based solely on the color of their skin. But Kiel didn't jump to that conclusion. As he put it in a radio interview: "I know how it's such a large and impersonal system. You know, debt buying companies and other banks might never meet their customers. You're literally a name on a spreadsheet to these companies."[1]

So how did these companies know which customers were African-American so they could specifically target them? Well, as Kiel suspected, they didn't know what color their customers were. They weren't targeting their African-American customers at all. Their African-American customers, no matter what city they lived in, just had fewer resources when it came to paying their debts compared to their white counterparts – even when both groups, on average, made the same amount of money.

Kiel described it this way: "In that income bracket, whites, on average, have five times the wealth as black households."[2]

While there is a lot of discussion about income inequality in the United States, there is less attention paid to wealth inequality. What is the difference? Income is what you earn on an annual basis from work or investments or any other source that generates money for you. Wealth, on the other hand, is whatever you own, separate from your income, that has some value, that you could turn into money if you had to – the equity in your house, the car you fully paid for, your retirement fund, your savings account, even your furniture and jewelry are part of your "wealth."

So, while a white household and a black household might each have the same amount of income, white households have on average sixteen times more wealth than African-American households.[3] The reasons for this are several, but when you compare low-income white families with low-income African-American families, as Kiel did, one thing stands out: For most of us, it takes time to build wealth - even a modest amount. As in, generations.

So even the lowest-income white person, living in a low-income neighborhood in a home that isn't worth very much, has likely benefited from whatever small amount of wealth her parents or grandparents were able to accumulate. Maybe she received some help with the down payment for her modest home. Or when she found herself in financial trouble, she called her parents or grandparents to get an interest-free loan or a gift of money to cover the shortfall. Or when a family member passed away, she received a financial windfall, however modest. Or she has other white friends she could borrow money from without any expectation that she would pay them back with exorbitant interest penalties.

Channa Joffe-Walt, interviewing Paul Kiel on NPR,

summed it up:" If you ask people, 'Could you borrow $3,000 from a friend or family member in an emergency,' white people are much more likely to say yes. Poor whites, a white person living in abject poverty, has roughly the same ability to borrow $3,000 in an emergency as a middle-class black person."[4]

These huge differences in wealth, even when incomes are equal, are in large part the result of centuries of active racist policies on the part of our government and businesses. And while such active racism still exists, the fact that large businesses that have no idea what skin color their customers are can still discriminate against African-Americans without even intending it gives one pause.

You can then begin to understand that as a lower- or middle-income white person who feels himself to be just getting by financially - stressed out by too many bills, endless work, trying to send the kids to college - even with all of it, you still have it easy compared to the black person earning the same amount of money. By virtue of your whiteness, you very likely have more resources on which to draw.

Equal opportunity notwithstanding, we are not equal in opportunity. With absolutely no discrimination taking place, the legacy of discrimination continues to put black and brown people at a disadvantage, through no fault of their own, nor through any fault of yours. This is one aspect of racism in America in the twenty-first century. What might be called Racism 3.0. Now we finally return to one of my very first questions: Does my white-person experience with law enforcement, along with Jill's and Tom's, have any connection with the police experience of people of color – and if so, what is the connection?

Racism 3.0

If slavery was Racism 1.0 and the subsequent era of Jim Crow was Racism 2.0, then we have over the past forty years entered a new era of racism in America – Racism 3.0

Unlike versions 1.0 and 2.0, in which racism was sanctioned through formal laws and plainly visible, this latest iteration is far subtler, more insidious, and even invisible, allowing those of us unaffected by it to imagine that racism is a thing of the past. There are no more color laws. What most white Americans see, as they go about their daily lives, are formal declarations by all of our major institutions of government and business assuring us that they do not discriminate on the basis of "race, sex, creed, religion, color, or national origin." We know, and all of our friends and neighbors know, to judge everyone by the content of their character, as Martin Luther King had instructed us, not by the color of their skin.

That racial progress has been made seems indisputable. We have coworkers of every color, nationality, gender, and sexual orientation. Black athletes and entertainers have highly visible and successful careers, and we elected the first black president – not once, but twice.

Facts to the contrary – that there are still crime-ridden sections of our cities where we fear to go, largely populated by poor black people, and that our prisons are filled far beyond their proportional numbers with African-Americans and Latinos—we attribute to social and psychological problems that are beyond our ability to fix.

The apparent ability of a small percentage of people of color to join us in the middle class seems to bear out our intuitive sense that racism is a thing of the past. All people of color need to do is buy into the American Dream that we have embraced as both the cause and result of our current well-being: work hard and play by the rules and you will get ahead. Take responsibility for yourself and change your circumstances. There is nothing in your way.

The fact that so many people of color have been unable to join us in our safe neighborhoods, good schools, and - relatively speaking - bright prospects must be, we surmise, because they are trapped in a cycle of self-defeating despair and self-loathing. These are personal failings that no amount of government spending or social programs can fix. And our own goodwill is testimony enough to our lack of responsibility for these ongoing social woes.

That there are significant cracks appearing in that narrative, even for white people, is concerning, but not yet compelling to us. Where our parents may have been able to afford a home, send kids to college, and have a decent retirement on a single (usually male) income, the fact that we find ourselves with two incomes, both essential to our middle-class lifestyle, is more a function of women's equality than the growing economic disparities in this country, isn't it? (We tell ourselves.)

Even if we acknowledge that there is something seriously wrong with the fact that a single person working forty hours a week for minimum wage will find it nearly impossible to support himself, let alone a family of four, to say nothing of trying to save for retirement or a child's college education, we still chalk it up to the American narrative that one's success or failure is entirely a matter of individual will, skill, and smarts. We deserve what we get, or don't get, here in America. The "system" is essentially fair, we convince ourselves.

Yet, even as we see some (an increasingly small percentage) of our fellow Americans moving from humble beginnings to middle-class or even wealthy lives, we find ourselves running faster and worker ever harder just to maintain the status quo of our enviable existence. We note in passing that the increasing wealth and income gap between the richest Americans and everyone else is growing, despite our personal best efforts to narrow it. The gap now is as large as it was before the Great Depression of the 1930s and continues to grow,[5] despite the hard work and striving of hundreds of millions of us.

Against this backdrop, the invisible factors that drive these disparities are exponentially multiplied if you are a person of color, and law enforcement represents the leading edge of this increasing difference in the quality of life and the possibility of having at least as good a life, if not a better life, than our parents did.

First-Order Racism in Law Enforcement

Although all our government agencies, from the federal government down to the smallest local law enforcement agency, have clear policies proclaiming their adherence to nondiscriminatory practices in the treatment of the public that they serve, direct and active discriminatory practices still abound.

While you most likely heard the news sound bites of the Department of Justice (DOJ) report summarizing the blatant targeting of black residents of Ferguson, Missouri, by police officers in the wake of the Michael Brown shooting, you might have passed this off as an exceptional case of a small-town police force in a red state taking the law into its own hands.

Sadly, this is not the case.

In the past ten years, the U.S. Department of Justice (DOJ) has conducted investigations of more than twenty law enforcement agencies across the country, from the relatively small (Ferguson) to the largest (Los Angeles, Chicago, Seattle, Oakland), in states both red and blue, in agencies with an ethnic and gender diversity of officers and those without much diversity.

The results are startling and reveal what the DOJ calls "patterns and practices" that violate the constitutional rights of all citizens in the most egregious and fundamental ways, but inevitably fall most heavily on people of color.

To get a flavor of what is happening on the ground, daily, in American cities both large and small, let's consider a representative summary of the recent DOJ investigation into the Newark (New Jersey) Police Department.

Newark, New Jersey Report (2014)

- *Stops for "suspicion" only.* Seventy-five percent of the Newark Police Department (NPD) stops of pedestrians - "Terry" stops that require police to meet the low threshold of having "reasonable suspicion" of a crime before they stop someone - were conducted without even reaching that low standard. That is, police simply accosted citizens on the street ("seized" them in the language of the Fourth Amendment) with no "suspicion" and subjected them to illegal searches and seizures.
- *Singling out black residents.* Police stop and arrest Newark's black residents at a rate far higher than that of white residents. Simply put, not only are three-quarters of police pedestrian stops illegal, but they disproportionately target black residents. And in many cases, the arrests themselves are illegal. The citizen had committed no actual crime.
- *Retaliating against individuals who question police actions.* In violation of the First Amendment, NPD officers have detained and arrested individuals who lawfully object to police actions or behave in a way that officers perceive as disrespectful.

- Using unjustified and excessive force in violation of the Fourth Amendment. In more than twenty percent of the NPD force incidents reviewed, the force as reported appeared unreasonable and thus in violation of the Constitution. Further, there has been substantial under-reporting of force by NPD officers, and most NPD use-of-force investigations have been too inadequate to support reliable conclusions about whether an officer's use of force, including deadly force, was reasonable.
- *Subjecting individuals to theft by NPD officers in violation of the Fourth and Fourteenth Amendments.* The investigation revealed evidence of theft of citizens' property and money by officers, specifically in the NPD's specialized units such as the narcotics and gang units, and in the prisoner processing unit at the Green Street Cell Block.[6]

In short, the Newark police were acting more like an armed gang terrorizing the local citizens than a police force sworn to serve and protect them. They subjected wholly innocent citizens to random stops and searches, illegal arrests, retaliation if they objected, illegally using excessive and even deadly force - and then stole from them, both on the street and in the process of arresting them. And while they did not subject only black citizens to this regime, they subjected far more black citizens to such terror than whites.

The exact same types of findings can be found in DOJ reports on law enforcement agencies in Oakland, California; Maricopa County, Arizona; East Haven Connecticut; New Orleans, Louisiana; and Cleveland, Ohio, to name just a few.

In the case of Cleveland, Ohio, the DOJ noted that it had identified virtually all of these illegal behaviors by the Cleveland police in an earlier 2002 investigation. In 2004 it had come to an agreement with the department to implement sweeping changes and terminated the agreement in 2005 on the assumption (but with no independent confirmation) that these reforms had occurred. Twelve years later in the 2014 report, the DOJ commented: "It is clear, however, that despite these measures, many of the policy and practice reforms that were initiated in response to our 2004 memorandum agreement were either not fully implemented or, if implemented, were not maintained over time."[7]

So even though the federal government and the Cleveland Police Department were fully aware of their illegal use of deadly force and excessive force, it continued, unabated, for another ten years before a public outcry jump-started another federal investigation of the force. Under the circumstances, there is no reason to assume that effective reforms have occurred at this point.

There have been similar "consent decrees" signed between many law enforcement agencies and the DOJ in which the agency agrees to make a variety of reforms, but there are ongoing questions as to how many of these decrees have actually been implemented and maintained. Current DOJ investigations into law enforcement in both San Francisco and Chicago in the wake of their questionable use of deadly force are ongoing.

In summary, police agencies nationwide, regardless of the political persuasion of their local or state governments, are actively engaged in daily egregious violations of citizens' civil rights. These violations are not attributed to a "few bad apples," according to the DOJ, but to a force-wide pattern of abuses. And these abuses generally fall most heavily upon people of color in these communities.

Recall the twelve New York City minority police officers who sued the department for the illegal use of arrest quotas and retaliation against officers who refused to meet those quotas. In addition to being pressured to arrest citizens for the most insignificant of matters (jaywalking, being homeless), they noted that minority communities inevitably bore the brunt of these practices.

NYPD Officer Adhyl Polanco: "When you go hunting, when you pull any kind of numbers on a police officer to perform, we are going to go to the most vulnerable. We are going to go to the LGBT community, we are going to go to the black community. We are going to go to those people that have no vote, that have no power. If we start doing what we are doing in midtown Manhattan, a phone call to the mayor's office is going to be made and that's gonna be the end of it."[8]

NYPD Officer Kareem Abdullah: "All they want us to do is go out there and lock them up. It's easier to get numbers out there because you work in this type of [minority] community."[9]

NYPD Officer Pedro Serrano: "They tell you this to your face. Blacks and Hispanics between [the ages of] 14 to 21 must get stopped."[10]

The problem with all of the investigations by the DOJ is that they only occur in response to high-profile, high-publicity instances of questionable police conduct. They are reactive, not proactive. With 18,000 law enforcement agencies in the United States, it is entirely possible to conceive, based on these sample cases, that a large percentage of law enforcement agencies are engaged in similar practices that have simply not generated the same level of public outrage and subsequent federal attention. How would we ever know? These are shadow programs with no formal policies, no written instructions - just a way of policing that even the police themselves often don't acknowledge and may not be aware of.

In Racism 3.0, while there are many laws banning outright discriminatory practices by public agencies, these same agencies engage in agency-wide illegal abuses of power directed at citizens based on the color of their skin. Because these practices are not legally sanctioned and mostly take place in communities of color, they are largely invisible to white members of the community. Brien Farrell, the white attorney in California who worked with law enforcement, said he never heard or saw any of these abuses in his largely white community. Because most police forces have either no oversight or any formal mechanisms for effective accountability to the public, extraordinary abuses can continue indefinitely without repercussions. Because these abuses are most often perpetrated against low-income people of color with few resources and no voice in their local community politics, the abuses are largely invisible to those who could effect change most easily: the middle-class white majority.

It is hard to conceive of the daily terror that poor communities of color live under on a daily basis, but a sampling of illustrations from the DOJ's report on the Ferguson Police Department give some idea of the daily abuse our fellow citizens suffer in the shadows, as most of us walk and drive about unimpeded. What is also worth noting is that none of these illegal practices are, by force of law, limited to communities of color. Law enforcement has the means and the ability to engage in these same abuses against the rest of us. They just seldom do. And as America becomes more and more divided economically, the specter of the police acting against poor communities of whites becomes a real possibility.

Arrested for Dancing

One of the most common abuses of police power in Ferguson was the "Manner of Walking" arrest. This law makes it a crime to walk in the street if there is an available sidewalk, or if not, requires one to walk along the side of the road, against traffic. In practice, it provided a means for the FPD to stop, question, and arrest African-Americans in Ferguson almost at will. The DOJ describes one episode:

"One afternoon in September 2012, an officer stopped a 20-year-old African-American man for dancing in the middle of a residential street. The officer obtained the man's identification and ran his name for warrants. Finding none, he told the man he was free to go. The man responded with profanities. When the officer told him to watch his language and reminded him that he was not being arrested, the man continued using profanity and was arrested for Manner of Walking in Roadway." [11]

The DOJ described the multilayered violation of this citizen's civil rights in this way: "FPD's suppression of speech reflects a police culture that relies on the exercise of police power –however unlawful – to stifle unwelcome criticism. Recording police activity and engaging in public protest are fundamentally democratic enterprises because they provide a check on those "who are granted substantial discretion that may be misused to deprive individuals of their liberties." [12]

The report continues: *"Even profane backtalk can be a form of dissent against perceived misconduct. In the words of the Supreme Court, '[t]he freedom of individuals verbally to oppose or challenge police action without thereby risking arrest is one of the principal characteristics by which we distinguish a free nation from a police state.' Ideally, officers would not encounter verbal abuse. Communities would encourage mutual respect, and the police would likewise exhibit respect by treating people with dignity. But, particularly where officers engage in unconstitutional policing, they only exacerbate community opposition by quelling speech."* [13]

In another case (June 2014): *"An African-American couple who had taken their children to play at the park allowed their small children to urinate in the bushes next to their parked car. An officer stopped them, threatened to cite them for allowing the children to "expose themselves," and checked the father for warrants. When the mother asked if the officer had to detain the father in front of the children, the officer turned to the father and said, 'you're going to jail because your wife keeps running her mouth.' The mother then began recording the officer on her cell phone. The officer became irate, declaring, 'You don't videotape me!' As the officer drove away with the father in custody for 'parental neglect,' the mother drove after them, continuing to record. The officer then pulled over and arrested her for traffic violations. When the father asked the officer to show mercy, he responded, 'No more mercy, since she wanted to videotape,' and declared 'nobody videotapes me.' The officer then took the phone, which the couple's daughter was holding. After posting bond, the couple found that the video had been deleted."[14]*

These incidents are so absurd, it is hard to know whether to laugh or cry over the unnecessary insult, injury, and harm caused. But they are mild compared to the FPD treatment of other purported "criminals."

Here's one example: *"In the summer of 2012, an officer detained a 32-year-old African-American man who was sitting in his car, cooling off after playing basketball. The officer arguably had grounds to stop and question the man, because his windows appeared more deeply tinted than permitted under Ferguson's code. Without cause, the officer went on to accuse the man of being a pedophile, prohibit the man from using his cell phone, order the man out of his car for a pat-down despite having no reason to believe he was armed, and ask to search his car. When the man refused, citing his constitutional rights, the officer reportedly pointed a gun at his head, and arrested him. The officer charged the man with eight different counts, including making a false declaration for initially providing the short form of his first name (e.g. 'Mike' instead of 'Michael') and an address that, although legitimate, differed from the one on his license. The officer also charged the man both with having an expired operator's license and with having no operator's license in possession. The man told us he lost his job as a contractor with the federal government as a result of the charges."*[15]

Here's another example: *"In January 2013, a patrol sergeant stopped an African-American man after he saw the man talk to an individual in a truck and then walk away. The sergeant detained the man, although he did not articulate any reasonable suspicion that criminal activity was afoot. When the man declined to answer questions or submit to a frisk – which the sergeant sought to execute despite articulating no reason to believe the man was armed – the sergeant grabbed the man by the belt, drew his ECW [taser], and ordered the man to comply. The man crossed his arms and objected that he had not done anything wrong. Video captured by the ECW's built-in camera shows that the man made no aggressive movement toward the officer. The sergeant fired the ECW, applying a five-second cycle of electricity, and causing the man to fall to the ground. The sergeant almost immediately applied the ECW again, which he later justified in his report by claiming that the man tried to stand up. The video makes clear, however, that the man never tried to stand – he only writhed in pain on the ground. The video also shows that the sergeant applied the ECW nearly continuously for 20 seconds, longer than represented in his report. The man was charged with Failure to Comply and Resisting Arrest, but no independent criminal violation."*[16]

These individual stories underscore the statistics the DOJ compiled:

- Despite making up 67 percent of the population, African-Americans accounted for 85 percent of

FPD's traffic stops, 90 percent of FPD's citations, and 93 percent of FPD's arrests from 2012 to 2014.

- African-Americans are 2.07 times more likely to be searched during a vehicular stop but are 26 percent less likely to have contraband found on them during a search. They are 2.00 times more likely to receive a citation and 2.37 times more likely to be arrested following a vehicular stop.

- African-Americans have force used against them at disproportionately high rates, accounting for 88 percent of all cases from 2010 to August 2014 in which an FPD officer reported using force.

- African-Americans account for 95 percent of Manner of Walking charges, 94 percent of all Fail to Comply charges, 92 percent of all Resisting Arrest charges, 92 percent of all Peace Disturbance charges, and 89 percent of all Failure to Obey charges.

- African-Americans are 68 percent less likely than others to have their cases dismissed by the Municipal Judge, and in 2013 African-Americans accounted for 92 percent of cases in which an arrest warrant was issued.[17]

A recent report by the ACLU put these statistics into a national context: "Racial disparities in sentencing are consistent with a larger pattern of racial disparities that plague the U.S. criminal justice system from arrest through incarceration. There are stark racial disparities in police stops, frisks, and searches. ...Blacks and Latinos are arrested at disproportionate rates and are disproportionately represented in the nationwide prison and jail population. For example, blacks compose 13 percent of the general population but represent 28 percent of total arrests and 38 percent of persons convicted of a felony in a state court and in state prison. These racial disparities are particularly pronounced in arrests and incarceration for drug offenses. Despite similar rates of drug use, blacks are incarcerated on drug charges at a rate 10 times greater than whites. Blacks represent 12 percent of drug users, but 38 percent of those arrested for drug offenses, and 59 percent of those in state prison for drug offenses. Although blacks and whites use marijuana at comparable rates, blacks are 3.73 times more likely to be arrested for marijuana possession. In some counties, blacks are 10, 15, even 30 times more likely to be arrested."[18]

The fact is that most police departments do not actively collect data that might show a pattern of racial profiling. But even if they did, and even if they implemented policies to stop their unconscious selective law enforcement against people of color, there are plenty of color-blind policies that reinforce the continuing use of police powers against those same people. Only now, they appear to be "neutral. Welcome to Racism 3.0

Second-Order Racisim—Color-Blind Enforcement Through Market Forces

It might seem like an even playing field when it comes to the color of your skin, if not the thickness of your wallet. But while we are now acknowledging that the amount of wealth a family has plays a huge role in achieving economic success, more so than native intelligence and/or hard work, we fail to acknowledge that those monetary resources have been allocated in a discriminatory and racist fashion over generations and that, now more than ever, play an outsized role in our relative success or failure and that of our children.

So, while we white people can look at ourselves and say,

"I didn't inherit anything; I earned every penny," we discount all the benefits that allowed us to achieve what we achieved: the stable home in a safe neighborhood, the stay-at-home mother, the high-quality public schools we attended, the extracurricular activities, the social contacts, the college education, and on and on. These are the indirect benefits of wealth, however modest, accumulated over generations.

To help white students better understand the effects of generational wealth on one's ability to live a productive and outwardly successful life, Berkeley High School in Berkeley, California, had students engage in a race. First, they all lined up at the starting line. Then the teacher instructed:

- If you live in a safe neighborhood, take a step forward.
- If you live in a dangerous neighborhood, take a step back.
- If you feel physically or emotionally safe in your home, step forward.
- If you feel physically or emotionally unsafe in your home, step backwards.
- If there are times when you have not had enough food at home, take a step back.
- If you have always had plenty of healthy, nutritious food at home, step forward.
- If your family owns their own home, take a step forward.
- If your family rents their home, take a step back.
- If your father or mother graduated from college, take a step forward.
- If your father or mother didn't go to college, take a step back.
- If a family member has been arrested and spent time in jail, take a step back.

- If your family will be able to help you pay for college, take a step forward.
- If they cannot help you pay for college, take a step back.

Then they started the race.

You don't need much imagination to know what the starting line looked like after these questions. Most of the white kids had a huge head start. Most of the black kids were playing catch-up at best, and given equal intelligence and equal ability and effort, could have never caught up to the white kids. So even if you have no actual wealth advantage as a white person (no parental money, no friends that have money, etc.), you have, despite all your apparent hardship, indirect but very substantial and personal benefits due to your whiteness.

Maintaining racism needn't require any racist laws in our country. All we need to do is treat everyone equally and the results will be racially skewed by virtue of generations of unfair advantages conferred upon those with white skin.

White Guilt, Black Resentment, and Social Programs

When my wife first started her career, one of her first jobs was in social services, providing early childhood care to low-income families in Oakland, California. She wasn't doing this because she felt sorry for the poor black people in the ghetto of East Oakland. She was doing it because she identified with those black people. She had severe dyslexia, so she was always placed in the "dummy" classes in school. More often than not, she was the only white person in an entire "dummy" class of black and brown people. She knew what it felt like to be considered stupid and less than everyone else. She felt that these academic rejects who happened to have darker skin were "her" people.

But when she did her rounds, visiting unwed teenage mothers totally unprepared to care for themselves, let alone a newborn baby, she was frequently met with anger and resentment. She didn't understand why her good intentions and material aid (diapers, formula, etc.) were greeted with scorn and hostility.

The response to her good intentions was not surprising, but sheds light on the current complexity of black/white relations at a time when systemic racism still abounds, but individual racists are much harder to identify (though less so now with the election of Donald Trump). People on both sides of the color line now find themselves in a mind-boggling game of trying to understand and anticipate each other's unspoken intentions, both conscious and unconscious, and then respond in a way that preserves one's sense of dignity and self-respect.

In the classroom, my wife was accepted as an equal by her darker-skinned classmates because the context (they were all in the "dummy" class) made for a level playing field. She could share her lunch with any of them and no one took offense.

But stripped of that equalizing context, in the role of social worker, she was just another white woman taking pity on "us poor black folk" who, not unreasonably, resented her charity even as they desperately needed it.

The psychology of charity and gift giving as a means of asserting one's superior status over the receiver was first recognized by Thorstein Veblen in his foundational work, *The Theory of the Leisure Class*, in which he coined the term "conspicuous consumption" to describe the tendency of the wealthy to purchase costly goods that were not functionally better than their cheaper counterparts, but served as "status markers" of wealth and social standing.

The corollary of this is "Conspicuous Compassion," in which the giver elevates his own social standing in the eyes of others by generously (and publicly) giving (because he can) to those less fortunate – which, by the same mechanism, confirms their low standing as the needy receivers. Geoffrey Miller, the evolutionary psychologist, grounds this type of giving in evolutionary terms,[19] theorizing that it has a high value when it comes to increasing your reproductive chances and those of your offspring. Being charitable is indicative of qualities women want in a mate – one who is caring and generous. If being charitable increases your stock in this regard, then it is better to give than to receive. So is it any wonder that in the minefield that is black/white relations today that well-meaning white people can find their offers of help met with resentment and even outright refusal, while black political leaders insist that more resources, better schools, and more jobs are necessary? This is not to say that white giving is always based on confirming white superior status, or that in accepting aid black people always feel insulted and demeaned. It just means that both of these psychological positions are in play in our attempts to create a more fair and equitable society.

In contrast, I think of my kids and all the children of my white friends (low to high income) and how they don't view any help they receive as a confirmation of lower status. Quite the opposite. Because they are privileged, they experience getting help as a natural and expected entitlement. They deserve all the help they get. And so they take these gifts as their due. In that sense, giving then becomes a tribute to their status, rather than an insult. In either case, the giving of aid and the receiving of it is a fine needle to thread without the added baggage of history and social meaning derailing the pragmatic effect of equalizing opportunity.

Feeling white guilt? Nobody likes to do anything out of

guilt. And nobody likes to have something done for them out of guilt or pity. It feels much better on both sides if you instead act out of compassion. Compassion stems from empathy, from understanding that we are ultimately "the same" in our humanity. Guilt comes from a sense of shame about who you are and what you have. It is hard to feel compassion for someone else when you feel shame about yourself. You are more likely to feel resentful for having been made to feel guilty. It's hard to accept help from someone you think is just taking pity on you. You are more likely to feel patronized and insulted.

At one time, we believed that we needed to make up for those four hundred years of disadvantage with affirmative action programs designed to recognize that history and advance some of those at the back of the line to at least be given the opportunity to get ahead. But because the Constitution demands "equal" treatment before the law, even if there has been a preceding four centuries of unequal treatment, such preferential programs have been deemed unconstitutional. Moreover, affirmative action smacks of guilt rather than compassion. Compassion would require us to help *all* those suffering from past injustices, not just a select few, and not just people of color. So, we now exist in a "color-blind" society, where we are not actively racist. We don't need to be. Racism is simply "a default setting," as Ta-Nehisi Coates puts it. All we need to do is nothing and the system perpetuates itself.

This is the invisible, systemic, and non-discriminatory discrimination of Racism 3.0. No individual need ever feel they are racist. Yet racism is simply a fact of life, like the air we breathe. No one of us is responsible for it, so none of us feels compelled to do anything about it.

We can easily discriminate against people of color based on financial resources under the guise of treating everyone "the same." We can even point to all the poor white people who are treated just the same as poor black people as evidence of the "fairness" of the system. But these examples suggest exactly the opposite: On the one hand, the relatively small percentage of whites who are subjected to the same mistreatment as blacks is simply the exception proving the rule, and on the other hand, it shows us that, privileged white people that we are, we are equally in danger of losing our white privilege and become "raced" black if we fail to take advantage of all those advantages we have already been accorded.

That race in America is not so much about skin color as it is a way for one group of people to assert their will over another group is a foreign notion to most of us. We have years of history that teaches us that we have discriminated against black people on the basis of their skin color. But the discrimination was not because black people have black skin, but *because* we needed some means to justify our discrimination in the first place, and skin color was the most obvious justification for treating other human beings as less deserving than us - because they were not like us.

Consider other examples of discrimination in other countries and throughout history. In World War II, the Nazis obviously could not tell who was Jewish and who was not. They had to comb through records that listed religion affiliation and then make Jews wear the Star of David on their clothing so they would be identifiable.

Likewise, in India, lower-caste members do not look different from their upper-caste fellows, but caste is often signified by a particular last name. In Rwanda, the differences between Hutus and Tutsis are not skin color but subtler physiological differences, and even these are not definitive given the intermarriage between the two groups. Racism, at its core, is not based on race at all, but on whatever derogatory differences one can ascribe to a group that one wishes to dominate.

In his book, *How The Irish Became White*, Noel Ignatiev describes in general how "…people are members of different races because they have been assigned to them."[20]

"The Irish who emigrated to America in the eighteenth and nineteenth centuries were fleeing caste oppression and a system of landlordism that made the material conditions of the Irish peasant comparable to those of an American slave. They came to a society in which color was important in determining social position. It was not a pattern they were familiar with and they bore no responsibility for it; nevertheless, they adapted to it in short order."[21]

Thus the Irish went from being the second-class citizens of the British Empire to "white" Americans, equal to their fellow English, German, and Nordic Americans in due course. Likewise, other southern European (Italian/Spanish) and Jewish immigrants gradually "traded up" to honorary "white" status in America.

Looked at this way, race changes from a noun to a verb, as Civil Rights attorney and legal scholar Lani Guinier uses it.[22] People are "raced," initially by the dominant culture, but then they can sometimes "race" themselves irrespective of their skin color. That is, even if one does not have black skin in America, one can identify socially, emotionally, psychologically, and materially with being "black" as a signifier of "lesser-than" status - though, to some degree, they will still retain the advantages of their non-blackness.

Likewise, African-Americans (and Hispanics and Asians) can identify as "white" insofar as they are "granted" honorary white status by virtue of their education, wealth, celebrity, athletic ability, or power on an individual basis, while still retaining some of the disadvantages of having physical identifiers of a lesser-than minority. Meanwhile, the group as a whole may still be relegated to all that goes with being a despised minority.

This understanding of race as a fungible creation was

highlighted most famously when black author Toni Morrison described Bill Clinton as "our first black president." This was interpreted by the press as a compliment with respect to Clinton's down-home personality, humble beginnings, and common touch. But as African-American journalist Ta-Nehisi Coates wrote in 2015, Morrison's depiction of Clinton described the coordinated and systematic effort to criminalize him in much the same way blacks are criminalized by their skin color.[23] The idea that race is not a passive "fact" but an ongoing and destructive activity which we Americans have engaged in now for some 400 hundred years, is not something we consider. And so, Coates points out, it allows us to see ourselves "as heroic do-gooders,"[24] rather than the perpetrators of that which we claim to abhor.

All of this elicits in well-meaning progressive middle-class whites a complex series of responses to the apparent reemergence of racism in the second decade of the twenty-first century. For many of us, we take for granted that, except for white supremacist groups, most of America is not racist.

Didn't Barack Obama get elected, not just once, but twice? Check.

And aren't all the Jim Crow laws repealed and overturned? Check.

Doesn't every job posting say we are an equal opportunity employer and we do not discriminate on the basis of race, religion, or gender? Check.

And don't I treat African-Americans as I would anyone else, per Martin Luther King's dream, according to the content of their character, not the color of their skin? Check. (Unless, of course, they are walking towards me on the street at night.)

Now we are being told that racism still exists and is as pernicious and virulent as ever, even though there are no racists left to excoriate and no Jim Crow laws to overturn. At this point, most of us throw up our hands and conclude that the problem is no longer our responsibility because we have made America color-blind. Individually we are not racist. (Even though we have no black friends or neighbors and our children's schools are predominantly all white – again.) Our businesses are no longer racist. The government is no longer racist. So where is the problem?

Most of us conclude the problem lies with black people themselves. We imagine that because there is nothing standing in their way of doing all that we have done to get where we are: work hard in school, get a college degree, find a job or start a small business, work hard, claw up some corporate ladder, buy a house, pay a mortgage, etc. No one helped me because I was white. Therefore, black people must be incapable of overcoming their history of being held back by others by holding themselves back. It's certainly not me (or anyone I know) holding them back.

For most of us well-meaning white Americans, our thought process ends there. We are good people. We have tried. We treat all people fairly. What else can we do?

If you dare to question your assumption that black people are still mired in lives of poverty, crime, and incarceration at levels far beyond those of whites because of their own personal failings, you are faced with only one other conclusion: there is racism built into our economic, education, legal, and political systems that is so subtle, yet entrenched, that we white people don't even notice it.

Brien Ferrell, the white attorney who had worked intimately with police officers for 24 years, described his shock at learning how his fellow minority task force members (some of whom lived in the same city as Ferrell) had been treated by police: "None of those things happened [to my family], nor were any of those stories ever shared. Nothing like them." Here is someone working at the nexus of the twenty-first century iteration of racism and he had no clue that this was going on in his own community.

Today racism is all in the shadows. No racist attitudes, laws, or lynchings required. Instead we can let the invisible hand of the marketplace do its unbiased and entirely impersonal work when it comes to reinforcing racial disparities in everything from education to employment.

If poor black people live in poor neighborhoods where their low-value homes generate low property taxes, which in turn inadequately fund their poor-quality schools, whose fault is that?

If their poor fathers can't find jobs because of their poor education and turn to petty drug dealing to get by, get arrested, can't afford a good attorney (because they are poor), and then are forced to plead guilty and go to jail (whereas even a poor white person can borrow money for a private attorney and get a plea deal that requires no jail time) – and then leave their families even poorer than before – whose fault is that?

We didn't do it, we think. But we have two options here when it comes to assuming any responsibility for the plight of our fellow Americans. We can acknowledge that we are not individually the "cause" of this systemic racism insofar as not one of us has any direct control over such disparities, but we can assume responsibility for changing the system that creates both white privilege and black mistreatment on a host of levels.

When we truly understand the underpinnings of other option - that being "raced" black is arbitrary and not based on skin color - we then know that it could be us next. Even if you don't believe that you have any responsibility for changing this unjust system, you might want to change it, because if you don't you will find yourself on the wrong end of being "raced black" no matter the color of your skin.

Canary in the Coal Mine

When I first conceived of this book, I understood the plight of African-Americans in relation to law enforcement as the canary in the coal mine. Because of their marginalized status, black Americans were simply easier targets for law enforcement to bully. They had relatively little voice, no political power, and few resources. But what I also understood from my own interaction with law enforcement was that being abused, humiliated, brutalized, and even killed was certainly not limited to black people and that any one of us could be targeted – not just individually, but as a group. And that whatever group you might conceive of could become a target.

I saw the mistreatment of blacks by law enforcement as a warning that the rest of us were at risk for having our rights violated in whatever way they could be if we didn't take some action to correct these abuses that our fellow Americans were suffering. I later learned that this metaphor of the canary in the coal mine had been used in much the same way fourteen years earlier by Lani Guinier and Gerald Torres in their book, *The Miner's Canary*.

While their work only touches on the relationship between communities of color and law enforcement, it applies the same metaphor on a much broader scale, suggesting that the distress of our minority communities is a warning (and a potentially valuable source of energetic political change) that we are all in danger of succumbing to the toxicity of our current politics. Communities of color are just the first and most obvious sign that something is seriously amiss in our civic life.

What Guinier and Torres go to pains to point out is that once you accept that the dominant hierarchy "races" you black or white in America, it is clear there are plenty of poor whites (and brown people) who are, for all intents and purposes, "raced" black. They are stuck in a grinding cycle of poverty and crime from which they cannot escape, and it is not because they are all somehow individually defective human beings. The environmental challenges (in the largest sense: social, political, economic, educational) are overwhelming, and only the lucky and/or exceptional escape the downward pull of desperate and depressing conditions.

But, as Guinier and Torres point out, poor whites, because they are white, have bought into the prevailing American myth that their failure to achieve the American Dream is solely a personal failure, not a systemic problem. Or if it is systemic, then the system is denying them their due by unreasonably favoring people of color.[25]

Of course, poor white people are going to be much more likely to "drink the Kool-Aid" of what Guiner/Torres call the "meta-narrative of American Individualism" – because they are not marginalized as an identifiable group, except by class. But in America, white people don't see themselves as lower class no matter how poor they are. Part of being white is being middle class, even if you live in poverty. You still get to watch the same TV shows, go to McDonald's, and walk down the street without being stopped and frisked, just like every other white person.

Guinier/Torres give an example of a white felon, Bill Harwood, who was on a work release program in a Smithfield Foods meat-packing plant where the worst jobs were given to blacks, the next worst to Mexicans, and the best jobs to whites. But Harwood, as a felon, was put in with the black employees. He was "raced" black. Harwood said the work stunk. "But at least I ain't a nigger. I'll find other work soon. I'm a white man."[26]

Guinier/Torres comment: "If everyone is an independent individual, then how does Billy Harwood explain his personal failure? ...He can either internalize his failure as an individual or blame someone else – most likely a person of color."27

And as is abundantly clear from the 2016 presidential election, in which disaffected white voters turned out en masse to support Donald Trump - a candidate spewing racist slurs, militaristic bluster, and insults against anyone not agreeing with him - blaming a minority group for their failure rather than inequities in the system saves face and provides an outlet for frustration and anger, however misplaced.

Minorities, on the other hand - having had long experience with the dominant culture, of which they are most definitely not a part, keeping them from achieving their personal goals - find it much easier to see that the fault lies more in the "rigged" system of power unfairly allocating rewards and punishments than in some personal failing.

This is not a rejection of assuming personal responsibility for oneself, but for taking personal responsibility for changing the conditions in the mine rather than "putting a tiny gas mask on the canary."28

Trickle-Down Racism

The example that opened this chapter, of perpetuating racism by punishing those who have fewer economic resources and who (coincidentally) tend to be people of color, extends in many directions. But I will provide examples of those that specifically impact the criminal justice system in keeping with the focus of this book.

In March 2016, *The Washington Post* published an article by Nick Selby, a police officer turned software entrepreneur, on a study his company conducted that disputed the widespread occurrence of racial profiling. The study did not dispute that such profiling does exist, but that in some - perhaps many - cases, it is economic class profiling that is occurring, not racial profiling.

The study is compelling in that it adds another helpful piece of statistical evidence, this time provided by a company with roots in law enforcement, that racism has morphed into class warfare which is perfectly acceptable to many Americans, despite the fact that it falls disproportionately on people of color.

The study analyzed traffic stops in a city in Texas. It found that blacks and Hispanics were not pulled over any more than whites, as a percentage of the population, but they were given much higher fines when they were stopped. Black women were fined, on average, $204 more than white women.

Breaking this down further, Selby discovered that the higher amounts were most often due to additional citations. The most common added violation for black people was driving with a suspended license, which is very expensive. For Hispanics, it was driving without a license.

Why do these minority drivers have suspended licenses or no licenses at all? Most often because they are poor. "Low-income workers in a region with no public transportation are more likely to have equipment violations on their older cars. When they get a $200 ticket for a broken headlamp, for example, they're more likely to be unable to pay. ... unpaid citations here become arrest warrants. [Unpaid] fines basically double, and the driver's license is often suspended. Next time he's stopped, the driver is cited for that violation and/or driving with a suspended license."[29]

This is exactly the same pattern found in a study conducted in 2015 in California.[30] More than four million California drivers have suspended licenses (17 percent of all drivers), and more than $10 billion of outstanding fines are on the books.

With cash-strapped states seeking more revenue, there is

an increased emphasis on the enforcement of traffic citations. Additional fees (which are not, strictly speaking, tax increases and so they are more politically palatable) are added on to minor offenses, which dramatically increases the original fine. For example, the cost of being ticketed for talking on your cell phone in California while driving is $76. But after the additional penalties and fees are added on (which you cannot avoid), the true cost of the ticket is $250.

If you are a minimum-wage worker and you choose to pay your rent rather than pay your ticket, additional penalties are added, a warrant for your arrest is issued, and eventually your driver's license is suspended. If you are stopped again, you are arrested and your car towed. If you can't afford bail, you sit in jail, lose your job and, if you can't pay the tow company hundreds of dollars, lose your car as well.

The net effect, of course, is to further impoverish those who are already struggling financially – who just happen to be black and Hispanic. There is no need to target minorities for selective enforcement; the historical economic disparities that already exist make that unnecessary. They are "self-selected" by their lack of resources, which we exacerbate by making affordable public resources such as public transportation nonexistent or so inconvenient as to be a meaningless alternative.

The substitution of color-blind economic bias rather than racial bias achieves the same result. The only difference is that all the rest of us, both black and white, who are not poor, can blithely go about our happy lives assuring ourselves that we are not racist - while the "non-racist" application of color-blind laws quietly, insidiously, inexorably makes its way into our own tenuous piece of the American Dream.

Examples and Solutions

In 2016, California implemented a "traffic citation amnesty program" that allowed hundreds of thousands of people with unpaid, outstanding tickets as well as the resulting suspended drivers' licenses to settle with the state, start fresh, and resume driving legally. The program lasted for eighteen months and resulted in hundreds of thousands of drivers getting their licenses back with more than $35 million in fines collected.[31] Nationwide, there are many local and state police agencies changing their traffic ticketing policies to take into account the income level of the person ticketed to allow for alternative forms of payment (e.g. community service). This has reduced the number of arrest warrants for non-payment of traffic citations and ended the practice of ticket quota systems for generating state and local revenue.[32] All of these changes help to reduce the "color-blind" economic discrimination that continues to fall most heavily on people of color. Most often, the cost of a traffic citation and the options which might take into account a person's income level are decided at the state level. Contact your state representative to learn if your state offers alternatives to the crippling cost of a traffic infraction for low-income people and the devastating impact of their unpaid tickets. Often, there will be one or two state legislators who have taken on this cause. Find out who they are and ask how you can help support their efforts to reduce this "invisible" discriminatory practice.

Other methods of so-called "policing for profit" are the ticket and arrest quotas that create arbitrary incentives to lock people up for just about anything. In 2014 in Illinois, a state law was passed that banned the use of ticket quotas for officers and prohibited their job performance from being based on the number of citations issued.[33]

In 2017, the Pretrial Justice Institute (university.

pretrial.org) released the first ever nationwide evaluation of pretrial systems in all fifty states. Overall, they gave the United States a "D" in pretrial justice. Only one state, New Jersey, received an "A" for its recently passed bail reform legislation.[34]

The New Jersey law provides for individual assessments of both flight risk and danger to the community and uses monetary bail as a last resort for ensuring defendants show up for trial. As a result, the number of people awaiting trial in jail in New Jersey dropped by one-third between 2015 and 2017, while its overall crime rate dropped 14 percent in 2017 and violent crime dropped 7 percent,[35] suggesting that releasing qualified defendants to the street did not result in a surge of crime. In California, a "no-cash" bail reform law was just passed that requires judges assess the risk of the person charged fleeing or committing additional crimes if released. Some critics believe this may actually increase the number of people in jails, while others see it as a potential major step in reducing an income-based system of pretrial justice.

We all have implicit bias, which, by definition, we are unconscious of. However, for those of us who are not police officers, it is not a potentially life-and-death matter for us or the community we work in. Implicit bias training is being implemented in various police departments, but unless it is evidence-based, there is no guarantee that these well-intended efforts will bear fruit. The Center for Policing Equity (policingequity.org) offers a rigorous program that includes a comprehensive evaluation both before and after training to look for measurable differences in racial bias and to build more effective means of combatting bias in policing.

Beginning in 2012, police departments in Oakland and Stockton, in addition to four other California cities, engaged in pilot projects to transform their departments' culture, policies, and results in a wide-ranging set of initiatives. Each

program is tailored to the needs of the communities they serve, so it is not a "one-size-fits-all" approach, but the projects all have the same guiding principles – what Stockton Chief of Police Eric Jones calls principled policing:
- Safeguarding the Community
- Living Our Oath
- Respecting and Protecting Rights
- The Badge as a Symbol of Pubic Faith
- Reducing Crime While Increasing Trust[36]

These programs were implemented by a consortium of participants including the California Partnership for Safe Communities, the Chicago Police Department, the California Department of Justice, Trustandjustice.org, Yale and Stanford universities, and multiple community groups in the cities involved. It has a strong component to address implicit bias. But what stands out in these projects is that creating change in one area (implicit bias) involves comprehensive police reform with the support of multiple stakeholders, including organizations from outside the targeted community.

Thus far, the results have been encouraging. Oakland, which had a police department plagued by scandal and poor relations with its black community, saw a thirty-eight percent drop in officer-involved shooting injuries between 2012 and 2015.[37] Between 2009 and 2014, use-of-force incidents dropped by more than eighty percent![38] In 2016, for the first time in more than twenty years, not a single citizen was killed by the Oakland Police Department.[39] Ending racial profiling, though, seems to be more challenging yet. A Stanford study of Oakland P.D. stops showed that the police are still four times more likely to search the cars of black motorists than white motorists.[40] Even so, there was an eighteen-percent improvement in the discrepancy in the first half of 2018.[41]

Stockton, on the other hand, continues to experience

citizen deaths at the hands of police at a high rate,[42] though the overall crime rate in the city has dropped.[43]

Despite these encouraging numbers, the problem of implicit bias seems to be particularly resistant to police reform efforts. Researchers have yet to identify surefire ways to reduce its pernicious effects.

To combat implicit bias in your local police department, find out what sort of implicit bias training is required of officers. Is it one-off training? How is it reinforced by policy? Are citizen/police interactions being tracked and analyzed by race, sexual orientation, or other demographics that can reveal racial profiling patterns? Is this training part of a larger program to enhance community relations and mutual respect between the police and your community? For a better understanding of implicit bias in policing, visit the Stanford Open Policing Project at openpolicing.stanford.edu, or for a narrative account of the problem, read this New York Times report: www.nytimes.com/2015/10/25/us/racial-disparity-traffic-stops-driving-black.html?partner=rss&emc=rss&smid=tw-nytimes&smtyp=cur&referer=t.co/AtjP6DmNMC.

CHAPTER EIGHT

(Very) Organized Crime

Steal a little and they throw you in jail
Steal a lot and they make you king
      —Bob Dylan

What country are we in?
      —Russ Caswell (after having his motel
         seized by the Drug Enforcement Agency)

$5,200,000,000[1] Total value of assets taken from U.S. citizens by federal law enforcement officers in 2014

$3,900,000,000[2] Total value of assets taken from U.S. citizens by burglars in 2014

It's Saturday Morning

You've got your coffee and you just sat down at your computer to do some online bill paying. After that you're going out to buy a used car you found on Craigslist for your seventeen-year-old daughter. You check your mortgage and see with both relief and satisfaction that you have only a few more payments to make until you own your home outright. Thirty years later and you're almost there.

Then there is a loud banging on your door and yelling. What the hell can that be, you think. The banging continues; the yelling too. You jump up and get to the door. You open the door and four armed men burst into the house. They throw you down to the floor and start ransacking your home. They find the $7,000 in cash that you withdrew yesterday for that used car you were going to buy. They find your wallet, your credit cards, and your checkbooks. An hour later they leave, taking your money, your wallet, and checkbook along with a quarter of an ounce of marijuana they found in the back of your daughter's dresser drawer. Is this a home invasion? A robbery gone wrong?

No. It's your local police. Do they arrest you? No. Do they arrest your 17-year-old daughter for possessing less than an ounce of marijuana? No.

Hours later you get back online to deal with your bills and discover that you have no access to your accounts. When you call the bank, you learn that your savings account has been emptied and your checking account has been frozen. You have no money and what little money you had in your checking account is off limits to you. You can't access your own bank account. Did someone get hold of your passwords and hack your account? Is this the cyber-crime you've been hearing about?

No. It's your local law enforcement. The people who are protecting you and your property from criminals. They've got a court order allowing them to empty out your bank accounts.

Several weeks later you receive a letter in the mail notifying you that your house, which you have just spent the past thirty years paying for, will be seized and forfeited to the federal government. There must be some mistake. This is your home, bought and paid for. Who could do this?

Yes, you guessed it. The district attorney has seized your home for being part of a criminal enterprise. What criminal enterprise? Three weeks earlier your 17-year-old daughter sold less than an ounce of her marijuana to a school friend who, it turned out, was an undercover policewoman. Your home is part of a "criminal enterprise" and subject to seizure.

Does this sound far-fetched? An exaggeration, an impossibility? It's not. This and even more outlandish, outrageous, and unbelievable acts of state-sanctioned theft are occurring every day all over America. It's called civil asset forfeiture, and how we arrived at the point where such acts are standard law enforcement practice is a tale of good intentions, political cynicism, and judicial malfeasance at the highest level. Understanding how this is possible in the United States, where the property rights of citizens are supposedly considered sacrosanct, showed me why, when I was arrested, the detective had more interest in my mortgage than my alleged crime; how the police were able to empty my bank accounts before they had even charged me with a crime; and how they were able to keep all my money, regardless of how I had earned it or if I was even convicted of any crime.

Smuggling on the High Seas

The story begins in the earliest days of the republic. The young government was starved for taxes (there would not be any federal income tax for another 137 years). A significant source of federal income was tariffs on imported goods, all which arrived by ship, the only means of transoceanic travel. Even then smugglers understood that it was wise to insulate themselves from their smuggled goods, so they would hire crews to run U.S. Customs patrols. When caught, the actual owners of the goods and the ship were nowhere to be found, so they could not be charged with any criminal act. The United States Government, with the approval of the Supreme Court, followed British legal precedent, which allowed for the ship and the goods themselves to be confiscated and considered "guilty" insofar as they (the goods and ship) were part and parcel of a suspected crime, even if the actual criminal could not be brought to justice.

In the arcane world of legal theory, this is known as a legal fiction. That is, if you are able to arrest a person for the crime of smuggling and they are convicted, the assets they acquired as a result of their criminal activity or the resources used to commit the crime can be criminally forfeited to the government. But if you can't arrest the person committing the crime, the inanimate objects can still be found guilty of a crime. Since you can't very well ask an inanimate object to defend itself, the government gets to presume it is guilty (as opposed to a person's presumption of innocence), and it is incumbent upon the owner to show up and prove their specific assets were acquired legally and/or not party to any criminal act.

Likewise, it is nonsensical to send a ship (or in modern times, cash, cars, boats, and houses) to jail. So the government considers such matters civilly, which deals with monetary damages, as opposed to criminally, which potentially involves jail time. The item at issue is forfeited to the government. But – and this is critical – unlike a criminal proceeding in which you are considered innocent until proven guilty, in a civil asset forfeiture, your assets are considered guilty until proven innocent. And not guilty beyond a reasonable doubt, but guilty based on a much lower standard of proof called "preponderance of evidence." That is, the appearance of guilt is enough to "convict" your property of participating in a crime. So, the fact that your 17-year-old daughter sold a joint to a friend in your home is considered enough evidence to take away your home. Your home is guilty of "participating" in the crime.

For one hundred and thirty years, this loophole in America's constitutional right against unreasonable search and seizure of property was almost exclusively limited to confiscation and forfeiture of smuggled goods, specifically in maritime law. Then there was a brief expansion of civil asset forfeiture during Prohibition when law enforcement took possession of cars used in bootlegging operations. This was a foreshadowing of what would come to pass fifty years later as the war on drugs began to expand.

Forfeiture Comes to the Homeland

In 1970, Congress passed the Comprehensive Drug Abuse Prevention and Control Act. This Act included a provision authorizing the government to seize drugs, drug manufacturing and storage equipment, and items used to transport drugs without necessarily charging any person associated with any of these items. Then, in the late Seventies, Congress passed legislation broadening forfeiture laws to include proceeds from drug transactions and real property.

At this point, this applied only to federal law enforcement. Moreover, any confiscated assets or the profits from selling them were placed into the government's general fund, so there was no direct monetary incentive for a particular agency - the DEA, the FBI, etc. - to seize citizens' assets. They never benefitted directly from any assets they might seize.

Now it's Personal

In 1984, this all changed. Congress created a special fund, the Asset Forfeiture Fund (AFF), which would hold all seized assets and authorized those funds to be used to directly fund the war on drugs. Then, with the understanding that many drug investigations and arrests were conducted by local law enforcement at the city, county, and state levels, they allowed local law enforcement to "partner" with federal agencies so that they would receive eighty percent of the assets seized, with the feds keeping twenty percent for administering the program.

Suddenly, law enforcement at every level could directly benefit from the assets they seized. These financial incentives proved irresistible. Need a new undercover police vehicle? The $80,000 BMW seized from an alleged (but never charged or convicted) drug dealer would do nicely. Need $100,000 to send the police chief and his top brass to a conference on drug interdiction in Hawaii? Seize and sell the home of a person growing ten marijuana plants to treat her Parkinson's disease.

While the entire rationale behind the war on drugs was (and is) just as flawed as alcohol prohibition was decades before, if you accept the flawed premise that the government should control consensual acts among consenting adults, then seizing the houses, cars, boats, and cash allegedly derived from illegal activities as a way of depriving suspected criminals of their profits makes perfect sense.

It certainly made sense to Congress and President Ronald Reagan. It didn't seem to trouble lawmakers that if your assets were honestly earned, you could only recover them by hiring an attorney to contest the seizure, something that might be impossible if you just had your bank accounts emptied and your property taken. Somehow everyone assumed that law enforcement would only seize assets from the bad guys, even if they couldn't prove the bad guys had committed a crime. And, according to drug war rhetoric, these seizures were going to cripple the large criminal organizations that controlled the drug trade. They were never intended to be enforced against the kid on the corner selling nickel bags of pot to his friends.

At this point, you start to get an idea of where this is headed. Instead of just being limited to seizing the goods of smugglers far from the reach of American law enforcement, the federal government was now empowered to seize the assets of American citizens who were most definitely within the reach of law enforcement – but who, for whatever reason, could not be criminally charged. Nor did they need to be charged, let alone convicted, for the government to keep their hard-earned property.

Now the person in question lives in the United States, is innocent – and law enforcement knows this – but has just been stripped of all monetary means by which they can contest this illegal seizure of assets. What happened to the rights against unreasonable seizures, to due process, to the presumption of innocence, and to petition the government for a redress of grievances? Gone, gone, and gone.

Democrats and Republicans alike were happy to jump on the politically convenient war-on-drugs bandwagon, which presented Svengali-like drug dealers as somehow forcing innocent law- abiding Americans into not only parting with their hard-earned money but somehow forcing them to ingest vast quantities of drugs against their will. They lauded civil forfeiture as a tool that would be used solely against drug kingpins to deprive them of their millions in profits and the boats, planes, and vehicles used to smuggle drugs into the country.

None of these representatives of the people seemed to consider the possibility that these new sweeping law enforcement powers were now applicable to *anyone*, and fundamentally undermined the most basic private property rights of Americans who had committed no crimes. Nor did they consider the extent to which these laws might be used against those same innocent Americans they were trying to protect from the supposed scourge of drugs - as a way to pad the coffers of law enforcement agencies nationwide, doing an end-run around the normal government funding mechanisms designed to make agencies accountable to the public.

The loophole now became a cavernous drive-through, grab-all-you-can exception to the Fourth Amendment. State governments quickly realized that they could pass their own forfeiture laws so that their local police could potentially keep one hundred percent of the proceeds of seized assets, no new taxes required.

And why limit asset seizures to the war on drugs? State and federal legislatures added hundreds of new crimes (even if no actual person was ever charged with said crimes) under which asset forfeiture could now take place. Everything was now fair game, from drunk drivers' vehicles to wildlife poachers' guns, to hotels and homes owned by innocent citizens where drug dealers just happened to conduct business. To say nothing of cash-carrying citizens driving the nation's highways.

Prior to 1990, most forfeitures had to be approved by a judge, so there was at least some small degree of oversight of the process. In 1990, Congress passed a law to permit the seizing agency to keep all cash it seized without any judicial review, provided no one contested the seizure. It could also keep any other property it seized with a value of up to

$500,000 with no judicial review. This further incentivized all law enforcement agencies to find ways to "convince" citizens, especially those who insisted that their property had been improperly seized, that it was in their best interests not to contest the seizure. This was most effectively realized by writing the law so that if a citizen could come up with the money to fight the seizure in court and lost, they would not only lose the seized asset but would now be liable for both the government's attorney fees as well as their own. Naturally, the number of citizens with the financial means to engage in such a battle - especially when their financial assets were also seized - were few and far between.

Craven Justice

The Supreme Court, the ultimate backstop when it comes to protecting the American people's fundamental constitutional rights against the momentary demagoguery of politicians, turned their backs on their sworn duty and let these gross insults to our basic rights continue unopposed.

In the case of United States v. Bennis (1996), Tina Bennis had her car seized and forfeited by the government after her husband was arrested in their vehicle for having sex with a prostitute. The car was deemed guilty of abetting the crime. Bennis, who was co-owner of the vehicle, sued, contending that she should not be punished for actions taken by her husband without her knowledge or (obviously!) her approval. ("You're going to get laid? By a prostitute? Sure honey, take the car.")

This was one in a long line of decisions in which the Supreme Court, in a five-to-four decision, upheld the twisted logic of the "thing" being guilty of a crime regardless of whether the owner participated or had any knowledge of the crime committed by the thing itself, let alone actually being convicted of the crime. Writing for the majority, Chief

Justice William Rehnquist did not even attempt to justify the reasonableness, fairness, or ultimate constitutionality of these forfeiture-gone-wild laws, merely stating: "We conclude today, as we concluded 75 years ago, that the cases authorizing actions of the kind at issue are "too firmly fixed in the punitive and remedial jurisprudence of the country to be now displaced,"[3] essentially saying, "We may be wrong, but at least we are consistent!"

With the benefit of 20/20 hindsight, it is difficult not to see both the Congressional actions and the judicial inaction as some of the most shameful and cynical examples of the politics of fear overwhelming the constitutional guarantees protecting citizens from a tyrannical government.

First Congress capitalized on a politically manufactured fear of drugs (and drug users) as the great Satan to pass extreme laws that were ostensibly designed to apply to large-scale criminal organizations, but which had virtually no limits or restrictions on who they could be used against. Then the Supreme Court, bowing to the same political pressures, declined to uphold even the most basic constitutional rights against these blatant violations of all Americans' civil rights.

On the ground and in the everyday life of Americans, these changes in our fundamental rights have played out and continue to play out in truly astounding ways.

Legalized Government Extortion

In what has become the classic piece of investigative journalism on forfeiture, Sarah Stillman of *The New Yorker* detailed the forfeiture scam in the small Texas town of Tenaha.[4]

Highway 59, running through the center of Tenaha, is a secondary highway going all the way from the Mexican border to Canada and is well-used by drug smugglers. But the police in Tenaha discovered that there was no need to limit their traffic stops to searching for drugs or drug money. Anyone passing through town for any reason was a potential target.

In the case of Ron Boatright, Linda Henderson, and Henderson's two young children, they were on their way from Houston to Linden, Texas, where Henderson had grown up. They were planning on buying a used car in Linden and so they had brought about $6,000 in cash with them.

After stopping in Tenaha for gas, they found themselves being followed by the local police and then pulled over for driving in the left-hand passing lane but not passing. After they were briefly questioned, the officer asked Henderson and Boatright if he could search their vehicle, to which they agreed. He quickly discovered the $6,000 located in the center console of the car.

At that point, they and the children were taken to the Tenaha Police Station, where they were offered a deal by the local district attorney: Either sign a waiver "voluntarily" giving up their cash or face felony charges of money laundering and child endangerment, which meant they would immediately be thrown in jail, and, Stillman writes, "their children would be handed over to foster care."[5] The basis of the charges, according to the police report, was that they "fit the profile of drug couriers" and they were driving from Houston, "a known point for distribution of illegal narcotics." And the children, they stated, were supposedly decoys "meant to distract the police as the couple breezed down the road, smoking marijuana"[6] (no marijuana was found in the car, although the arresting officer claimed to have smelled it).

Boatright described her reaction to Stillman: "'Where are we?' Boatright remembers thinking. 'Is this some kind of foreign country, where they're selling people's kids off?'"[7]

This use of so-called waivers is not unique to Tenaha. Local jurisdictions throughout the country are using these waivers as a way of extorting money in exchange for not criminally charging the victims for crimes that, in many cases, they never committed in the first place. But knowing you are innocent is small comfort when faced with the prospect of jail, bail, legal fees and, given the obvious illegitimacy of the entire process, even the chance of being found guilty on top of losing the money you just had taken from you. Not surprisingly, many people simply decide it is better to cut their losses, sign the waiver, and get the hell out of Dodge, so to speak.

Henderson and Boatright signed the waiver, turning over all of their cash.

In the unlikely case that you decide to fight to get back money that is rightfully yours, the government will continue to attempt to extort even a portion of what they have seized – even when they have no case.

Vincent Costello was traveling from New York to Florida to renovate a foreclosed home he had purchased. He had $32,000 in cash to pay for the work. He was pulled over in South Carolina for having a cracked windshield. The officer claimed he smelled marijuana and asked if he could search the vehicle. Costello, knowing he had no drugs and believing he had nothing to hide, agreed to the search.

Finding the $32,000, the police seized it, claiming that anyone driving from New York to Florida with that much cash must be going to buy drugs and that Costello appeared "nervous." Costello hired an attorney to contest the seizure. The government offered to return half the money. At that point, Costello was desperate and agreed to the settlement. However, after paying legal fees of $9,000, he ended up with only $7,000 of his original $32,000.

Even if you get all your money back, it still comes at a price beyond the time and legal fees.

Jose Guerrero was visiting his brother's home in Georgia when police questioned him in his car. According to officials, they had been surveilling Guerrero's brother's home in a separate investigation. Under questioning, Guerrero acknowledged he had approximately $13,000 in cash in the car. The police brought in a canine unit to search for drugs. When the dog "alerted" for drugs, the police had the authority to search the car without a warrant and seized the $13,000 even though no drugs were found. The government asserted that the money was intended to buy drugs, though they didn't even have probable cause to suspect this was the case.

Guerrero found an attorney who agreed to take the case pro bono. At first the government offered to give him back half the money, but Guerrero declined. Three years later he received the entire amount back on the condition that he would not sue the police or prosecutors for violating his civil rights. He took the deal. According to his lawyer, the legal fees alone would have exceeded $50,000.

In April 2016, a grand jury indicted an Oklahoma sheriff for extortion and bribery for seizing $10,000 from two men and then offering to not charge them with any crime if they agreed to sign over the $10,000. The sheriff's lawyers claimed that the indictment was "politically motivated" by civil forfeiture reformers.

According to *The Washington Post*, the government uses civil asset forfeiture procedures "to extort money out of innocent individuals without the messy need to actually show that they did anything wrong or wrongful."[8]

Legalized Government Theft

Russ Caswell was sixty-five years old in 2009 when the government seized the motel that he and his father before him had owned for more than 55 years. It had no mortgage on it and was worth an estimated $1.5 to $2 million, which is perhaps why the DEA chose to seize it in the first place.

The motel, located in Tewksbury, Massachusetts, had been the location of some fifteen drug transactions resulting in arrests over a period of fourteen years. In every case, Caswell had cooperated with the police, doing whatever they asked and taking steps to prevent further drug transactions from taking place on his property. Needless to say, there was no way for him to control the activities of those who rented rooms from him. Those fifteen drug arrests were tied to less than one-hundredth of one percent of the more than 200,000 room rentals that occurred during that 14-year period.

Nonetheless, the DEA was able to seize Caswell's property, charging it (since Caswell had clearly committed no crime) with facilitating these drug transactions. It was up to Caswell to prove his motel was innocent of this facilitation. It's not easy to prove a negative.

Caswell fought the forfeiture, and after four years the government agreed to give up its claim. Caswell describes the seizure as "legalized theft."[9] Conservative columnist George Will described it as "a process of government enrichment that often is indistinguishable from robbery."[10]

Punishment Without a Judge, Jury, or Even a Trial

Jeff Hirsch and his brothers owned and run a successful distribution business on Long Island, New York, providing corner stores with cigarettes, candy, and other sundries. Many of their customers paid them in cash, so the brothers regularly make cash deposits at their local bank. They'd been doing this for twenty-seven years.

Imagine their shock when they went to the bank one morning in 2016 to make a deposit only to discover that the federal government had frozen their account and ended up taking every cent of the $447,000 that was there.

The Hirsches' crime? Well, there was no crime. The government has the authority to seize citizens' bank accounts if they show a pattern of cash deposits that appear to evade the $10,000 cash deposit reporting requirement even if there is no evidence that the money was acquired illegally. There is no law against depositing $9,999 cash in your bank account. There is just the assumption that if you are making such deposits it must be to avoid reporting it to the federal government because it was illegally earned. But many entirely legitimate businesses deal largely in cash and make small deposits for all kinds of reasons.

The Hirsches were aware that they were avoiding the requirement, not because they had anything to hide but because their previous bank had closed their account because the bank didn't want to do the required paperwork for each deposit over $10,000. So, the Hirsches began breaking up their deposits into smaller amounts so the bank wouldn't have to deal with the onerous reporting to the feds. Did the government investigate the Hirsches or their business to determine if they were engaged in some illegal activity? No. Did they contact the Hirsches and require them to explain their pattern of deposits? No. They just took the money.

Having committed no crime, the Hirsches had to try and continue conducting business with no money. To get their money returned, they had to hire an attorney and an accounting firm to audit their books to prove to the government that it was legally earned. The audit alone cost them $25,000.

If this isn't punishment, it's hard to imagine what is. If having to spend $25,000 in accounting fees to get back money that is rightfully yours isn't punishment, then what is? If having a business that you have spent your entire life building held hostage by the government for more than two years isn't punishment, then what is?

But the Hirsches were lucky. The Institute for Justice, a public interest law firm, took their case, and after more than two-and-a-half years, the brothers had their money returned to them. But as the *New York Times* pointed out in an article on civil asset forfeiture in banking, "The median amount seized by the IRS was $34,000, according to the Institute for Justice Analysis, while legal costs can easily mount to $20,000 or more. ...The government can take the money without even filing a criminal complaint, and the owners are left to prove that they are innocent. Many give up."[11]

If you give up, then your money or any other property (except real estate) that the government has taken is administratively forfeit, which simply means that the seizing agency doesn't even have to go before a judge to keep your cash. They act as the judge, jury, and executioner when it comes to taking and keeping your money. Innocence and guilt often play no part in the process. You either have the money and the will to fight or you lose what is rightfully and legally yours. Being innocent and one thin dime won't even get you a cup of coffee in the bizarre world of civil asset forfeiture.

Official Dereliction of Duty

Even if we believe that police culture and policies leave much to be desired, most of us still assume that the police themselves are sincerely trying to catch the "bad guys." But civil forfeiture brings even that basic assumption into serious doubt.

In 2015, John Malcolm of the Heritage Foundation, a conservative think tank, testified before the Pennsylvania Judiciary Committee on Abuses of Civil Forfeiture.[12] He provided an amazing laundry list of the ways in which forfeiture has twisted police priorities to benefit themselves very personally rather than the public they are entrusted to serve.

In Nashville, Tennessee drug enforcement officers were ten times more likely to pull over drivers as they were leaving the city than entering. The reason? It is much more likely that the vehicle entering the city will contain drugs, while the vehicle leaving the city will have cash. Of course, stopping vehicles which contain cash defeats much of the purpose of the war on drugs: to stop the drugs themselves. "If you pull over a car full of drugs, that's of little value to a police department. But if you wait for the drugs to be sold, then pull over cars that meet your drug courier profile as they're leaving a major city, they're much more likely to be filled with cash,"[13] Said Radley Balko, writing in the Washington Post. So in Nashville, police target the cash and ignore the drugs.

In 2008, the Las Cruces, New Mexico, district attorney was caught on video speaking about how police in his city target high-value vehicles parked near bars (in this case a 2008 Mercedes-Benz) and then wait for the unsuspecting driver to emerge from the bar so they can arrest her for a DUI and seize her car to sell at auction. Sometimes they don't even bother with an arrest, or they may not ever get a conviction, but they will keep the car.

The officer who arrested Jennifer Boatright and Ron Henderson in Tenaha, Texas, received a $10,000 bonus paid directly out of the forfeiture fund he spearheaded.

In the case of the seizure of Russ Caswell's motel, a DEA agent admitted under oath that "financial gain played a significant role in determining which properties would be selected for forfeiture. Mr. Caswell's property, which he owned outright...was a target too lucrative to pass up."[14]

These high-dollar examples, though, are the exception. When the idea of civil forfeiture first caught the attention of lawmakers, it was touted as the ultimate tool to use against large criminal organizations with huge resources to bribe officials and invest in expensive planes, boats, and technology to bring in illicit drugs. By being able to seize their assets, if not the drugs themselves, law enforcement could at least cripple these powerful groups financially, making it harder for them to conduct business.

Fast forward to 2016. In Philadelphia, the average cash forfeiture amount was $550. In Georgia, $650.[15] Hardly the bank accounts of drug kingpins. These small amounts are basically nothing more than shakedowns of citizens who will never contest such seizures – because even if they win, they will lose. The cost of fighting for $600 is far more than $600. But there is no cost to law enforcement. It's all upside. However, if you are a person of modest means, $600 may be your rent money, your food money, or your car payment. Now it's gone.

Drawing on numerous reports and studies,[16] it is estimated that thousands of police departments around the country use asset forfeiture to fund up to twenty percent of their annual budgets. Even better for them, the forfeiture money is completely outside of any legislative control or oversight. So you have law enforcement treating themselves to sports tickets, flying themselves out for further "training" in Hawaii, paying local prison inmates to build a private home, and even purchasing the services of prostitutes and marijuana (you'd think they could get the marijuana for free).[17]

Police aren't out there chasing the bad guys; they're out there chasing the money.

Violation of Police Code of Conduct
Corruption

The police officers' Code of Ethics include the following promise: "I will never act officiously or permit personal feelings, prejudices, animosities, or friendships to influence my decisions. With no compromise for crime and with relentless prosecution of criminals, I will enforce the law courteously and appropriately without fear or favor, malice or ill will, never employing unnecessary force or violence and never accepting gratuities."[18]

In March 2013, investigative reporter Phil Williams got hold of dashcam video showing local Tennessee law enforcement agents alternately threatening and then negotiating with a truck driver to tell them where the cash was hidden in his eighteen-wheeler.

At first, they threatened him with arrest if he didn't tell them. But then the video goes on to show the officer assuring the trucker that "money laundering is a federal offense. The good thing is we don't deal with the feds. So, if you tell me it ain't your money...I'm not asking you if you have knowledge about it [the money]. And I won't be asking you if you have knowledge about it. All I'm asking you is, where's the money? I don't even care where you got it. I just want the product."[19]

Finally, the officer made his final offer: "You sign these forms saying you don't know anything about it. You're disclaiming it, it's not yours, and it's done."[20] The driver finally relented. The money was hidden in the refrigerated section of the truck. The police collected almost $500,000 in cash and the driver got to go on his way.

In Stillman's *New Yorker* article, she describes a traffic stop that netted more than $620,000, all of it neatly wrapped up as Christmas presents, given that it was in late December. The woman driving the vehicle was jailed for one night in Tenaha and then released.

It's hard to call these amounts of money "gratuities" – more like winning the drug dealer lottery jackpot – but they certainly seem to encourage officers of the law to overlook at lot of wrongdoing they are supposed to be "relentlessly prosecuting without fear or favor." In other countries, this type of quid pro quo is commonly called corruption.

Entrapment: Pretext Stops, Reverse Stings, and "Smelling Marijuana"

Of all the cars on the road, how is it that police regularly stop drivers who have substantial cash? First, they tend to stop drivers who are either from out of state or driving rental cars. No doubt, some of these people are actually intent on buying drugs or have just sold drugs, but many of them are carrying cash for all kinds of other legitimate reasons: they are going to buy a used car; they are moving and have their nest egg with them; they are tourists and brought along their "fun" money. Whatever the reason, cops know that these types of vehicles are more likely to have substantial cash on board. But here in America you can't just pull someone over for no reason. They have to have committed a crime. Right?

No worries. Back in 1996, the Supreme Court affirmed that "pretext stops" –traffic stops manufactured by police with the goal of investigating another crime of which they have no evidence (such as carrying cash with the intent to buy drugs) - were legal.

So, if the police want to pull over an out-of-state vehicle to learn if the driver is carrying any cash, they pull the driver over for "driving in the passing lane (but not passing)," as happened to Linda Henderson and Ron Boatright in Texas. Or they stop you for speeding five miles an hour over the speed limit, or for an "improper lane change." If the police want to stop you, they will find a way even if you have done nothing wrong. They can always find a pretext.

But stopping you is only the first step. The officer cannot search your vehicle for cash or drugs without probable cause, or unless you give her permission. So, as in the case in Tenaha, Texas, the arresting officer wrote in his report that he "smelled marijuana." The fact that no marijuana was found in the car doesn't matter. If the officer thinks he smells marijuana, he has probable cause to search the vehicle.

If the officer fails to detect some faint odor of nonexistent marijuana, he may bring in a drug sniffing dog. Drug dogs are notoriously unreliable when it comes to detecting drugs.[21] Nonetheless, the Supreme Court affirmed that a drug dog's alert for drugs was also sufficient probable cause to allow a police officer to search you and your vehicle without a warrant. In many of the cases described previously, the dog alerted for drugs, a search was done, but no drugs were found. But either the officers already knew the driver had cash or cash was discovered in the search.

Once the police find your cash, they will often have the dog sniff the cash for drug residue, which will further "prove" that you are a drug dealer. What they don't mention is that 80 percent of all U.S. paper currency has a detectable residue of drugs on it, usually cocaine. Moreover, it has been shown that drug dogs respond to subtle verbal and non-verbal cues by their handlers to "alert" even when no drugs are present.[22]

All of this most closely resembles the stuff of mediocre television drama: the classic setup. And indeed, from pretext stop to the smell of nonexistent marijuana, to the presumption that any cash must be for a drug buy, it's cheap theatrics. But in the U.S., home of hyperbolic TV drama, it's entirely real. In this case, the bad actors are the police.

Perhaps the most egregious "pretext" stops occur in Philadelphia. The Philadelphia police, in partnership with the city district attorney, has one of the most robust civil forfeiture operations in the entire country. In fact, Philadelphia seized more than $6 million in assets compared to Los Angeles's $1.2 million, and Los Angeles has six times more people.

While the bulk of the money seized is in cash, about thirty percent comes from homes the police have seized from local residents. Police target low-level drug users in the hope that the drug sale will occur in a home that they can then seize.

Take the case of Markela and Chris Sourovelis. Their twenty-two-year-old son sold forty dollars of heroin to an undercover cop in the Sourovelis's home. The parents had no idea their son was selling drugs. He had never been in trouble with the law. He had no criminal record at all. Nor was he the owner of the family's home. Nonetheless, a month after his arrest, the police showed up and seized the Sourovelis home without notice or warning. The Sourovelises were now homeless and at risk of losing the home they had spent years working to buy.

Mary and Leon Adams had lived in their home in Philadelphia for more than 50 years. Their son, Leon Jr., also lived with them. Unbeknownst to the parents, Leon Jr. was selling small amounts of marijuana, in $20 increments. He sold several batches to a police informant on the porch of his parents' home. The police came and arrested Leon Jr. and then a month later showed up at the Adams's with a "seize and seal" order, telling them they had ten minutes to collect whatever they could and leave their home forever. The city was charging their home with "facilitating a drug transaction." The parents, having committed no crime, were not charged. Leon Sr. was suffering from pancreatic cancer at the time.

The war on drugs has always promoted itself as targeting drug dealers rather than drug users, who were portrayed as innocent, weak-willed victims of the dealers. As such, police most often conducted undercover drug buys to ensnare the dealer, no matter how low down on the totem pole he was.

With the advent of asset forfeiture, that changed. Now it made much more sense to do a reverse sting in which the police play the role of the drug dealer and arrest the buyer. Why? Because the buyer has actual money the police can seize. Describing the many ways asset forfeiture has warped police priorities, an article in the *Arizona Law Review* states that if the goal of civil forfeiture is "preventing crime and putting major offenders away [this is] inconsistent with practices such as reverse stings because they target relatively low-level, non-trafficking drug offenders who are subject to less severe criminal penalties than those arrested for drug sales and do not affect drug supply. Instead, law enforcement targets buyers rather than sellers because buyers tend to have more cash on hand subject to forfeiture."[23]

Finally, one of the more creative asset forfeiture schemes was reported by Radley Balko, writing for the Huffington Post. He described how a Wisconsin drug task force arrested Joel Greer on drug charges, with bail was set at $7,500. When his mother spoke to the police about bailing him out of jail, they advised her to "bring cash," which she did. But upon arriving at the police station, the police accused her of bringing "drug money" even though she had ATM receipts showing that she and other family members had just withdrawn the funds from various bank. The cops trotted out the drug sniffing dog to smell the money and it alerted – no surprise to the police, of course. They seized her bail money. It took Greer more than four months to recover her money. This was just one of several such cases involving this particular drug task force.

In 2014, *The Washington Post* ran a four-part series exposing the many facets of the failed civil asset forfeiture laws now in place. Following the series, two former directors of the Department of Justice's Asset Forfeiture office wrote the following in a letter to the Post:

"...civil forfeiture is fundamentally at odds with our judicial system and notions of fairness. It is unreformable. ...The program began with good intentions but now, having failed in both purpose and execution, it should be abolished."[24]

Taking Back Our Civil Rights

All that is plainly wrong, unfair, corrupt, and criminal about civil asset forfeiture must be ultimately and formally recognized by upholding our constitutional rights in the face of these violations. The fundamental point is not just about upholding our rights (though this is important), but understanding and appreciating that our constitutional rights are nothing more (and nothing less) than formal statements about what we all know to be the differences between right and wrong, between fairness and abuse, between corruption and honesty – not just in civil forfeiture, but in any aspect of our relations to each other and to our government. For all their complexity, at heart our constitutional rights reflect our most basic and best ideals about how we treat others and wish to be treated.

Despite the Supreme Court's failure to strike down these unconstitutional government powers, public outcry and new justices with different perspectives can result in judicial course corrections. Alternatively, politicians can pass legislation prohibiting such abuses even if the Court declines to affirm citizens' rights.

Both of these approaches can complement and reinforce the other. High-profile lawsuits can result in judicial victories, and losses can inspire grassroots campaigns to change the laws themselves. Both are happening in the area of civil asset forfeiture. State legislators in New Mexico and Nebraska have banned civil asset forfeiture outright. Unfortunately, law enforcement in these states continues to disregard state law by partnering with the federal government and receiving back eighty percent of the forfeiture funds that are jointly seized.

Examples and Solutions

When it comes to asset forfeiture, New Mexico became the first state to ban it outright. Previously in New Mexico, law enforcement was entitled to keep 100 percent of forfeiture in addition to an average of $2.4 million per year from the federal equitable sharing program. That changed when a coalition of civil rights groups was able to convince the legislature to pass sweeping reforms before local police were able to mount significant opposition.

Now assets can only be seized in criminal cases and, more importantly, only be taken after a criminal conviction if they're associated with the crime and if law enforcement successfully fights for them during a separate trial in criminal court. Additionally, the proceeds go into a general state fund, not directly to law enforcement, ending the direct benefits to the police which drives so much of their forfeiture activity. Finally, the law bans the practice of turning over assets to the federal government, unless they are worth at least $50,000.

Any or all of these policy changes can be implemented on the local level, meaning that you can advocate for them with your city council, county supervisor, and at the ballot box when you vote for the city or county district attorney as well as other local officials. Here is a checklist of law enforcement financial incentives that need to end:

- End quotas for tickets and arrests.
- Limit fines for people of low income.
- Prohibit courts from requiring individuals to pay the cost of correctional and probation fees.
- Stop courts from issuing additional fines and arrest warrants for failure to appear for traffic court.
- Prohibit police from seizing assets unless the person is convicted of a crime and his assets are proved to be part of that crime.
- Prohibit police from receiving funds from any forfeited assets, with those funds instead going to a general fund.
- Require that police fines and civil settlements are paid out of the department's budget, not the general fund of the city or county.
- Find out where your local representatives and the police stand on the issue of asset forfeiture, and advocate for change. For more information visit campaignzero's policing for profit webpage at www.join campaign zero. org/end-policing-for-profit.

CHAPTER NINE

Apologies, Respect, and
Procedural Justice

*I'm not concerned with your liking or disliking me.
All I ask is that you respect me as a human being.*
—Jackie Robinson

*Our systems are, perhaps, nothing more than an
unconscious apology for our faults, a gigantic scaffolding
whose object is to hide from us our favorite sin.*
—Henri Frederic Amiel

*All men make mistakes, but a good man yields when he
knows his course is wrong, and repairs the evil. The only
crime is pride.*
—Sophocles

Apologies

In his bestselling book, *Just Mercy*, civil rights attorney Bryan Stevenson (who is African-American) tells the story of his near-fatal encounter with the police outside of his Atlanta apartment.[1] It was close to midnight and he had just pulled up in front of his apartment after a long day at work. Playing on the radio was a special on Sly and the Family Stone, one of Stevenson's favorite groups. Like many of us would in a similar situation, he remained seated in his car through several of his favorite songs. It was several songs later that he noticed "flashing police light approaching."[2]

To his surprise, the police car pulled up about twenty feet in front of his parked car. He thought it odd since there was nothing happening on his street. It was a one-way street and he was parked facing the right way. The police car had come down the street from the other direction, against the one-way traffic. Only when they lit up their spotlight and shined it directly on him did he begin to consider that they were there because of him.

After a minute, with the spotlight still trained on him, the police emerged from their vehicle. They weren't in regular uniforms but were dressed in military-style clothing, all black with vests. Stevenson decided he should get inside his apartment, still thinking that the police were there on some other business.

As Stevenson describes it, as soon as he got out of his car, the officer closest to him pulled out his gun and screamed, "'Move and I'll blow your head off!'"[3] But in his shock and fear, Stevenson couldn't understand what the officer was saying.

The officer ordered him to put his hands up, which he did. He had never had anyone pull a gun on him before. He thought about running, but decided that wasn't a good idea. Involuntarily, he found himself saying to both himself and the police, "It's all right. It's okay. It's okay. It's okay."

The second officer came around behind him and shoved him up against his car and pulled his hands behind his back. They started to question him. What was he doing in this neighborhood? (He lived there.) What was he doing in his car? (Listening to the radio.) Neighbors started filtering out of their houses to watch the scene. The second officer started searching through his car, looking in his glove compartment, going through his work papers. As a lawyer, Stevenson knew the search was entirely illegal, but he said nothing.

White neighbors started calling out the officers to "ask him about my missing vacuum cleaner. Ask him what happened to my cat."

After about 15 minutes, the police confirmed that Stevenson had done nothing wrong and there were no warrants out for his arrest.

"I asked them to apologize and they wouldn't. The officer who left said, 'You should be lucky you got away. Next time we'll get you.' ..."It was surreal and terrifying."[4]

Then there was the case of Cheye Calvo. He was thirty-seven years old in 2008 and the mayor of Berwyn Heights, a small town in Prince George County, Maryland.[5] However, this was largely a volunteer position. His fulltime work was at an educational foundation in nearby Washington, D.C.

It was early evening on July 29th of that year when he took his dogs, black labs, out for a short walk before he got ready to attend a community meeting in town. Returning from his walk, he brought in a package left at his front door and went upstairs to change for the meeting.

Minutes later he heard his mother-in-law scream. Looking out his window, he saw armed men rushing his front door. The police blew open his front door with an explosive device and started firing their weapons. Except Calvo had no idea it was the police. He screamed at them not to shoot.

They ordered him to come downstairs with his hands up. He came down in his underwear. The police grabbed him, handcuffed him, and forced him to his knees. He thought he was about to be killed."[6]

Both of Calvo's dogs were dead, shot by police immediately upon entering the house. For four hours, the police searched his home, tracking the dogs' blood everywhere. For four hours, they held Calvo and his mother-in-law without a search warrant, which didn't show up until hours after they had stormed the house. They found no drugs, no money, no evidence of any crime whatsoever.

The raid, it turned out, was based on a FedEx delivery containing marijuana that had Calvo's address on the package. The package was part of a scheme in which addresses of innocent citizens were used to mail drugs that were then intercepted by a local FedEx employee before the actual delivery could occur. The county drug task force had intercepted this package. In fact, they had intercepted several packages and knew about the use of innocent community members' addresses. Even so, with no additional investigation, an officer, disguised as a delivery person, had left it on the front porch of Calvo's home. Once the package was retrieved by the unknowing Calvo, the raid could commence.

As journalist Radley Balko takes pains to point out in his summation of the case, "Even after they realized they had just mistakenly raided the mayor's house, the officers didn't apologize to Calvo or Porter (Calvo's mother-in-law)."[7]

Several days later, the county sheriff called Calvo to let him know that he and his mother-in-law were no longer considered suspects, but he "made sure to explicitly tell the mayor that the call should not be interpreted as an apology."[8]

Several months later, one of the county's top government officials said that because the police had been cleared of any wrongdoing, "that was the only apology necessary – and in fact they deserved praise for clearing Calvo's name after nearly killing him."[9]

Brien Farrell, the City of Santa Rosa police attorney who served on the Sonoma County policing task force, described his work on a subcommittee exploring how police should respond to so-called "critical incidences" in which lethal force is involved (the policy they developed was never adopted):

"...that little policy would call for whichever police agency was involved in meeting privately with the family and expressing condolences, acknowledging their loss, and in an appropriate way saying how sorry they were that they had lost a loved one. Not assuming civil liability. Not assuming criminal liability. Listening to the family."

"...sometimes, after the fact, you discover that their loved one didn't threaten the life of a police officer either, but that's not what was perceived by the officer in the moment. ...It doesn't matter which case it is. The *family* didn't threaten the life of an officer. And in both cases, there has been a tragedy, so why not show respect and dignity?"[10]

Time and time again, after the most terrifying and traumatizing experiences at the hands of the police, the victims are less interested in justice, or in compensation, than in an apology. Yet that is often the one thing they never receive.

In my one previous run-in with the police, many years earlier, this was made terribly clear to me. On a spring morning in 2004 in Sonoma, California, my doorbell rang. I don't know what day it was exactly, but I know it was a weekday because I had just dropped off my daughter at her K-6 Spanish immersion school and my son was already at his preschool.

I was working from home that day, as I had the luxury of

doing in the small business my ex-wife and I operated. I wasn't expecting anybody, so I guessed it was either Mormon missionaries or Seventh Day Adventists handing out literature. Telling either of them I was happily Jewish was a sure way to quickly end a potentially long proselytizing session.

I opened my front door and there were two men on my front step, casually dressed, middle-aged, and definitely not religious zealots.

"Are you Larry Bearg?" they asked.

"Yes."

They flashed their badges. "I'm detective so-and-so," said one. (When confronted by the police, you almost instantly find yourself unable to remember even the simplest details, overwhelmed by adrenaline and fear, even if you have done absolutely nothing wrong.)

The other detective introduced himself, then said, "We want to talk to you."

"Sure."

I couldn't imagine what this could be about, but I had nothing to be concerned about. I was a law-abiding citizen. Perhaps it was about one of my employees?

"We are investigating you for child pornography and child molestation."

I laughed. I thought they were joking. The statement was so bizarre, so foreign, so incredibly absurd that my spontaneous unfiltered response was to laugh.

"You think this is funny?" It wasn't a question.

Standing there at my front door, the detectives explained to me that they had photographs of me with a young girl sitting naked in my lap, looking uncomfortable, even scared.

I couldn't understand what photographs they could possibly be talking about. I had never had some naked young girl sitting on my lap, much less had someone photograph me with some young girl. I was sure they must be confusing me with someone else.

They kept talking, asking me questions. "Did I have a daughter?"

"Yes."

"Did you do 'things' with her?"

"Most definitely not."

"Did you take pictures of her naked?"

A lightbulb went off in my head, like you see in the cartoons. It really was like that. Again, I laughed (not a good idea).

I knew why they were here. This was back in the days before digital cameras and camera phones. Back when you dropped your canisters of film off at a processor to be developed. You went back a week later and picked up your photos.

Months before, I had dropped off some family photos to be developed. I had gone back several times to pick up my photos, but each time I asked, the elderly woman who ran the photo department said that she couldn't find my photos. Eventually I had forgotten about them.

These were the photos to which they were referring. As for who took this photo of my daughter sitting naked on my lap, I remembered that as well. Like many families, we were sure we had the cutest, most amazing, most fantastic children who had ever been born and we wanted to document them in all their glory. We were always taking photos. Lots of photos.

My three-year-old son, Dylan, like all three-year-olds, wanted to play with the camera that his dad, mom, and even his sister were constantly holding, looking through, and clicking. Despite my misgivings about having his sticky, grimy fingers on the camera, I finally gave in and showed him which button to push to take a picture. I sat my naked daughter on my lap (we had just had a morning hot tub, a daily ritual in our house as they grew up) and Dylan clumsily clicked the shutter a few times, pretending to look through the viewfinder. I never actually considered he had managed to find us in the frame or had in fact taken photos of us. But he had! These were the photos to which the detectives were referring.

As I explained the circumstances of these photographs to the detectives at my door, they wanted to know if we spent a lot of time "naked" as a family. We did.

"Do you have family photos documenting that?"

I did.

"Could we see them?"

"Sure." (In retrospect, this was a terrible mistake. I have since discovered that the most common police investigative tactic is to ask suspects for additional information under the guise of "helping to clear you" of any wrongdoing, when in fact they are seeking confirmatory evidence to charge you with a crime and you are giving up your right to "remain silent" as a natural inclination to prove your innocence.)

I invited the detectives into my house. I pulled out our family photo albums, which I had lovingly compiled, and showed them photo after photo of our kids naked in the backyard, naked at the dinner table trying to blow out their birthday candles, dancing naked in the living room.

They looked at the photos and said they would continue their investigation and left. Then, without notifying me, they went to my daughter's school, had her pulled out of class, and interviewed her, a seven-year old, with no other adults present, about any abuse she might have experienced.

Next, they contacted my ex-wife. At this point we were not yet divorced, only separated. While statistics on the prevalence of ex-spouses falsely accusing their ex of child abuse are hard to come by, estimates are that they run from 5 percent to as high as 35 percent of all such abuse reports.[11]

Fortunately, my wife, estranged though we were, was not

so embittered that she would lie about this, and expressed to the detectives that, knowing me well, there was no way I would ever sexually or otherwise abuse my children.

Even though I knew I had done nothing wrong and that my estranged wife had defended my character and confirmed our casual family nudity, I was still fearful. I felt I was caught up in some alternate reality in which the reality in which I lived was looked at suspiciously, as an act or some sort of deception. Everyone has heard the cliché, "It's hard to prove a negative." While there was certainly no evidence of my being a child pornographer (the photo of my daughter on my lap notwithstanding), it was clear that the police could accuse me of anything if they so wished.

I called an attorney friend and asked his advice. "Wait and see what happens," he told me.

After several weeks, I called one of the detectives and received the good news. They had found nothing that suggested I was abusing my children or that my photos were pornographic in nature or intent.

What a relief! The first thing that came to my mind was that I wanted to retrieve those photos, which were private, personal, and non-pornographic.

"No," he said.

"But they are my photos, my property," I suggested.

"We keep these things," he said.

Intimidated, I thanked him and hung up. I called my attorney friend.

"Don't I have rights? I'm innocent! Those are my photos and they are my property. I don't want those private family photos sitting in some police file for anyone to see. They have no right and no reason to keep them. I didn't commit any crime."

"Call Steve," he suggested. Steve was another friend of mine, an attorney who worked for the County of Sonoma.

No doubt he had connections he could call on to get my photos back.

I called Steve and explained the situation to him. He said he would make some calls.

Several days later, after the calls had been made, I called the detective again and asked for my photos back. He suggested I come by the Hall of Justice where he worked. He would meet me in the lobby.

The lobby was busy. He took me to a less crowded corner. I admit I felt a little smug. I knew people. I could make the levers of power work in my favor. He would be apologetic. Maybe even be ashamed at trying to violate my rights as a law-abiding American citizen.

"Do you have my photos?"

He looked at me without any sign of offering an apology.

"Do you think this was bad?" he asked me.

"What?" I had no idea what he was talking about.

"This was nothing. If you fuck with me, I will make your life a living hell. You will lose your kids, you will never get over this. Do you understand me?"

"Yes,"

"Good."

I left.

I called my attorney friend at the county. I was outraged. I was righteous. "How could this be? This was wrong. Wasn't it illegal? Wasn't there something to do? How could they keep *my* photos? *My* private property.

"Larry," he told me, "I know you think you have rights. You think that there are laws that protect you and that they are applied fairly. I know you did nothing wrong and those photos are yours. But there is something you need to understand: When it comes down to it, we live in a police state. You can fight it, but is it really worth it to you? They *will* make your life hell. You could lose your children. I advise you to let it go. It's not worth it."

At that time in my life, I didn't have the courage, resources, or knowledge to fight that battle. I let it go. But the absolute arrogance of the detective, his flaunting of his power, even in the face of my innocence, was stunning. The complete absence of any sort of humility, or an acknowledgment of having suspected me of something I didn't do, was breathtaking. Where was his humanity, I wondered?

What makes it so hard for the police to apologize when - as in the cases of Bryan Stevenson and Cheye Calvo - they have made unequivocal errors in the execution of their duties? Errors that are neither small nor insignificant to those who experience them. Errors that are life changing.

Here we step off into the realm of human relations. There is no law requiring the police to apologize for their mistakes. And there is no constitutional right for any of us to receive an apology. An apology has no material value. It will not change what has happened, nor make up for abuse, indignity, or trauma in any visible or material way. Its value is invisible, yet entirely real. An apology often becomes the most important act someone can do for someone they have wronged. This is especially true when the person or group perpetrating the harm is in a position of power relative to the person suffering the injury.

If you consider times when you have been hurt by someone's behavior and then received an apology, it is easy to grasp why the apology is of great importance. Receiving a sincere apology (insincere apologies are a whole other discussion) makes you feel that the person who harmed you recognizes and regrets the harm they caused. You are validated as a human being. It is both the recognition and the regret of an apology that indicates the offending person is sharing in our pain that thereby lessens it. An apology is an implicit acknowledgement of our mutual humanity. A heartfelt apology is heartfelt because the person apologizing is recognizing the hurt in themselves that they have caused in you.

As the injured party, when you are wronged you feel diminished and demeaned. When someone apologizes, they are implicitly acknowledging their own vulnerability by admitting that what they did was wrong, even though, at the time they did it, they believed it was the right thing to do. That expression of regret levels the playing field in terms of how each of you feels about yourself and each other. Even if the person who hurt you is more powerful, their apology joins their vulnerability of being sorry to your vulnerability of being hurt. An equilibrium in restored. A relationship is repaired.

So, if an apology is generally a positive thing for all those involved, why do we, and more specifically the police, have such a hard time offering one?

The scientific literature on apologies sheds some light on why this is the case.

In a 2002 article in the *Journal of the American Academy of Psychiatry and the Law*,[12] the authors offer a three-part definition of an apology:

- An acknowledgment of the offense so that the victim's account is verified. (Saying "That's not what really happened" is not an apology.)
- Admitting what you did was wrong and that you have no defense, justification, or other excuse for your actions. (Saying "I did it, but..." is not an apology.) Implicit in this acknowledgment is that you will also accept the consequences of your actions, whatever those may be.
- In acknowledging your mistake, you imply that you will not repeat it. (Apologizing with the expectation that you will repeat the same offense and again apologize is not a true apology.)

The impact on the victim of such apologies, research shows, is an increased sense of justice and positive sentiments toward the perpetrators. In other studies, if the offender does not make appropriate amends or the victim does not accept those amends (forgives the offender), then the rest of the community may retaliate against either the victim or offender for failing to facilitate the reconciliation between the two parties. All of this sounds like a strong case for both sincere apologies and forgiveness.

Other benefits that come from apologizing are diffusing the anger of victims and other members of the community; restoring one's reputation in the eyes of the victim and other people (it takes moral courage to apologize); regaining acceptance of the community; and repairing personal relationships. Apologies may even reduce our own sense of guilt.[13]

So why do we *still* find it hard to apologize?

To answer that question, researchers had members of various groups either apologize, refuse to apologize, or do nothing, and then measured their feelings of self-worth, power, control, and independence.

What they found was revealing. Those who refused to apologize reported higher levels of perceived power.[14] (Note that this is "perceived," not necessarily actual, power.) In another study, the researchers found that apologizing and refusing to apologize both elicited greater feelings of control and power – and a sense of consistency in personal thought and action – than those who did nothing. Also worth noting: The non-apologizers also showed higher self-esteem. Apologizing is humbling. You tend to feel a bit bad about yourself.

Their findings say nothing about how the victims felt about this refusal to apologize, nor about how this might play out in social contexts of long-term intimately related communities. But in the short term, refusing to apologize clearly showed some unexpected personal benefits to the offender. The researchers concluded: "These findings point to potential barriers to victim–offender reconciliation after an interpersonal harm, highlighting the need to better understand the psychology of harm-doers and their defensive behavior for self-focused motives."[15]

If we place police in this short-term context and within the context of their own subculture of bullying, which is defined as the abuse of power, then it quickly becomes apparent why it would be both difficult and even perceived as harmful to apologize to those they have harmed.

By definition, if an apology levels the emotional playing field between the offender and the victim, the offender experiences a loss of power relative to the victim over whom he exercised power. Given that the current police paradigm is all about asserting and maintaining both power and control in every citizen/police interaction, any diminishment of that approach, in any context, would be anathema to law enforcement.

The countervailing benefits of an apology - that it increases the victim's sense of justice and makes for more group harmony - would also have little apparent value to police, at least in the short term. They already see themselves as separate, apart, and isolated from the rest of the society. If they don't feel they have any stake in the community's sense of justice in regard to their interactions, apologizing has no positive effect. There is no relationship that needs repairing. Apologizing can only reduce the coercive power and control they are trying to maintain.

Lastly, we return to the idea of cognitive dissonance. Having certain strongly held beliefs about oneself, particularly those publicly promoted by the police - that they protect and serve the community, that they only exercise their powers against the "bad guys" who deserve what they get, and all those other justifications listed previously, make it immensely uncomfortable to acknowledge, in the form of an apology, that those laudable standards are not always upheld. Writing about the psychology of apologies, journalist Cindy May comments: "By refusing to apologize, we deny any incongruity between belief and action, thus preserving a sense of authenticity and self-worth"[16] - even if the rest of us can see the ever-widening gulf between those beliefs and the actions that result.

An apology - so humbling, so human, and such an integral part of who we are - reflects a whole world of shame, denial, fear, and anger on the part of the police. And we have to consider how we have helped make it so hard for them to express this most human of responses to those we have hurt yet claim to care about.

In his book, *The Power Paradox*[17], social scientist Dacher Keltner describes how power is given by a community rather than taken from a community. The paradox lies in the fact that power is gained by helping others achieve their goals, by being generous, by showing respect and kindness. But once power is realized, there is the tendency to attribute it to one's own exceptional qualities, to become selfish, to feel entitled.

Once power is achieved, those in power often forget all those qualities that brought them to power in the first place, and a sense of common purpose and community morphs into one of isolation and alienation. This paradox, Dacher writes, results in those in power committing "...acts of incivility [that] violate sacred rules of respect..." When those in power no longer respect those over whom they have power "the social fabric wears thin."[18]

If we are accorded power to serve others and then abuse it by using it to shame and disrespect them, the results are the opposite of what the power was originally intended to do. We may still have power, but now it is maintained by coercion rather than cooperation. It is held by fiat, not by common accord.

The death of Philando Castile in Minnesota at the hands of the police and the subsequent shooting deaths of five Dallas police officers (July 2016) at a protest over Castile's death show too clearly and painfully how thin our social fabric has worn when power is viewed as corrupt by those who are subject to its excesses.

The inability of law enforcement to apologize when it has clearly wronged someone is indicative of a culture that knows that in many instances its power is not granted by the community it serves, but taken from a community that deserves better.

Respect and Dignity

Apologies, respect, dignity, and fairness seem to be concepts that have no formal place in the law, our system of justice, or our constitutional rights. Yet they are fundamental to our way of life. These "soft" ideas are the informal under-standings that are the actual basis for the formal statements that we hold so dear - those cited in our Constitution - and all that they stand for. Yet it is how these formal laws and rights are interpreted and applied that either manifest our best intentions or give rise to our worst selves. Standing alone, without these "soft" ideals as guiding forces, our formal statements become mere platitudes that ring hollow in the face of on-the-ground truths.

The idea of respect - which hopefully precedes apology (if we are respectful of people, we will have fewer apologies to make) - is so basic to our lives that most of us rarely consider it at all. I recall reading those apocryphal news stories that always featured some black teenager shooting another black teenager "because he disrespected me" (according to the shooter quoted in the news report). I remember thinking, *So you shoot someone because he looked at you the wrong way? Those (black) people are crazy.*

I apologize now for my complete ignorance about how black people in America have had so little respect over the centuries that a lack of respect for someone who has had none can quickly become a life-or-death issue.

Respect is not such a "soft" concept after all.

Why is respect - which, like an apology, provides no material gain to the recipient nor loss to the giver - such a life and death matter? Because it is the invisible currency by which we recognize that others have value, simply by virtue of our common humanity. To be disrespectful is to make someone less than human. It's hard to be more abusive than that.

Sociologists describe two types of respect.[19] The first, categorical respect, is respect granted to those we accord membership in our community. That community can be defined as broadly as all human beings (or even as the entire natural world, as environmentalists strive to do), or narrowly, such as only our nation, our religious group, or our political affiliation. Respect is given to those who are in the category we define as worthy of respect however we define it.

The second type of respect is contingent. When we say to someone, "You need to earn my respect," we are speaking of respect contingent upon their showing themselves "worthy" of respect by whatever measure we consider of value: Do they have more knowledge and skills applicable to the task at hand than others in the group? If so, then they are accorded relatively more respect than less able members. If the task at hand is athletic, then the better players will be more highly respected than those of lesser skill. If you are a musician, the better you play your instrument the more respect you will receive based on that skill.

Categorical respect encompasses contingent respect insofar as to earn contingent respect you must first be granted categorical respect as a general member of a given community. Then, based on whatever attributes are deemed relevant in that group, you will be accorded a degree of contingent respect within the group.

The experience of having categorical respect is described as "having a voice, being heard, and participating in the wider community."[20] On the other hand, contingent respect is experienced as "having an influence and an impact"[21] within the group. So, while you may be given categorical respect as a member of a community, you may not have much or any contingent respect - that is, influence relative to other members. As you can see, these two types of respect are not entirely unconnected or distinct. For example, if you have no influence in your community (contingent respect), are you, in fact, a member of that community at all (categorical respect)? That is, if you are a member in name only, then are you really a member?

On the face of it, not receiving respect of either type might seem inconsequential. After all, if you respect yourself, who cares what others think or how they treat you? But not granting others respect is far from an act of benign neglect. In its expression, it is an aggressive act of devaluing a person. And when the community at large sanctions that devaluation both in its laws and in its culture, lack of respect is simply the abuse of power: bullying.

Thus, when law enforcement denies people the categorical respect they deserve as fellow human beings when they are demeaned and humiliated, which may be entirely legal* but nonetheless a complete disavowal of the ideals we claim to hold dear in the United States, then we have betrayed ourselves.

In America, we have not only made convicted criminals

---

* As the Supreme Court explicitly stated in the Atwater v. Lago Vista case described on page 208

unworthy of basic respect as human beings,* we have extended this disrespect to those who simply interact with law enforcement before any determination of guilt or innocence is made. In the public mind, such people are already guilty. And if they are guilty, they are not entitled to respect. Thus, when someone is beaten and shot, "he got what he deserved,"[22] as one online commentator said of seventeen-year-old Deven Guilford's killing by Officer Jonathan Frost. He was undeserving of respect by virtue of his attempt to assert his rights because (as one version of police powers has it), the police must be obeyed no matter their lack of respect for the rest of us.

Respect is the precursor to justice and fairness. As social psychologist Ronnie Janoff-Bulman and her colleagues described it, without respect, and having placed "others" outside the bounds of what we consider our community, "people [in this case, law enforcement] can perpetrate heinous acts of degradation, extreme humiliation, and physical violence. ...They [these 'others'] are now outside of our *scope of justice* [original emphasis], barred from the protections of community membership, and thereby perceived as justifiable targets for exploitation and violence."[23]

When we treat all citizens with respect, there is an implicit recognition of their value as coequals. In recognizing others' value, there is a reciprocal response from them to recognize our implicit and equal value as fellow community members. When it comes to law enforcement, granting all citizens respect does not reduce the power accorded law enforcement (unless the power itself is being illegitimately exercised as in the case of Deven Guilford). Rather, it legitimizes that power by placing officers within the

---

* As exhaustively detailed in Michelle Alexander's The New Jim Crow. We continue to punish criminals long after they have "paid their debt" to society by denying them access to jobs, education, social benefits, voting rights, etc., essentially making them permanently less human than the rest of us in meaningful daily humiliating ways.

community rather than separate and above it - above us.

By its very nature, granting respect tends to foster respect in return. By the same token, withholding respect is not passive, but active. It is respect's evil twin: disrespect. When we disrespect others, we don't just withhold respect, we attribute to them the opposite of what respect conveys. "Labels such *as ruthless, devious,* and *aggressive*[24]" are commonly used to describe those we have symbolically or actually "cast out" of our communities.

Once we have decided that certain individuals or groups are "the other," and do not deserve our respect, we don't just ignore them, we demonize them, attributing selfish, dishonest, aggressive, and harmful intentions to them, while our community has only "the best of intentions": honest, well-meaning, trustworthy, and cooperative.

According to researchers Janoff-Bulman and Werther: "When the out-group is an enemy – viewed as threatening and with hostility [as police culture now views much of the citizenry] – these perceptions of bad intentions take on a particularly antagonistic, negative tone and becomes hardened perceptions of the other."[25]

Is it any wonder, then, that those who feel a lack of respect from the police most acutely - black people particularly - will, in extreme cases, respond in kind with the ultimate disrespect: violence? The killing of police officers in Dallas and Baton Rouge is not surprising. "In the face of these perceptions, it is typical for communications to plummet and conflicts to escalate."[26]

Stepping back from what has become an escalating conflict between the police and parts of our national community can only begin if a mutual categorical respect is actively pursued and renewed on a daily basis. The idea of law enforcement giving citizens fundamental respect is not new, but has of late become a popular, if not yet widely implemented, practice. It is called procedural justice.

Examples and Solutions

Procedural justice is the simple idea that if a community believes that law enforcement is acting fairly, honestly, and with good intentions, they will be far more likely to respect the police, cooperate with the police in helping them do their jobs, and respect the law in the first place.

The procedural justice part of this equation is the specific steps or procedures law enforcement can take in their daily interactions with a community to foster this reciprocal sense of trust and respect. The theory of procedural justice is based on work by Yale Professor Tom Tyler, dating back to the early 1990s.

Tyler posits some fundamental concepts that underlie procedural justice, the most critical being that of police legitimacy. Legitimacy, according to Tyler, has three components: "The first is public trust and confidence in the police. Such confidence involves the belief that the police are honest, that they try to do their jobs well, and that they are trying to protect the community against crime and violence. Second, legitimacy reflects the willingness of residents to defer to the law and to police authority, i.e. their sense of obligation and responsibility to accept police authority. Finally, legitimacy involves the belief that police actions are morally justified and appropriate to the circumstances."[27]

There are several critical assumptions embedded in Tyler's formula for legitimacy. The first, he takes pains to point out, is the difference between legitimacy and legality. Legitimacy is "the *judgments* [emphasis original] that ordinary residents make about the authority of the police to make decisions about how to enforce and maintain social order."[28]

In contrast, legality is a legal standard as determined by

the local, state, and national legislatures and then interpreted and applied by police departments, district attorneys, and the courts. Legitimacy is conferred on the police by the public they serve on a day-by-day, case-by-case basis. Just because police behave legally does not necessarily mean they have legitimacy in the eyes of the citizens they serve. As we have seen in so many of the sad narratives I have related, all manner of police-inflicted humiliation, abuse, punishment, and violence are perfectly legal, but certainly not legitimate, in the eyes of many people.

Legitimacy, then, is simply another way of describing what is a constant theme in all these citizen/police encounters: not just doing what is legal, but doing what is right. Tyler writes: "...the argument being advanced here is that there is an additional benchmark *(beyond purely legal considerations)* [original emphasis] for evaluating police practices: the impact of a policy and practice upon perceived police legitimacy within the community.[29]"

So how do police achieve "legitimacy?" The actual law enforcement procedures that result in legitimacy in the eyes of those they serve are not particularly mysterious.

- Listen to people. This not only includes street-level citizen/police interactions, but actually soliciting community input on police policies and procedures. People are generally more cooperative and respectful of authority if they feel their concerns are being heard and acted upon."[30]

- Be transparent about rules, procedures, and laws. People have an innate sense of fairness and want to know that the laws are being applied fairly and equitably to everyone.

- Treat people with respect. "The issue of inter-personal treatment *consistently emerges as a key factor* [emphasis added] in reactions to dealing with legal authorities."[31] Respect is the ultimate coin of our democratic values as translated into how the law is enforced. Without according citizens respect, the law has no legitimacy.

- "Show you care about the person's well-being."[32] Again, showing care for the community you interact with, even in the face of disregard by others, commands respect. It both sets an example and legitimizes one's authority.

All of Tyler's research shows that when police apply these principles of procedural justice, their perceived legitimacy increased. When law enforcement has more legitimacy in the community they serve, policing becomes safer and more effective.[37] When policing is more effective, communities have less crime and feel protected and served by the police rather than bullied, abused, and mistreated.

It is hard to know whether to laugh or cry over the fact that it takes a professor from Yale to develop an "approach" to policing that is nothing more than treating the people they are sworn to protect and serve with the dignity and respect they deserve. It's not rocket science.

It seems tragic, absurd, and even ironic that here in the United States a basic recognition of our human rights requires an impressive sounding moniker (procedural justice) and specific procedures for how to accord citizens the most basic respect to which they are entitled. Likewise, it seems discouraging to have to "prove" that treating others with respect has value because it lowers crime rather than because treating others with respect has its own inherent value. Presumably, one could also show that living in a totalitarian police state also lowers crime, but is that an argument we want to make for how we police citizens in our country? Plenty of Americans seem to think so.

While I have been arguing that we, as citizens of the United States, deserve and are entitled to respect and dignity in our interactions with law enforcement based on our sacred social contract – the United States Constitution – Tyler argues the same point from the other side: that even if such respect is not legally (constitutionally) required, it actually makes for better policing. He argues that when law enforcement honors our highest ideals of fairness and justice, rather than just the minimum legal requirement, it is not just the "right thing to do"; it is also the most effective and safest way to police.

So why is it that, twenty years after these ideas were first formulated, procedural justice is still the exception rather than the rule in the many thousands of police agencies around the country?

The answer, I believe, is because we, the members of our communities, have not stood up and insisted that the bedrock of all policing should begin with treating each and every citizen with respect and dignity. Back in 2004, I couldn't do it. But now I believe I must.

CHAPTER TEN

Moral Outrage and Enlightened Self-Interest

First they came for the Socialists, and I did not speak out—
Because I was not a Socialist.
Then they came for the Trade Unionists, and I did not speak out—
Because I was not a Trade Unionist.
Then they came for the Jews, and I did not speak out—
Because I was not a Jew.
Then they came for me—and there was no one left to speak for me.

> **—Martin Niemoller,** Pastor and concentration
> camp survivor

It's Easier to do Nothing

"Life isn't fair" is something I have told my children on repeated occasions when they have been faced with the inevitable injustices of living. Some of this unfairness seems like the weather - unpredictable, arbitrary, fickle, natural, and impersonal. The fact that we are born only to die - and that we know this fact - is grossly unfair. I remember sitting in the hot tub with my son when he was perhaps six years old. He asked me, "Why do we have to die?" What answer could I give? I said something that meant nothing. He cried pure and simple tears at this unalterable sad truth. There was nothing that would take away that unfairness.

In other cases, the unfairness in life seems shameful, wrong, personal, and mean. Being made fun of, insulted, discouraged, bullied, rejected, or denied by others. Life seems to offer plenty of natural and inevitable unfairness without the additional piling on of human-inflicted injustice. Yet I often offered up the same homily to my kids – "Life isn't fair" - as if these two types of injustice were equal, natural, and inevitable. Which they may be. But implied in the "Life isn't fair" discussion-ending statement is the conclusion that there is nothing that can be done to lessen the suffering that we inflict on each other - that the unfairness and injustice experienced by us and our fellow human beings is just something to be accepted and borne, like death and taxes.

I had started out with the idealism of youth, imagining I would help change the world for the better in some small way. But somewhere along my path I gave that up as a prime directive and instead focused on me and mine. America was all about opportunity, working hard, taking risks, and getting rich. I assuaged whatever guilt I had by convincing myself that I was at least promoting something I could morally believe in, even if moral considerations in the day-to-day battle of business (gain customers, buy cheap, sell high, destroy the competition, make a profit) seemed anything but honest or moral. Doing well always took precedence over doing good. And I could always rationalize that my doing well was good, though as an unintended secondary effect. At least I wasn't selling cigarettes or machine guns, I thought.

What I gave up questioning was the contradiction and hypocrisy of pretending to do good in a system that was increasingly unfair and unjust. I simply accepted the system itself and the gross inequities that resulted as inevitable, like the weather. I would just have to be on the right side of those inequities, so I and my family could prosper, even if those who worked for me could not. I could always justify that at least I provided them with health insurance (until it got too expensive), an above-minimum-wage income (but not much above), and a job that paid the bills (better than no job). Thinking of myself as passably moral in an unjust and immoral system was easier than trying to justify doing nothing to change the system itself.

Fortunately (or unfortunately), I was never so successful that I ever had to rationalize my millions against my employees' slightly-better than poverty wages. But even earning $150,000 a year compared to their $23,000 required some rationalization. That I had certain advantages going for me, such as a stable middle-class upbringing, a college education largely paid for by my parents, and family friends who help fund my startup business were chalked up to "Life isn't fair." Nothing I could do to change that. Except in this case, I justified all of my advantages and relative rewards.

Cynical, yes. But like most of my peers, advantaged as we were, we didn't feel advantaged. We felt tired. We felt stressed. We felt beat up by forces beyond our control. No matter how fast I ran, it seemed that others who were smarter, better financed, and luckier were running faster. Those I knew who had jobs, good jobs in corporate America, were working harder for the same money, and then they were fired or laid off. And those who kept riding the wave of the American Dream certainly felt that they deserved everything that came their way: family money, good fortune, success. It all must certainly be the result of their superior talents, skills, and hard work – or just dumb luck. Never mind that there were and are millions of Americans who are smart, skilled, and work hard who never make a fraction of what we fortunate few do.

Oh well, "Life isn't fair" always helped to justify their enviable positions. In truth, we had no illusions that we were doing anything to make the world a better place. If we did, it was purely incidental to our main focus: taking care of me and mine.

Only when I was humbled by my own failures did I start to question my unquestioning acceptance of my "Life isn't fair" credo, which justified my own advantages and good fortune and others' misfortune. Only when I was arrested for growing medical marijuana was I shocked in ways that I could not have foreseen, causing me to reassess my adherence to the convenient and self-serving American narrative: land of opportunity, equality, freedom, and justice, as if that were the entire unblemished story.

I realized that as a middle-class white person with some financial resources, I got off easy in a system of justice that is too often anything but just. I had a wife who had money to bail me out. I had parents who could loan me the money to hire an expensive defense attorney. I still had a house I owned that was worth something (though with a large mortgage that, thankfully, kept the police from seizing it). I could have just accepted it as "the way things are" and taken my lumps and moved on with my relatively privileged life, unconcerned and relatively unaffected by the unfairness that was now, suddenly, made visible. It had always been there, right in front of me. But before, it was just easier not to see. Seeing it would have made it necessary to do something about it. Or at least find more creative ways to dismiss it. Better to not see it at all.

For some reason, which I do not understand, I just couldn't do it. Part of it certainly stemmed from my own sense of being personally wronged. I had been fine with the unfairness of the economic system so long as I felt that, relatively speaking, I was still on the winner's side of the table. That is, there may have been large corporate interests with huge financial resources that I could never compete with that were trying to destroy my livelihood, but that would be acceptable as long as I could make a modest middle-class living. I could assure myself that I was better off than the other 75 percent of Americans who averaged about $50,000 a year and were getting seriously screwed by the system, as far as I was concerned. But that was their problem, not mine.

When it came to the injustices in policing, I was simply oblivious to it. Whatever injustices there were took place in communities and neighborhoods that may have been geographically near, but were psychologically and emotionally in some other country. They didn't touch me. My arrest changed all that. When I got over my own sense of being personally wronged, I found myself incensed that *anyone* in America could be treated like this.

I finally knew, firsthand, about moral outrage.

It's not About me (or you)

While I have offered suggestions for taking action to correct what are blatant injustices in our policing, I have also been forced to consider why I avoided taking any action to address these wrongs for so long. What is the psychological tipping point between complacency in the face of injustice versus a will to act? Moral outrage is one such tipping point.

Generally speaking, moral outrage is considered to be a feeling of anger over injustice inflicted upon others whom one does not have a direct vested interest in - not yourself, your family, or your friends. Simply strangers. It is considered odd, among some social scientists, that one would have any concern for anyone other than oneself and a few intimates. (Apparently, they are unfamiliar with the idea of categorical respect as broadly applied to all people.) Among this group are unreconstructed Darwinians who strive to find a selfish and self-serving basis for every altruistic and generous human impulse, as if any personal benefits of being kind to others (such as social acceptance or elevated status) negated the entire and ultimate goodness of the act itself. So, if we assume Gandhi or Martin Luther King undertook their ostensibly selfless work for purely selfish reasons of self-aggrandizement, does that make them any less heroic? I think not. To be sure, there are easier ways to raise one's social standing.

In light of this theory, I suppose that you could consider my moral outrage an attempt to recapture some of the status I have lost as a result of my arrest and my failure to make millions (or at least inherit millions) as many in my social circle had. Whatever its roots, moral outrage generates social action to address the injustices inflicted on our fellow human beings.

The other aspect of moral outrage theory that I find puzzling is that moral outrage is regarded as synonymous with both anger and punishment. Yet in both cases, anger and punishment have nothing to do with moral outrage and everything to do with feelings of personal injury and self-righteous indignation – very much the opposite of Moral

Outrage. The hot anger we feel when we have been personally harmed and the desire to strike back at those who have hurt us is rooted in a small sense of self, which has been attacked. We are simply trying to prop up our injured self-worth.

Moral outrage, on the other hand, is not so much about anger, though that may be an initial reaction, but about shock and a deep-seated feeling that what has sparked our outrage is just plain wrong. You are not angry about it because anger does not last. It burns out quickly unless, like a fire, it is continually fed. Moral outrage is cooler, steadier, and more constant. It is a feeling of rejecting the status quo of what is manifestly wrong and demanding change. Not punishment, but change. There may be punishment as a signifier of change, but without changing the status quo, punishment is meaningless. Nor, as punishment would suggest, is it about blame. Punishment and blame go hand-in-hand. He who gets blamed gets punished. But moral outrage is less about blame and more about change. Blame and punishment are retrospective. They are focused on what has been done and what the consequences for past misdeeds should be. Moral outrage is forward looking and concerned with changing the future rather than reliving the past.

Some theorists on moral outrage are quick to point out that you can never be morally outraged at your own behavior but only at the behavior of others, as if being morally outraged implies that you are blameless and it's "those other guys" who are morally impaired. I would suggest it is quite the opposite. When we are morally outraged, our own immoral behavior is implicated as well. And, in fact, it is the recognition that we are as guilty as anyone else of allowing these injustices to go unchallenged that forces us to act. We see ourselves in those we call out. None of us are innocent.

A related theory of moral outrage is that it is the human

social equivalent of animal territoriality. A 1997 paper by a UCLA professor sums it up neatly: "Infringements in the rights and privileges in the social and symbolic worlds in which humans live are the equivalent of encroachments on territory among animals, and moral outrage can be understood as the human expression of what we perceive as territorial behavior in animals."[1]

It is exactly these "rights and privileges" that make up our social and symbolic worlds that are enshrined in our Constitution, which those revolutionaries were willing to fight and die for - and which are in jeopardy of being lost today. It was their moral outrage that fueled their fight. What is puzzling is why so few of us today feel any sense of urgency or agency when it comes to the loss of our "territory" of rights as we understand them.

Are we all just too cynical, tired, and beaten down by the system we have embraced as unfairly fair? Or are we just guilty of the immortal mindset of our teenage children: *This will never happen to me.* Or maybe we are distracted by the narcotic effect and seductive powers of the intermittent reinforcement bombarding us every minute of every day by social media. We are nodding out at our phones and tablets while all around us Rome is burning.

Or perhaps it is just the stories we keep telling ourselves and each other that allow us to believe what we want to believe. A recent study by a group of social psychologists, including Tom Tyler of "Procedural Justice" fame, explored why, with the worsening economic and social inequality in America, relatively few can be bothered to do anything about it. They theorized that most Americans who are disenfranchised do nothing about it because they have been substantially influenced by what the authors describe as a "system-justification mindset."[2] That is, they believe a story that justifies the inequities they experience as natural and inevitable, aka "life isn't fair."

Those who could most easily effect change in the system, the well-off, are even less inclined to pursue any changes because these justifications serve their narrow self-interest.

In the first study they conducted, they divided participants based on their family income. Then they measured how strongly the different income groups endorsed system-justifying ideologies (basically rationalizing their own wealth or lack thereof as reasonable, fair, and appropriate) and also measured their emotional distress over this inequality, defined as either moral outrage or guilt over undeservedly having more money than most others. Then they asked the participants if they favored a variety of programs that would redistribute wealth more equitably.

Not surprisingly, the students whose families were the most well-off tended to endorse the system-justifying story more readily and also had more guilt about it than less well-off participants. However, feeling guilty did not lead them to support the redistribution of wealth more equitably. Only experiencing distress in the form of moral outrage correlated with taking an active position on making things fairer. The key difference here is that sadness and guilt are inward focused emotions, while sympathy and anger are outward focused. Wrote the study's authors: "…it is only those emotions that are outward focused that are predictive of support for redistributive policies."[3] Moral outrage focused on wrongs done to others leads to social action. Feeling guilty about your own good fortune leads to feeling guilty.

In the second study, they wanted to understand how the stories we tell each other (and ourselves) influence our degree of moral outrage or lessen it by justifying unfairness and inequality. They selected only students who had high family incomes to measure how narratives justifying their wealth affected their willingness to help less fortunate people.[4]

The participants were given different stories to read, some

of which were rags-to-riches stories about how individual effort, talent, and perseverance brought them success (high system justification). Other stories were tales of people suffering in difficult circumstances that were not within their control. As the researchers described it: "The high-system-justification condition underscored the belief that success is a function of effort and ability; the low-system-justification condition reminded subjects that many people are unfairly disadvantaged and that being impoverished does not mean that one lacks merit or deserves to suffer."[5]

Then they measured the subjects' levels of emotional distress and their willingness to favor redistributive economic programs.

As expected, the narratives that justified their wealth made them less likely to feel either guilt over their good fortune or moral outrage over the plight of those with less."[6] Or in plain English, if you are repeatedly told that your successes (and your failures) are entirely your own doing – and that the circumstances of your birth (race, wealth, access to education, healthcare, security, safety, and just plain luck) have no bearing on your life outcomes - then you will feel neither an obligation to change the system nor a willingness to question it or your own assumptions about your good fortune.

The authors conclude: "We assume that people care about justice, at least to some degree, and are bothered by potential departures from fairness. In order to maintain their perceptions of the world as just, however, people do not necessarily strive to make changes that will increase the overall amount of fairness and equality in the system. Rather, they often engage in cognitive adjustments that preserve a distorted image of reality in which the world is a fair and just place."[7]

Of course, the different stories that the research participants read were all true. Which is to say, it is not all one way or the other. Yet here in America, there can be no denying that unfairness and inequality are at an all-time high and the chances of going from rags to riches is less likely than it has been for at least sixty years.[8] And rather than have the stories we tell ourselves reflect our reality, we continue to tell ourselves only one story, which grows less true by the day. We rationalize our success, and perhaps more disturbing, we rationalize the suffering of others as their lot in life. And so we do nothing.

I can't blame my peers for not being morally outraged by the injustice that swirls around them. Life is hard, even for the middle class. For those fortunate enough to be free of the daily grind of merciless work schedules to pay mortgages, compounded by intense familial obligations, feeling guilty is a minor inconvenience at most. And though many of them may support social and economic justice in theory (by voting for Democratic and progressive candidates), it never crosses their minds to personally donate any of their incredible talents or financial resources to create the change they claim to favor. They are much more concerned with finding ways to add to and preserve their already considerable wealth and privilege. Because their hearts are in the right place, they think, their time and wallets don't have to be.

Only moral outrage seems to provoke action, and action is what creates change. It's easy to make someone feel guilty. But how do you make them look at someone's else's pain, so removed from their gentle life, and find not despair, cynicism, or hopelessness, but a fellow-feeling of there-but-for-the-grace-of-God-go-I?

Put Yourself in Someone Else's Shoes

This can also be described by the antiquated term "enlightened self-interest." Thus, if moral outrage prompted by the mistreatment of one's fellow citizens seems a foreign concept, then perhaps concern over the fate of one's fellow Americans *because this might become your fate* will be one's call to action. Enlightened self-interest: While you may not care about the suffering of others, the potential for that suffering to be visited upon you is a pragmatic, if not noble, motivation to act.

With the advent of cell-phone cameras, YouTube and police body cameras, it becomes harder and harder to make those "cognitive adjustments" that allow us to go on about our happy lives, blissfully ignoring the suffering all around us.

As former New York City police officer and current Brooklyn Borough President (and African-American) Eric Adams describes it: "A lot of America, for the most part, wanted to drive their car and their manicured lawns and just wanted to know that you dealt with the crime whichever way you wanted to or had to. But when those photos and images came into their living room, the reality is that when people had to see it, see someone shot in the back, see someone choked out, they had to see someone being beaten, it forced them to say, 'something is wrong here.'"[9]

Some – such as writer and professor Matt Johnson, who is also black - don't have the luxury of waiting for moral outrage or the spur of enlightened self-interest to manifest itself. In this not-so-subtle calling out of white American privilege, he writes: "I understand why those who feel they aren't directly affected by this issue would be tempted to react to the complexity of what's going on by scapegoating or dismissing recent events [the police shootings of unarmed black men] as isolated incidents. We all have full, demanding lives. No one wants to add the burden of dramatically changing how our society is functioning to their daily duties. But I don't have that privilege. What I have is black children."[10]

Thanks, Matt, for the wake-up call. I hear you. I don't have black children, and I do have privilege, but that is small comfort. Neither of us have our unalienable rights. I want to reclaim them. And I can't sit by and hope that you do it for me.

CHAPTER ELEVEN

The House We Live In

Sanity may be defined as a synthesis of insanities.
—Bertrand Russell

The condition of alienation, of being asleep, of being unconscious, of being out of one's mind, is the condition of the normal man.
—R. D. Laing

The Third Rail of Local Politics

John Malcolm of the conservative Heritage Foundation suggests one of the many problems with civil asset forfeiture is that it provides funding for the police that is outside the control of the normal legislative process. That is, unlike the normal process by which a county or city government funds the police department based on certain publicly justifiable law enforcement goals and priorities, civil asset forfeiture allows the police to fund themselves directly from seized assets, with no government or citizen oversight. So, in theory at least, one of the ways that local law enforcement remains accountable to the public is that their budget must be approved by local elected officials who can exercise oversight by funding the law enforcement priorities of their constituents or withholding funding.

If only this were true.

In 1997, former San Jose Police Chief Joseph McNamara convened a symposium on drug policy at the Hoover Institute, where he was a fellow. At one of the panel discussions, he presented a scenario in which the police had received a tip that a major drug dealer was holding a large stash of crack cocaine in an apartment in a public housing project, protected by armed gunmen. What would the chief of police do?

On the panel were the Los Angeles chief of police, the San Jose mayor, the San Francisco district attorney, and a federal judge. L.A. Chief of Police Bernard Parks said he would send in a heavily armed SWAT team.

McNamara asked: Even at the risk of unarmed innocent residents of the housing project getting shot?

"Yes," Parks replied.

McNamara then asked: What if it were marijuana, or prescription drugs, or even bootlegged alcohol?

The SWAT team was always the answer.

Next McNamara asked the mayor, who in this scenario was the chief's boss, if she would be comfortable with sending heavily armed officers into a public housing complex to seize these drugs, whatever they might be, given the risks involved and the potential benefits of such a bust. The mayor responded that it was not her job to question her chief, but to support whatever decisions he made.

Next up, San Francisco's district attorney, Terence Hallinan, said he too would not second-guess the police. Finally, McNamara asked the federal judge if he would approve a "no-knock" warrant, essentially allowing the police to storm the building without giving the suspects either a chance to peacefully surrender or other residents an opportunity to take cover. Like all of the previous officials, he said that even though judges were tasked with ensuring that citizens' Fourth Amendment rights were protected, he rarely, if ever, would question what the police were doing when it came to warrants and Fourth Amendment exceptions.

In short, none of the elected officials or an independently appointed judge tasked with overseeing policing and protecting citizens' rights were willing to take any role at all in questioning police tactics, let alone engaging in oversight or demanding police accountability. And these were elected officials and a judge from comparatively liberal California.

When it comes to local control of our police, our elected officials consider it political dynamite, better left untouched. As long as they don't intervene, they cannot be held accountable. If they can't be held accountable, they won't suffer any political fallout. Even better, they can place the blame for any community anger solely on the police themselves, who are, as just described, virtually unaccountable to any of our politicians or even directly to the voters.

A Sonoma County supervisor who declined to go on the

record because of fear of law enforcement retaliation told me that they (the county supervisors) never used "the power of the purse" to insist that Sonoma County Sheriff's Department Office be held accountable to their constituents' concerns. They just approved whatever budget the sheriff asked for. The reason was simple: If they did push back, they risked law enforcement retaliating by delivering slower response times to the community or even an investigation into the supervisors themselves. And since the only constituents who might complain about policing were well-off white voters, who rarely had complaints, there was virtually no upside to exercising any type of law enforcement accountability. It would only be politically damaging.

Also, although the Sonoma County sheriff is an elected position, there has not been a contested sheriff's election in the county for more than twenty years. (This finally changed in the 2018 election.) It appears that come election time, the various local law enforcement agencies get together behind closed doors and decide who will be the single unopposed candidate for sheriff for that cycle. He then runs for the office as the only "choice," gets elected, and then runs the department as his own personal fiefdom, unchecked and unaccountable to anyone in local government. Just as shocking, the voters of Sonoma County have never seen fit to challenge this fundamental failure of democracy. As Brien Farrell of the Sonoma County Policing and Community Task Force noted: "We had no power to implement any of our recommendations. The sheriff could accept or reject any or all of our report."[1]

Even at the most basic level of accountability - patrol officers being supervised by their superior officers – Norm Stamper, former Seattle chief remarks that police work, as vital and critical as it is in our communities "goes essentially unsupervised."[2] He adds that Americans would likely be shocked if they understood the degree to which policing fails to police itself for corrupt and abusive police officers.[3]

The fear of retaliation, along with the political risk of assuming any responsibility for local policing, is not the only thing that gets in the way of creating police forces that truly serve and protect their communities instead of themselves. Local police associations and unions are hugely powerful in setting the tone inside police departments and fighting to stop any reforms that might be implemented from the outside, should local politicians and citizens be so inclined.

A recent investigation into the workings of the San Francisco Police Department by a panel of independent judges and attorneys found that the department too often operated as an "old boys club,"[4] with a code of silence - a dominant culture that encouraged illegal and unethical behavior to go unreported and undisciplined - and a promotional structure based on nepotism, childhood friendships, and even particular high schools attended.[5]

In an ironic if unintended confirmation of all of these findings, the head of the Police Officers Association (POA), Martin Halloran, characterized the report thusly: "a biased, one-sided, illegitimate work of fiction."[6]

The *San Francisco Chronicle*, in an editorial, described Halloran's remarks as "a disgraceful response to a measured look that's so reasonable that parts have already been embraced during its yearlong preparation."[7] But without the political will, the editorial concluded that "the list of recommendations will languish."[8] Where would such political will come from?

From each of us.

Just across the bay, in Oakland, the city went through three police chiefs in as many months, and even as it has shown great strides in more fair-minded policing, it is mired in a scandal in which as many as thirty officers engaged in sexual relations with an underage prostitute over a period of several years. City officials and citizen groups are pressing for a new police commission made up of citizens that would have the power to investigate and discipline officers for misconduct, but as in San Francisco, the Oakland Police union is strongly opposed to any such oversight.[9]

And in a recent study that examined how officers are treated within their organizations in relation to how they treat the communities they serve, the more officers felt they were treated with respect and fairness internally, the more likely they were to treat citizens with the same respect and care.[10] Setting examples of procedural justice within a police organization supports the same goals when applied to the wider community. But as the strong opposition to reforms by police unions show, the police themselves are plagued by exactly the same lack of fairness and respect for each other that we want them to embody with us.

Imagine if you and your colleagues at work continually failed to meet your company's goals, disregarded the ethical standards you swore to uphold, and harmed the very customers you were supposed to be serving in the process. Then, when your boss insisted he was going to hold you accountable for all this, you and your colleagues' union rejected the very idea that you should be overseen or held responsible by anyone in any way, except by your own coworkers. You'd be fired before you finished your first sentence. And, as Norm Stamper points out, unlike almost any other profession, policing is about life-and-death decisions.[11]

There are more than 18,000 police agencies in the United States and every one of them is local. On the downside, this means there is no sweeping federal policy change that is going to fix policing or police culture nationwide. On the upside, it means that all of these agencies are susceptible to local grassroots citizen-driven political pressure. Policing can be changed, one department at a time, with the involvement of local citizens. The police department in Richmond, California, under the leadership of Police Chief Chris Magnus, is one such example, as detailed in Chapter 4.

Even if our Fourth Amendment rights have been stripped away by a misguided Supreme Court, we can still reclaim them by holding our local law enforcement to a higher standard - a standard of justice, respect, and fairness rather than a now thoroughly co-opted, if not corrupt, legal standard.

What might such a movement look like? There is no one path.

All over the country, citizens' groups are springing up to directly monitor the police in real time. They call themselves "Copwatch" and they fan out with their cell phones in hand to record the police as they do their jobs, a way of making police officers accountable both in the moment and, by recording them, after the fact, as well.

A more formal structure of civilian oversight is NACOLE, the National Association for Civilian Oversight of Law Enforcement. This group provides training, consulting, and instruction for both citizen groups and police departments in how to establish effective citizen oversight of the police, and enhance police/community relations.

More recently, the website campaignzero.org has offered a comprehensive overview of policing issues, relevant research, and policy initiatives to address all of these interconnected issues of implicit bias, use of force, asset forfeiture, police training, and more.

And, of course, there are public protests such as those that Black Lives Matters and wetheprotestors.org initiate, which are, regardless of your opinion of them, part of a long and honorable American tradition of free speech and public politicking going back to the country's founding.

These citizen activists can force change, but unless we take ownership of *our* responsibility for our local police and the larger context in which they work, we run the risk of further isolating, alienating, and polarizing our relationship to law enforcement. That would not serve anyone's interest. It's not enough to hold the police accountable. We must hold ourselves accountable, too.

The Forest and The Trees

In his speech at the memorial for the five Dallas policemen killed on July 7, 2016, President Obama laid it out: *"As a society, we choose to under-invest in decent schools. We allow poverty to fester so that entire neighborhoods offer no prospect for gainful employment. We refuse to fund drug treatment and mental health programs. We flood communities with so many guns that it is easier for a teenager to buy a Glock than get his hands on a computer or even a book.*

And then we tell the police, 'You're a social worker; you're the parent; you're the teacher; you're the drug counselor.' We tell them to keep those neighborhoods in check at all costs and do so without causing any political blowback or inconvenience; don't make a mistake that might disturb our own peace of mind. And then we feign surprise when periodically the tensions boil over. We know those things to be true. They've been true for a long time." [12]

We shrug, we look glum (for a moment), we make sympathetic noises, and then we go back to our lives as if nothing has happened. But, as the President said in the same speech: "...we ask the police to do too much and we ask too little of ourselves." [13]

Why do we do so little? Because it is hard, very hard, to take on the burden of changing that which seems so large, yet amorphous - so entrenched, yet invisible to us in our daily lives. It's easier, certainly, to lay blame on the "criminals" who deserve what they get - and if what they get becomes a bit too much to bear, what with cell-phone videos and all, then we can blame the police for being a bit to zealous in the execution of their duties. For most of us, it's easier not to look too closely. But I hope you will try and look closely, hard as it is.

The tree of law enforcement cannot be separated from the forest of issues of which it is a part. The metaphor of not seeing the forest for the trees applies here, but is insufficient. If we consider the problems of law enforcement in isolation, we will be discouraged and disillusioned when our efforts to reform it fall short of our goals. Yet when we consider the forest of other issues, all of which are both cause and effect of law enforcement's ills, we might become equally discouraged because the task will appear to be too overwhelming, too complex, too multifaceted to even attempt some change. Yet the knowledge of the relationship between law enforcement, economic fairness, racism, education, and social welfare can allow us to take comfort in being part of a much larger struggle, however humble, local, and limited our own efforts may be. No one of us can change a system, but each one of us can alter its trajectory, one small incremental change at a time.

The Stories We Live By

The crisis of law enforcement and the proposed solutions arrange themselves into familiar divisions between liberal and conservative ideological positions. My decidedly liberal view is plain. On the conservative side, which includes most law enforcement organizations, is a doubling down on everything from more power for police, less accountability, harsher laws, more jails, tougher sentences. It would be easy to dismiss the conservative view as misguided, ignorant, and anti-American, but as satisfying as that might be, it offers no way forward to work with those who, by their very numbers, cannot simply be ignored. The idea of defeating them, however politically appealing and necessary, can only, at best, result in a temporary and partial victory. The election of Donald Trump following the presidency of Barack Obama provides irrefutable evidence of that. In a democracy, we have little choice but to work with those with whom we deeply and fundamentally disagree. To work with them requires some understanding of them. To understand them, we need to know them. And to know them, we have to set aside our own way of seeing the world and seek to understand theirs. We need to understand their story.

Standing in Line vs. Communal Space

In 2016, sociologist Arlie Hochschild published a study which posits that conservatives and liberals have different "deep stories," each of which they use to explain the world to themselves and which undergird their political views. The conservative "deep story" is one in which they are patiently, stubbornly, and honorably waiting in a long line, at the front of which is the American Dream – not just a good job, and a home of your own, but the recognition from your country that you have done things the "right way." You have worked hard and suffered through hard times to achieve that dream. You have played by the rules as they have been laid out.

Then they see other people - black people, gay people, immigrants - cutting in line in front of them. Getting welfare and not working. Getting jobs and rights they don't deserve. How is that possible, they ask themselves? They aren't waiting patiently; they are getting special treatment. And who is giving them special treatment? It is none other than the government. The government, conservatives believe, is denying them what is rightly theirs in favor of helping other less deserving groups.

The liberal "deep story" is that of a shared common

public space where, through years of struggle, they have, with a small portion of everyone's hard work (taxes), built a beautiful playground in which people of all types can come and enjoy themselves. But then they see a few angry disgruntled fellows come and steal the swing set and the benches and take them back to their private dwellings where they hoard these benefits for themselves and a few others they consider part of their "group," while everyone else is now excluded.

As Hochschild explains, the deep story is a way of getting at some fundamental but otherwise nonrational experiential truth. It describes an inner experience in terms of image, symbol, and metaphor, giving words to our experience. It doesn't take into account "objective" facts or even reason, but reveals a felt reality. If we consider our stories, and others' as well, in that light, we can appreciate how they are both subjective *and* true for each of us.[14] Our story is the guiding metaphor we use to make sense of our experiences and our lives, and the lives of others.

Two Visions of The Family

Twenty years before, in 1996, George Lakoff, professor of cognitive and linguistic science at UC Berkeley, published another story seeking to explain the same phenomenon. Lakoff's story is couched in the metaphor of family. Conservatives have a "Strict Father" model of the family, while liberals have a Nurturing Parent model. When we consider the country as a family and apply these disparate parenting models to it, all the seemingly irrational and contradictory positions of liberals and conservatives turn out to have an unassailable internal logic particular to each position.

In the Strict Father world view, the highest good is defending the Strict Father Moral System itself in which the world is divided into good and evil. Evil must be punished and good rewarded. Good is defined as a natural hierarchy of power, with God at the top, then humans over nature, men over women, parents over children. Individual discipline, responsibility, and self-reliance are good and should be rewarded. Disobedience, disrespect for authority, and laziness deserve punishment.

Through this prism, all the seemingly contradictory conservative positions fall into place: Abortion, which kills "innocent babies," is immoral. The death penalty, which kills guilty "evildoers," is moral. Spending billions on the military to defend us against our enemies (who are, by definition, evil) is good government (moral). Spending billions to help undisciplined, lazy, and irresponsible poor people is bad government (immoral). Stopping self-reliant hard-working people (and corporations) from earning a living by imposing environmental regulations is immoral (after all, Man has dominion over the earth to do as he wishes). Being rich is the moral equivalent of being good as a natural result of being disciplined and self-reliant, so taxing the rich is punishing their goodness. Taxes are thus immoral. Everyone who is not a criminal should be free to own a gun because that is the only way good moral people can protect themselves against bad evil people. And criminals, naturally, deserve only punishment because criminal acts define a person as evil and deserving of punishment (never mind the research which shows that rehabilitation and restorative justice are far more effective in stopping crime and reducing recidivism).[15]

Thus, while it outwardly appears that low-income Republicans are voting against their own economic and environmental self-interest out of sheer stupidity, they are voting for their perceived moral self-interest which, they believe, despite all evidence to the contrary, will benefit them because they are morally deserving. As Lakoff and

Hochschild point out, these views are not irrational, they are pre-rational. We embrace a worldview, which is beneath our conscious awareness, and then we accept and discard the facts to fit that worldview, not the other way around.

As Hochschild described in her interviews with Tea Party members in Louisiana, they favored abolishing the EPA even as their communities were devastated by toxic chemicals and their friends, family members and coworkers were dying of all manner of pollution-related cancers. As Hochschild reports, regulating pollution conflicted with their "deep story" in which the evil of government regulation outweighed the unfortunate but necessary cost to one's health and the environment in the name of getting one's piece of the American Dream.

On the liberal side, Lakoff tells a story of the "Nurturing Parent," which in the realm of politics translates into being cared for, learning to care for oneself, and caring for others. This is achieved through the primary goal of fairness, which Lakoff says includes: "Helping those who cannot help themselves, protecting those who cannot protect themselves, promoting fulfillment in life, and nurturing and strengthening oneself in order to do the above."[16] This explains the same sort of stupidity that conservatives see liberals engaged in: wealthy liberals stupidly voting against their own economic self-interest by wanting more taxes on the rich and more spending on the poor. Pro-choice liberals claiming how they want more money for child welfare, education, and the like, but supporting the killing of innocent 'babies' through abortion - and then opposing the death penalty for guilty evildoers. In conservatives' system of moral accounting, liberals have everything exactly backwards. Liberals claim they want peace but encourage our enemies to attack us by advocating for less military spending. And so on.

A Dangerous World vs. Common Ground

In the twenty years between the emergence of these two stories (more formally described as theories), experimental psychologists offered their own data and theories (that are also a type of story) that attempt to explain experimental results. John Hibbing and his colleagues, along with many other researchers, focusing on our worsening political polarization, posited a biologically-based conservative trait described as "negativity bias." A negativity bias is science-speak for perceiving threats in your environment. It's the Murphy's law of psychology: Whatever can go wrong, will go wrong, and I'd better be worried.

Certainly, over millions of years of evolution, humans had to develop a very keen awareness of threats if they were to survive and thrive. So, we come by a "negativity bias" quite naturally. Yet some of us see threats everywhere we turn, while others see far fewer dangers. Once again, you can place fear of crime and those people deemed "criminals" high up in the "threat" column.

Negativity bias, as applied to political positions, breaks out into two main subcategories: threat and disgust. The evolutionary function of sensitivity to threat is fairly obvious and generally concerns avoiding the threat of physical harm from others. The evolutionary function of disgust "evolved in part to keep individuals safe from disease by motivating them to avoid disease-bearing foods ('That tastes/looks disgusting!'), substances, individuals and groups."[17] Our current president, Donald Trump, uses the word "disgusting" to describe those with whom he disagrees so often that it has spawned numerous articles about its significance to him and his followers.[18] Clearly, Trump has an intuitive sense of what will trigger his followers' nonrational emotional biases and support: Fear and loathing.

To measure this negativity bias, scientists have conducted eye-tracking studies assessing how long subjects looked at positive versus negative images and how quickly they fixated on positive versus negative images; another study had subjects rate negative images on a scale of negativity. In these studies (and many more), self-identified conservatives rated negative images more negatively than self-identified liberals. They looked at negative images longer and fixated on them more quickly. Similar results were recorded when measuring the electrical response of the skin (electrodermal response) when viewing negative images. Other longitudinal studies have suggested that children as young as four who exhibit a heightened negativity bias are much more likely to become political conservatives as adults, indicating that this bias, also described as "threat sensitivity," is a naturally occurring precursor to conservative political positions, not the other way around.[19]

As political scientist John Hibbing states, some people "believe that higher level decision-making, such as that involving politics, is the product of rational, conscious responses to the objective world and therefore not influenced by forces out of conscious awareness. This flattering view of human decision-making in the area of politics is most likely unwarranted."[20]

Liberalism as a Biological Imperative

Though there is less scientific evidence on the psychobiology and evolutionary roots of liberal politics, there still exists substantial evidence that evolution has bred us to be compassionate, generous, and caring of our fellow human beings even as we see them as competitors in a zero-sum game.

Evolutionary psychologist Geoffrey Miller devotes an entire chapter in his book, *The Mating Mind*, describing the individual and group survival advantages of being compassionate, generous, and moral, even at the cost to oneself.[21] We can see all around us, every day, how we balance our competitive hierarchical instincts to dominate our fellow humans with the need to cooperate with them to survive and thrive. We compete in business but cannot hope to prosper if we do not work cooperatively with others in the department and the company. We want our teams to win in every sport, which only occurs if the athletes make the highest levels of sacrifice for the greater good of the team. And in our parenting, one of the first things we teach our children is the value and necessity of sharing.

From an evolutionary perspective, Miller argues that women rank human kindness as the most valued trait when it comes to choosing a mate. It turns out, kindness towards others is sexy! It is also indicative of what kind of partner and father you might be. Psychologically, such traits manifest themselves as a general openness to unfamiliar experiences and a decreased fear response to potentially threatening situations.

Depending on your psychological orientation, you will likely identify with either a high negativity bias or a low negativity bias. Because you identify more strongly with one of these tendencies, the other just seems plain wrong. You have a pejorative reaction to it. We have our biases and we take these biases to be reality. Any view that conflicts with those biases we dismiss as just wrong and those who hold such views as plain stupid. We are strident in our dismissal of the opposing view because it threatens our very core, without which the world ceases to make sense. What we fail to recognize is that these are "as if" stories, and not "true." They are only partial pieces of our experiential reality, which we have filtered, reduced, and then rendered into some manageable facsimile of "truth." Thus, in the realm of policing we end up being either "soft on crime" or "tough on crime," as if those positions were mutually exclusive, which they are not.

All the "stories" described above take outward behaviors, opinions, and positions and attempt to find the underlying explanation that makes them a coherent whole. They all have strong similarities as if they were each describing the same phenomena, but peering through somewhat different sets of glasses – bringing a part of the picture into focus while the background remains blurry. Yet, as every one of these scientists take pains to point out, whatever story we have, none of our stories are consciously chosen, and we act and react based on these unconscious scripts. As Chief Justice Charles Hughes told fellow Supreme Court Justice William O. Douglas in 1939, some fifty-six years before George Lakoff's work, "…ninety percent of any decision is emotional. The rational part of us supplies the reasons for supporting our predilections."[22] And here he is speaking of the presumably most rational among us - Supreme Court justices. If these unconscious processes undergird all of their court decisions, what hope do the rest of us have in reaching across a chasm of perceptual differences of which both sides are completely unaware?

As Hochschild remarks, the deep story is an "as if" story. That is, it is not the truth, it just points towards some larger inexpressible truth in the form of symbols, i.e. language. In the realm of science, there are definitive standards for stories (scientific theories) that are accepted as "more true" than others. Those that are "more true" have measurable explanatory and predictive power of the physical universe we inhabit. But in the realm of human consciousness, the story that you choose does not have to correlate with any quantifiable physical reality. The story you choose is the one that makes sense to you, even if nothing else about the story does. No rational arguments will cause you to change your mind because, until some other story *feels true*, this is the only story you have for making sense of your experience.

At the end of his book, *Moral Politics*, Lakoff argues that there are strong non-ideological reasons to prefer liberal political positions. He argues that all of these different stories we live by are, at root, based on the experiential reality of human well-being. However, if your story loses touch with the experiential reality on which it is based, it no longer serves the function it was created to fulfill. Because the Strict Father worldview holds that maintaining its primacy rather than promoting human welfare is its prime directive, it ignores all evidence to the contrary, such as its failure to promote human well-being. Like a runaway train, it is no longer constrained by the tracks of direct human experience to keep it in check. Thus, as Arlie Hochschild describes, her Tea Party subjects could not reconcile the devastated toxic environment in which they lived with their unwavering commitment to rollback, rather than strengthen, the limited and largely ineffective environmental regulations that had allowed this devastation in the first place. They were willing to quite literally die for what they believed in, as the price they had to pay for a decent job. They couldn't imagine any other options.

What would it take for them (and us) to be able to see outside of our pre-rational self-reinforcing, limited, worldviews? We might begin by considering that that there is a story that we are all telling ourselves of which we are totally unaware. Viewed in this light, it's hard to condemn as stupid, ignorant, and less-than-human those with whom we disagree. It is the equivalent of telling the weather it is stupid for raining or the dog that is bad for being hungry. All of us are at the mercy of forces we do not control and have no awareness of.

Also, as Lakoff points out, we can't mock those opposing points of view unless we, on some level, understand them as parts of ourselves.[23] We hate them because we recognize them in ourselves and despise those parts of ourselves. The messiness of being human suggests that we all have both worldviews in our consciousness and that we even switch between them as circumstances and personal traits dictate. In business, which has a zero-sum, take no prisoners set of rules, we may very well employ a Strict Father worldview, while at home and in politics, we are Nurturing Parents. The knowledge that our strongly held beliefs (and of those who oppose us) are just stories we tell ourselves can free us to not take them personally. And if we do not take ourselves or others so personally, we can reach across that chasm of difference and find inklings of our other side and, perhaps, engender the same awareness in those we oppose.

Recently, I asked a man wise in spiritual matters why we humans treated each other so badly. He thought for a minute or two and replied: "Because we are unable to carry the burden of our darkness."

It is our own darkness that we attribute to "the other," whether the other is a criminal, a police officer, a conservative, or a liberal. Understanding that we all have these stories frees us to set them down, if only for a moment, and allow a sliver of light to penetrate between us and who it is we think we are, and between "them" and who it is we think "they" are. In that moment, something new, different, and unforeseen can emerge: a lifeline across that chasm of hopeless division, anger, and vitriol.

In so many communities in the United States, this terrible chasm separates the police and the policed. The positions harden, become entrenched, and the chasm widens. Yet, by our own actions, however small, we can begin to heal that rift, close the gap, and create something that we can be proud of: policing that truly does "serve and protect" us.

The House We Live In

None of us wants to see our dark side. It's humbling, if not humiliating. It's much easier to blame the other person. And in business, politics, or marriage – in any intimate relationship in which issues of dependence, vulnerability, authority, responsibility, and fairness are paramount – we all come up short at times. If we are unable to recognize our shortcomings and acknowledge them, our relationships, at least those that are based on the equality and freedom of both parties, will not last. Partnerships will dissolve, marriages will end in divorce, political compromise will be impossible. We will go our separate ways.

There can no more be an "ultimate" victory politically than there can be an ultimate victory in an argument with your spouse or your child. Any such "victory" results in the diminishment of someone you love. Their diminishment breaks the bonds of love and respect that bring us together. In our intimate relationships we don't seek "victory," we seek mutual recognition and respect for our inherent value as human beings. In politics, it should be no different. Hochschild describes how her working-class Republican Tea Party "friends" feel in relation to mainstream (and particularly liberal) politics: While they strive to lead honorable lives, they feel belittled, made fun of, insulted and demeaned. Good jobs are few for those without a college degree; the places they live are considered hopeless backwaters of cultural inferiority, and being white and religious makes you suspect and racist. They "suffer this sense of fading honor…"[24]

But here in the United States, we cannot go our separate ways.

Yes, we can divide ourselves into red states and blue states, into white and black neighborhoods and schools, into rich and poor communities, but we are still in the same house. We are like a couple in a fight that never ends. We walk past each other, eyes down, not speaking. We communicate tersely if at all. We dare not look the homeless person in the eye for then we'd have to acknowledge that they are a "person." We find friends who share our political views and simply don't discuss politics with those who don't see things our way. We dare not speak because we know that the only thing we will say is "It's all your fault." And though we feel powerful in our righteous indignation, we don't feel good, we don't feel at peace, we don't feel whole. We walk around angry, blaming, superior, and resentful in our righteousness.

We tell the police that they are heroes, but rarely, if ever, do police get to be heroes. Instead they carry the shame that we are unable to carry. The shame of denying day after day the respect and dignity to those we deem "less than": the mentally ill, the homeless, the poor, the minorities, the criminals. These are our scapegoats, even though they are OURS. But we can't admit that. It's too hard to admit all the ways we have failed those among us and that there, but for the grace of God, go I.

Instead, we comfort ourselves by insisting that we, individually, are good. We are not to blame. It's the system that is at fault, and who can change the system? Or if not the system, then it is most certainly the victim's fault. They had it coming. They deserved it. But, we assure ourselves, we most certainly do not deserve it. Or we assure ourselves that we do deserve all that we have because the system is fair. Even as we teach our kids, "Life isn't fair," but we don't lift a finger to make it more so. We can show them something different. And show our friends and neighbors in the process. And, perhaps, get them to join us in creating change in how our communities are policed.

No wonder the police feel angry, isolated, and betrayed. We give them a gun, a taser, a baton, and handcuffs to keep the most vulnerable in our country out of sight and out of mind. This is the house we live in. We can try and shut them all up in the rooms in our house, rooms we never have to enter: the prison, the ghetto, and the doorways, alleys, and underpasses where homeless people sleep. We roll up our windows and lock the car doors driving through certain neighborhoods or avoid them altogether. We breathe a sigh of relief as we pull into our three-bedroom house with the two-car garage. But we never consider that they are part of our community. They, too, are in the house we live in.

And they keep spilling out, on cell-phone cameras, in the news, and now, sometimes, in our own safe, white, prosperous neighborhoods.

The police problem is not a problem that exists in isolation from the rest of America, though it is often presented that way. It is merely one manifestation of all the ways in which we would rather not admit our individual and personal shortcomings - the way we justify what we know to be unjust and unfair - just so we can go on with our lives and not have to bother with those "other" people. But those "other" people are still here, in our house. They know it, we know it, and the police know it.

In America - in the house we live in - there is no divorce. There is nowhere to go, no other place to move. Red states will not defeat blue states, nor blue defeat red. If victory for some means defeat for others, ultimate victory will never be realized because there will always be some of us who will be denied the respect and dignity we deserve, so none of us will have peace.

We don't have to agree on everything.

In that same speech in Dallas, Obama said: *"Can we find the character, as Americans, to open our hearts to each other? Can we see in each other a common humanity and a shared dignity, and recognize how our different experiences have shaped us? And it doesn't make anybody perfectly good or perfectly bad, it just makes us human."*

Being human is hard. Very hard. It requires us to be humble in the face of our own limitations. It requires vulnerability. It requires the courage to admit our mistakes - and we all make them, all the time.

Law enforcement is the sharp end of the spear for of all those who truly and sincerely believe we are under attack from both within and without, and to let our defenses down is fatal. But just as when your only tool is a hammer, everything starts to look like a nail, so when your only tool is a gun (and a taser, a baton, and handcuffs), everyone starts to look like a criminal.

Can we turn law enforcement's swords into plowshares? No, and we wouldn't want to. Sometimes you need a sword. But wouldn't it be better if the police had more tools than just the sword on their heavy belts. Wouldn't the functional equivalent of a plowshare be some tools that would truly protect the vulnerable in our communities instead of locking them up, and, instead of just punishing those who need to be locked up, working to bring them back into the fold of our community as caring and productive people? The moral cost along with the economic cost of treating some of our fellow citizens as human garbage is making a mockery of our best attempts to carry on as if nothing is wrong.

For far too long, we have asked the police to do our dirty work and "take out the garbage" - the people we have decided are not part of our community. Untouchables. In so doing, we have made the police equally untouchable - despised, feared, rejected, and suspect. Contaminated by the very job we have demanded that they do, because we don't want to deal with it.

It is time we returned both groups to the fold. They may be bad by our standards. They may be bullies, criminals, and crazies, but here in America, they are OURS. And they deserve better. But to do that, we will have to own our own shame. More hard work is required.

Some pundits say that we have been duped by our politicians. We have been led astray by their fear-mongering – the war on drugs, the war on crime, and now the war on terrorism, all in the name of political power in the service of corporate economic interests. That makes us too stupid and our politicians too smart by half. We were never so easily duped.

We allow ourselves to be duped because it is easier than doing the hard work of democracy. And because it is hard to admit that the drug dealers and the drug consumers that create the dealers are us. Our sons, daughters, mothers, and fathers. They are not some separate alien perverted subspecies of human.

Our criminals, who we lock up in greater numbers than any other country in the world, are those same people. They are us. Imperfect. Flawed. More than half of them are nonviolent.[25] But they made a mistake and got caught. Studies show that we all break the law an average of three times every single day.[26] Often the only difference between us and them is they got caught. And more often than not, they got caught because they were poor or had dark skin or both.

But rather than face that truth, it is so much easier to cast them out, blame them for our evils, our shortcomings, our lack of compassion. It is the ultimate job of blaming the victim. And we give our police the impossible job of taking some of US and turning them into THEM - making sure they feel humiliated, degraded, and despised - as if that would somehow "teach" them something, when it only serves our need to feel better about ourselves because we are not them.

So we have the despised, the disgraced, the denied, the outcast. And then we wonder why they continue to break our rules. Why seventy-six percent of offenders re-offend and end up back in jail. We have designed a system so these results are virtually assured. Because we need them to lose so we can continue to feel like winners. And then we call it fair. We enjoy our privilege but fail to see how we are losing our rights. This is a hard pill to swallow, but it is something I know to be true of myself, and perhaps it is true for you. Consider it.

I think we have become a much more meanspirited country over the last forty-five years. The culture of police violence, the Us vs. Them mentality, the police militarization, and a basic disrespect for those they are sworn to serve and protect has not occurred in a vacuum. During this same period, we have seen growing wealth and income inequality, increasing poverty (especially among children), wage stagnation, and less and less funding for higher education. We have seen more money for prisons and increased health care costs, with fewer and fewer people able to afford health insurance. Reductions in welfare, reduced unemployment benefits. A war on drugs that disproportionately falls on racial minorities, already struggling with fewer resources as a result of past racial injustices. We are becoming a country of haves and have-nots with little in between.

The resulting anger, stress, anxiety, and fear are played out on all sides, every day. In bucolic small-town Sonoma, largely white, well-off, and with a booming Wine Country tourist economy, I am amazed when no one will let me in as I try to turn onto busy Highway 12 from one of the neighborhood side streets. They drive by, studiously ignoring me. How many times have I seen people blaring their horns and flipping each other off for some perceived disrespectful act. In beautiful, safe, successful Sonoma. And we have it easy compared to most of America.

It's mean out there. But it doesn't have to be.

We blame the poor for being poor, no matter how many jobs they hold. We let the mentally ill roam our streets, we let the homeless starve and freeze, and we stigmatize the eighty million of us who have criminal records. (That's not counting the many millions more who have been arrested but never convicted of any crime, yet are still stigmatized when they go to apply for jobs.) Is it any wonder that 76 percent of criminal offenders reoffend? (No other country even comes close to this level of recidivism). What other options do we provide? And then we criminalize behavior that stems from social ills and public health issues, not criminal acts, and tell the police to arrest these "criminals." Shame on us. Shame on me. Let's make a change.

And what tools do we give the police to deal with mental illness, homelessness, and poverty? Guns, tasers, handcuffs, and batons. Can it be surprising that they grow cynical, mean, abusive, and violent? The work we give them is, for the most part, not honorable, not heroic. It is shameful. And it is our shame with which we burden them. Let's take responsibility for our neighbors and let us "serve" the police in making our communities safe and secure for us all.

We have been lied to about the threat of some drugs – which at best are medicinal and at worst give people a few hours of euphoric relaxation – while other drugs, which do nothing except addict us and then cause cancer, remain legal. And so we waste more than $1 trillion on this pointless, ill-conceived "War on Drugs." We can instead advocate for treatment rather than jails, legalization rather than criminalization.

The lived Constitution - what we Americans conceive of as our rights as we go about our day-to-day lives - is not distant or separate from the written Constitution. The written Constitution is still the embodiment, the formal statement, of our mutual understandings of how we live together. It is a statement about our highest aspirations and our best hopes. We all want to be treated with respect and dignity. But that formal statement, lofty as it is, is easily turned into a mockery of itself by those consumed by fear and driven by hate.

It is up to us to keep it current, to renew it and make it reflect our lived ideals today. To protect our rights and make laws that reflect our best selves, we must engage with each other and our government just as we engage with our partners, our children, and our workplaces. With passion, with commitment, with the best intentions. This is uncomfortable, to be sure. Unlike engaging in the safe spaces of family and like-minded friends, it demands that we make ourselves vulnerable to those we most fear or with whom we disagree. This is not a battle we can win by arming ourselves with righteous anger and uncompromising aggression. It requires compassion, humility, and sincerity. But we cannot count on our government to do that for us. It will not. It cannot. To do nothing and hope that the chaos and violence swirling around us will never reach us or our neighborhoods is a delusion. Just ask Deven Guilford's parents.

To imagine that we can go through life untouched by the pain and suffering inflicted on others with our silent acquiescence is an illusion. The price we pay is a deadening of our souls and a denial of our common bond with our entire community, even those we seek to cast out. If we seek to cast them out, we should at least admit what we are doing and live with it rather than have the police carry our shame and guilt for us. There is no honor in such a bargain. It is a deal with the devil. And the devil is us: our worst selves.

To reclaim our honor, and our unalienable rights, we must act. Sitting idly by while fanatics and zealots wield the levers of power because we do nothing is no longer an option. Voting is not nearly enough. By the time we vote, our choices have been reduced to a poor facsimile of what most of us would call fair. Doing the hard work is what it will take. And it won't happen overnight. It will take years. But it can happen. We just have to act. If not us, then who? After all, this is the house we live in.

ACKNOWLEDGMENTS

This book could not have been written without the never-ending support of my incredible wife, Michelle Bayba, who has helped me through the darkest of times and shared my most joyful moments, and my parents, Steve and Gerrie Bearg, who have always encouraged me to do what I thought was right, even when they thought it was completely wrong (which it sometimes was). They have also been great readers of this book and of many other books they have shared with me. They are responsible for my love of books, ideas, and an abiding sense of right and wrong. I also thank my children, Dylan and Jordan, who accompanied me on this wild ride because they had no choice, but seemed to have not only survived but thrived under sometimes difficult and challenging circumstances and brought me so much joy in the process. Also, I thank Jeff W. and Jeff S. for being helpful readers, and Phil Cousineau, whose passion for my work and close reading and detailed notes gave me the direction and impetus to finish. Additional thanks to Bob Cooper for his editorial expertise and Jim Shubin for guiding me through the end of the publishing process.

Thanks also to the various folks who told me stories, and shared their experiences and ideas about law enforcement—Tom, Jill, Dave Dodderidge, Brien Farrell, Jay G., J.C., Omar F.—and to all those who have risked their own safety to capture dramatic citizen/police confrontations and then posted them online to draw attention to this critical issue in our lives.

THE AUTHOR

Larry Bearg, Ph.D, clinical psychology, worked with mentally ill young adults, founded several award-winning small businesses in the Bay Area, and raised two children in Sonoma, California. He currently lives with his wife in Richmond, California, and Orcas Island, Washington.

Video Illustrations

Introduction
Walter Scott, April 4, 2015: www.vimeo.com/124336782
Chapter 1
Eric Garner (New York City, NY):
  www.youtube.com/watch?v=LfXqYwyzQpM
Dwight Harris (Washington, DC):
  www.youtube.com/watch?v=FC24PbCJlXQ
Diaz Zeferino (Gardena, CA):
  www.graphics.latimes.com/gardena-police-shooting
Police Raid on Medical Marijuana Dispensary (Santa
  Ana, CA): www.youtube.com/watch?v=JTKTfUHfeKM
NYPD Officers speak out on arrest quotas
  www.youtube.com/watch?v=oK35y9-dTuw

Chapter 2

Officer Jason Van Dyke shooting Laquan McDonald
  (Chicago):
  www.youtube.com/watch?v=JqCMMRoyPE4
Tamir Rice Shooting (Cleveland):
  www.theguardian.com/us-
  news/video/2014/nov/26/cleveland-video-tamir-rice-
  shooting-police
Jason Harrison shooting (Dallas, TX):
  www.youtube.com/watch?v=EUp4bDa9M3o

Chapter 3
Sandra Bland (Prairie View, TX):
  www.youtube/jpSEemvwOn4

Chapter 5
Officer Scott Tobler (Sidney, Nebraska, June 27, 2013) to
  a couple

asserting their right to record him on video
www.youtube.com/watch?v=KBsUUlY_fXQ
Trooper Donald Fougere (New York City, September 25, 2015)
to a videographer outside trooper headquarters
Eric Garner (New York City, NY):
www.youtube.com/watch?v=LfXqYwyzQpM

Chapter 6
Deven Guilford (Eaton County, MI):
www.youtube.com/watch?v=RihIPKrznMs

Chapter 7
NYPD Officers speak out on arrest quotas
www.youtube.com/watch?v=oK35y9-dTuw

Chapter 8
las cruces da asset forfeiture video (Las Cruces, N.M.)
www.youtube.com/watch?v=7F8S0XY7-74
Asset forfeiture nashville tn videos
www.youtube.com/watch?v=In3inU5WBGw

Chapter 11
President Obama's Dallas Memorial Speech:
www.youtube.com/watch?v=xQPBPB8UDyQ

Chapter One

[1] www.youtube.com/watch?v=LfXqYwyzQpM

[2] www.youtube.com/watch?v=FC24PbCJlXQ

[3] graphics.latimes.com/gardena-police-shooting

[4] www.theguardian.com/us-news/2015/jun/09/the-counted-police-killings-us-vs-other-countries

[5] www.justice.gc.ca/eng/rp-pr/csj-sjc/jsp-sjp/wd98_4-dt98_4/p2.html

NOTES

Preface / Introduction

[1] "Operation Iraqi Freedom | Iraq" (PDF). iCasualties. May 28, 2010. Retrieved 10/10/2012

[2] There is no national government data collection of civilians killed by police. This estimate is based on unscientific reporting of *The Guardian.*

[3] The number of police killings, assaults, asset seizures, and stop and frisks are all in the thousands per year, with "officer-involved shootings" being the least frequent at an average of 2-3 per day, based on data from *The Guardian*'s police killings database: www.theguardian.com/us-news/ng-interactive/2015/jun/01/the-counted-police-killings-us-database

[4] www.copsalive.com/from-buddha-to-the-blue-line

[5] www.cnn.com/2017/07/14/health/police-confidence-gallup-polls-trnd/index.html

[6] Holmes, Malcolm D., and Smith, Brad W., *Race and Police Brutality: Roots of an Urban Dilemma.* SUNY Press, Albany, New York, 2008

[7] United States Census Bureau, 2014, census.gov

[8] www.nobelprize.org/nobel_prizes/peace/laureates/1986/wiesel-lecture.html

Chapter One

[1] www.youtube.com/watch?v=LfXqYwyzQpM

[2] www.youtube.com/watch?v=FC24PbCJlXQ

[3] graphics.latimes.com/gardena-police-shooting

[4] www.theguardian.com/us-news/2015/jun/09/the-counted-police-killings-us-vs-other-countries

[5] www.justice.gc.ca/eng/rp-pr/csj-sjc/jsp-sjp/wd98_4-dt98_4/p2.html

[6] www.pewresearch.org/fact-tank/2013/06/04/a-minority-of-americans-own-guns-but-just-how-many-is-unclear/

[7] www.theguardian.com/us-news/2015/jun/09/the-counted-police-killings-us-vs-other-countries

[8] Stamper, Norm, *To Protect and Serve,* Nation Books, New York, 2016, pg. 17

[9] Smith, P. K., and Sharp, S. (eds), *School Bullying: Insights and Perspectives,* Routledge, London, 1994, pg. 2

[10] Stamper, pg. 145

[11] *President's Report on 21st Century Policing,* pg. 11

[12] www.sonomacounty.ca.gov/Community-and-Local-Law-Enforcement-Task-Force/#duties

[13] Author Interview

[14] Ibid., pg. 11

[15] Stamper, pg. 15

[16] Alexander, pg. 7

[17] Roy Walmsley (November 21, 2013). World Prison Population List (Tenth Edition). International Centre for Prison Studies. Retrieved July 11, 2014.

[18] Reiman, Jeffrey, and Leighton, Paul, *The Rich Get Richer and the Poor Get Prison,* Routledge, London, 2016, pgs. 11-51

[19] Benforado, Adam, *Unfair: The New Science of Criminal Injustice,* Crown, New York, 2015, pgs. 272-286. Drug diversion programs: www.ncjrs.gov/App/Publications/abstract.aspx?ID=246652 *Restorative Justice Programs*: journals.sagepub.com/doi/abs/10.1177/0032885505276969. *Rehabilitation instead of punishment:* onlinelibrary.wiley.com/doi/abs/10.1111/j.0011-1348.2005.00001.

[20] *Final Report of the President's Task Force on 21st Century Policing*

[21] Balko, Radley, *Rise of The Warrior Cop,* PublicAffairs, New York, 2013, pg. xv.

[22] www.policefoundation.org/leading-culture-change;, and Early, Steve, *Refinery Town,* pgs. 66-92, Beacon Press, New York, 2017.

23 Balko, pgs. 162-163.

24 www.ci.richmond.ca.us/Archive.aspx?AMID=72

25 Author interview, July 2015

26 www.youtube.com/watch?v=oK35y9-dTuw

27 "PBS NewsHour" interview, November 25, 2015

28 Stamper, pg. xvi

29 Zimbardo, Phillip, *The Lucifer Effect: Understanding How Good People Turn Evil,* Random House, New York, 2007. Pg. 211

30 www.nytimes.com/2004/05/03/international/middleeast/03ABUS.html?th=&pagewanted=print&position=

31 Ibid., pg. 329

32 Balko, pg. 275

33 *Final Report of the President's Task Force on 21st Century Policing,* pg. 11

34 www.army.mil

35 www.policecrimes.com

36 Adorno, T. W., Frenkel-Brunswik, E., Levinson, D. J., Sanford, R. N., *The Authoritarian Personality,* Norton, New York, 1950.

37 McNamara, J. H., *Uncertainties in Police Work: The Relevance of Police Recruits' Backgrounds and Training,* in *The Police: Six Sociological Essays 163 (D. Bourdua ed. 1967)*

38 Stamper, pg. 190

39 Ibid., pg. 145

40 Author Interview

41 Ibid., pg. 70

42 www.womenandpolicing.com/violenceFS.asp#notes

43 *The Atlantic,* Vol. 317, No 1, Jan./Feb. 2016, pg. 26

44 www.ncbi.nlm.nih.gov/pubmed/18717895

45 www.citeseerx.ist.psu.edu/viewdoc/download?doi=10.1.1.329.7737&rep=rep1&type=pdf

46 www.policelink.monster.com/training/articles/1970-the-use-of-trickery-and-deceit-during-interrogation

47 www.sfgate.com/opinion/openforum/article/Why-cops-lie-2388737.php

[48] Ibid.

[49] Stamper, pg. 195

[50] www.youtube.com/watch?v=JTKTf

[51] Balko, pg. 230

[52] Ibid pgs. 283 -286

[53] Ibid, pg. 231

[54] Ibid. pg. 214

[55] Ibid, pg. 214

[56] *The Bohemian,* Vol. 36.48, April 8-14, 2015

[57] www.rmc.library.cornell.edu/gettysburg/good_cause/transcript.htm

[58] www.theatlantic.com/politics/archive/2016/07/dallas-police/490583

Chapter Two

[1] Author Interview

[2] Balko, pgs. 239-242

[3] Balko, pg. 240

[4] www.cnn.com/2015/11/25/us/jason-van-dyke-previous-complaints-lawsuits/

[5] Klinger, David, *Into The Kill Zone: A Cop's Eye View of Deadly Force,* Josey Bass, San Francisco, 2004, pg. 63

[6] www.youtube.com/watch?v=EUp4bDa9M3o

[7] Author Interview, July 2015

[8] "Listening Session on Policy and Oversight: Use of Force Investigations and Oversight" (oral testimony of Chuck Wexler, executive director, Police Executive Research Forum, for the President's Task Force on 21st Century Policing, Cincinnati, OH, January 30, 2015)

[9] www.whitehouse.gov/the-press-office/2014/11/24/remarks-president-after-announcement-decision-grand-jury-ferguson-missou

[10] Bureau of Labor Statistics, National Census of Fatal Occupational Injuries, 2013

[11] National Safe Council (nsc.org), 2015

[12] Policemisconduct.net

[13] www.policeone.com/use-of-force/articles/3468102-Shooting-center-mass-The-dangers-of-denial

[14] www.health.harvard.edu

[15] www.cbc.ca/news/health/police-officers-face-higher-stress-levels-1.1275191 and www.officer.com/article/12156622/2015-police-suicide-statistics

[16] Ibid.

[17] Stevenson, Bryan, *Just Mercy,* Random House, New York, 2014, pg. 290

[18] Carlen, Philip, Nored, Lisa, "An examination of Officer Stress: Should Police Departments Implement Mandatory Counseling?" *Journal of Criminal and Police Psychology,* June 2008, Vol. 23, Issue 1, pgS. 8-15

[19] Klinger, pg. 216

[20] www.nytimes.com/2014/12/09/opinion/the-cop-mind.html

[21] Stamper, Norm, *To Protect and Serve,* Nation Books, New York, 2016, pg. 215

[22] www.apmreports.org/story/2017/05/05/police-de-escalation-training

[23] www.policechiefmagazine.org/mindful-policing-officer-wellness-training

Chapter Three

[1] www.archives.gov/founding-docs/declaration-transcript

[2] www.constituteproject.org/constitution/United_States_of_America_1992

[3] www.npr.org/sections/thetwo-way/2014/11/25/366507379/ferguson-docs-how-the-grand-jury-reached-a-decision

[4] In a rare move and in an attempt to allay concerns about bias, McCulloch made public the mountain of evidence presented to the grand jury.

[5] youtu.be/jpSEemvwOn4

[6] www.cnn.com/2015/07/23/opinions/cevallos-sandra-bland-traffic-stop

[7] supreme.justia.com/cases/federal/us/434/106/case.html

[8] Ibid.

[9] www.archives.gov/exhibits/charters/declaration_transcript.html

[10] en.wikipedia.org/wiki/Reasonable_suspicion

[11] www.law.cornell.edu/supremecourt/text/392/1#writing-USSC_CR_0392_0001_ZD

[12] supreme.justia.com/cases/federal/us/392/1/

[13] www.nyclu.org/content/stop-and-frisk-data

[14] www.law.cornell.edu/supremecourt/text/412/218

[15] www.supreme.justia.com/cases/federal/us/412/218/case.html

[16] Alexander, Michelle. *The New Jim Crow,* The New Press, 2012, New York, pgs. 66, 67

[17] Department of Health, Education and Welfare, Federal Register 39, No. 105, Part 2 (May 30, 1974)

[18] Ker v. California, 1963

[19] Ibid.

[20] www.chicagotribune.com/news/opinion/chapman/ct-fourth-amendment-baltimore-police-searches-unconstitutional-perspec-20160812-column.html

[21] www.supreme.justia.com/cases/federal/us/374/23/case.html

[22] www.supreme.justia.com/cases/federal/us/374/23/case.html

[23] www.supreme.justia.com/cases/federal/us/468/897/case.html

[24] Balko, Radley, *Rise of the Warrior Cop,* PublicAffairs, New York, 2013, pg. 150

[25] www.supreme.justia.com/cases/federal/us/468/897/case.html

[26] supreme.justia.com/cases/federal/us/332/581/

Chapter Four

[1] www.supremecourt.gov/opinions/15pdf/14-1373_83i7.pdf

[2] Larabee, Leonard, *Conservatism in Colonial America,* Cornell University Press, Ithaca, NY. 1948, pg. ix.

[3] Ibid., pg. 8

[4] Ibid., pg. 8

[5] Benforado, pg. 162

[6] Douglass, pg. 8

[7] www.uscourts.gov/educational-resources/educational-activities/chief-justice-roberts-statement-nomination-process

[8] Benforado, pg. 162

[9] Ibid.

[10] Friedman, Barry, *Unwarranted,* Farrar, Straus, and Giroux, New York, 2017, pg. 130

[11] Ibid., 131

[12] Douglas, pgs. 261-262

[13] Ibid., 261-262

[14] Labaree, pgs.145, 153, 164, 165

[15] Ibid., pgs. 110-111

[16] Amar, Akhil Reed, *American's Unwritten Constitution: The Precedents and Principles We Live By,* Basic Books, New York, 2012, pg. 247

[17] Ibid, pg. 97

[18] Amar, pg. 97

[19] www.cecc.gov/international-agreements-and-domestic-legislation-affecting-freedom-of-expression

[20] The Ninth Amendment reads: "The enumeration in the Constitution, of certain rights, shall not be construed to deny or disparage others retained by the people."

[21] United States Constitution, Amendment IX, Ratified December 15, 1791

[22] Amar, pg. 303

[23] Douglas, William O., *The Court Years,* Random House, New York, 1980, pg. 8

[24] www.en.wikipedia.org/wiki/Pledge_of_Allegiance

[25] www.archives.gov/press/exhibits/dream-speech.pdf

[26] Both Barack Obama and Donald Trump used this phrase, which, given their substantial differences, should make us seriously question what the true meaning of "a nation of laws" really means.

[27] Notice how you never hear that politicians say that "We are a nation of justice." Even they can only tell so many lies with a straight face.

[28] Benforado, pg. Pgs. 96-107

[29] cbsnews.com/news/st-louis-no-1-on-dangerous-city-list/

Chapter Five

[1] www.supremecourt.gov/opinions/15pdf/14-1373_83i7.pdf

[2] caselaw.findlaw.com/us-supreme-court/471/1.html

[3] caselaw.findlaw.com/us-supreme-court/471/1.html

[4] caselaw.findlaw.com/us-supreme-court/471/1.html

[5] supreme.justia.com/cases/federal/us/490/386/case.html

[6] supreme.justia.com/cases/federal/us/490/386/case.html

[7] supreme.justia.com/cases/federal/us/563/731/

[8] supreme.justia.com/cases/federal/us/475/335/

[9] www.law.cornell.edu/supct/html/03-1261.ZPC.html

[10] www.reviewjournal.com/crime/courts/federal-scrutiny-missing-from-las-vegas-police-shootings

[11] www.reviewjournal.com/crime/las-vegas-police-release-report-detailing-use-of-force-statistics

[12] www.cops.usdoj.gov/pdf/deadly-force-statistical-analysis.pdf

[13] www.lasvegassun.com/news/2016/jul/17/las-vegas-is-a-standard-bearer-in-holding-police-a

Chapter Six

[1] Lloyd, Douglas, Easton County Prosecuting Attorney, Press Release, June 16, 2015

[2] Case 1:15-cv-01053, Doc #1, Filed 10/14/15, pg. 6

[3] Author interview, July 23, 2015

[4] Rawls, John, *Justice as Fairness: A Restatement.* 2001

[5] Case 1:15-cv-01053, Doc #1, Filed 10/14/15, pg. 4

[6] youtube.com/watch?v=ExE78amvpT4

[7] Ibid.

[8] Fitch, Brian D., Ph.D., "Understanding the Psychology of Police Misconduct,":*The Police Chief: The Professional Voice of Law Enforcement* July 2015

[9] Kahneman, D., Tversky, A., 1979. "Prospect Theory: An analysis of decisions under risk," *Econometrica,* 47:263-291

[10] Atwater v. The City of Lago Vista, www.law.cornell.edu/supct/pdf/99-1408P.ZO

[11] www.theatlantic.com/politics/archive/2014/12/how-police-unions-keep-abusive-cops-on-the-street/383258

Chapter Seven

[1] "This American Life," Transcript 573, Aired on November 27, 2015

[2] Ibid.

[3] www.demos.org/sites/default/files/publications/RacialWealthGap_1.pdf

[4] "This American Life," Transcript 573, Aired on November 27, 2015

[5] www.washingtonpost.com/news/wonk/wp/2015/05/21/the-top-10-of-americans-own-76-of-the-stuff-and-its-dragging-our-economy-down

[6] www.justice.gov/sites/default/files/crt/legacy/2014/07/22/newark_findings_7-22-14.pdf

[7] www.justice.gov/sites/default/files/opa/press-releases/attachments/2014/12/04/cleveland_division_of_police_findings_letter.pdf

[8] www.youtube.com/watch?v=oK35y9-dTuw

[9] Ibid.

[10] Ibid.

[11] DOJ Report on Ferguson Police Department, 2015, pg. 28

[12] law.justia.com/cases/federal/appellate-courts/ca1/10-1764/10-1764p-01a-2011-08-26.html

[13] DOJ Report on Ferguson Police Department, 2015, pg. 31

[14] DOJ Report on Ferguson Police Department, 2015, pg. 30

[15] DOJ Report on Ferguson Police Department, 2015, pg. 22

[16] Ibid, pg. 37

[17] Ibid., pg. 65

[18] www.aclu.org/sites/default/files/assets/141027_iachr_racial_disparities_aclu_submission_0.pdf

[19] Miller, Geoffrey, *The Mating Mind,* Anchor Books, New York, 2001, pgs. 321-327

[20] Ignatiev, Noel, *How The Irish Became White,* Routledge, New York, 1995, pg. 1

[21] Ibid., pg. 2

[22] Guinier, Lani, Torres, Gerald, *The Miner's Canary,* Harvard University Press, 2002, pg. 16

[23] www.theatlantic.com/notes/2015/08/toni-morrison-wasnt-giving-bill-clinton-a-compliment/402517

[24] Ibid.

[25] Ibid, pg. 58

[26] Ibid. pg. 76

[27] Ibid. pg. 94

[28] Ibid. pg. 12

[29] www.washingtonpost.com/posteverything/wp/2016/03/03/how-tracking-police-data-by-race-can-make-unfair-laws-look-like-the-cops-fault

[30] www.lccr.com/wp-content/uploads/Not-Just-a-Ferguson-Problem-How-Traffic-Courts-Drive-Inequality-in-California-4.8.15.pdf

[31] www.kcra.com/article/californias-traffic-ticket-amnesty-program-is-about-to-end/9198864

[32] www.joincampaignzero.org/end-policing-for-profit

[33] www.chicagotribune.com/news/local/breaking/chi-quinn-signs-into-law-bill-banning-police-ticket-quota-20140615-story.html

[34] www.chicagotribune.com/news/local/breaking/chi-quinn-signs-into-law-bill-banning-police-ticket-quota-20140615-story.html

[35] www.huffingtonpost.com/entry/state-bail-system-grades_us_59f78f90e4b0aec1467a2708

[36] www.uploads.trustandjustice.org/misc/ChiefJOnesPrincipledArticle.pdf

[37] www.s3.trustandjustice.org/misc/StrengtheningCommPolice_CAPSC.pdf

[38] www.sfchronicle.com/bayarea/article/Sharp-downturn-in-use-of-force-at-Oakland-Police-6481637.php

[39] www.oaklandmagazine.com/April-2017/The-Year-of-No-Shootings

[40] www.nbcbayarea.com/news/local/Racial-Profiling-Is-a-Problem-at-Oakland-Police-Department-Study-488719541.html

[41] www.ktvu.com/news/oakland-ends-racial-profiling-contract-with-stanford-as-it-hosts-a-town-hall-on-racial-disparities

[42] www.static1.squarespace.com/static/56996151cbced68b170389f4/t/57e1b5cc2994ca4ac1d97700/1474409936835/Police+Use+of+Force+Report.pdf

[43] www.ballotpedia.org/Fact_check/Did_Stockton,_California,_have_%E2%80%9Cits_lowest_crime_rate_in_the_past_15_years%E2%80%9D_in_2014%3F

Chapter Eight

[1] Law%20enforcement%20took%20more%20stuff%20from%20peop
le%20than%20burglars%20did%20last%20year%20-
%20The%20Washington%20Post.html

[2] Ibid.

[3] www.law.cornell.edu/supct/html/94-8729.ZO.html

[4] Stillman, Sarah, "Taken," *New Yorker,* August 12 and 19, 2013

[5] Ibid.

[6] Ibid.

[7] Ibid.

[8] www.washingtonpost.com/news/volokh-
conspiracy/wp/2014/10/26/the-too-long-arm-of-the-law-contd

[9] www.lowellsun.com/news/ci_26407418/after-nearly-60-years-
motel-caswell-checks-out

[10] www.washingtonpost.com/opinions/when-government-is-the-
looter/2012/05/18/

[11] www.nytimes. gIQAUIKVZU_story.html com/2014/10/26/us/law-
lets-irs-seize-accounts-on-suspicion-no-crime-required.html

[12] www.heritage.org/crime-and-justice/report/civil-asset-
forfeiture-good-intentions-gone-awry-and-the-need-
reform

[13] www.washingtonpost.com/news/the-
watch/wp/2014/11/12/policing-for-profit-in-tennessee

[14] www.heritage.org/research/reports/2015/04/civil-asset-forfeiture-
good-intentions-gone-awry-and-the-need-for-reform

[15] Ibid.

[16] Ibid.

[17] Malcolm, John, *Civil Asset Forfeiture: When Good Intentions Go
Awry,* heritage.org/testimony/civil-asset-forfeiture-when-good-
intentions-go-awry

[18] policecrimes.com/police_code.html

[19] www.youtube.com/watch?v=In3inU5WBGw

[20] Ibid.

[21] www.huffingtonpost.com/radley-balko/supreme-court-considers-
t_1_b_2063820.html

[22] Ibid.

[23] www.arizonalawreview.org/pdf/51-3/51arizlrev777.pdf, pg.

788

[24] Yoder, John, Cates, Brad, "Government Self-Interest Corrupted a Crime Fighting Tool into An Evil," *Washington Post,* September 18, 2014

Chapter Nine

[1] Stevenson, Bryan, *Just Mercy,* Random House, 2015, New York, pg. 39

[2] Ibid.

[3] Ibid. pg. 40.

[4] NPR interview on "Fresh Air," October 20, 2014

[5] His story comes from Balko, Radley, *Rise of the Warrior Cop,* pg. 310

[6] Cato Policy report November-December 2008

[7] Balko, Radley, *Rise of the Warrior Cop*, PublicAffairs, New York, 2013, pg. 311

[8] Ibid., pg. 314

[9] Ibid, pg. 315

[10] Interview with the author[11] Mikkelsen, E. J., Gutheil, T. G., Emens, M. (October 1992), "False sexual abuse allegations by children and adolescents: contextual factors and clinical subtypes," *Am J Psychother,* 46 (4): 556–70 PMID 1443285.

[12] Regehr, Cheryl, Gutheil, Thomas, "Apology, Justice, and Trauma Recovery" Nov 3, 2002, *J Am Acad Psychiatry Law,* 30:425–30

[13] May, Cindy, "The Advantages of Not Saying You Are Sorry," *Scientific American,* July 2, 2013

[14] onlinelibrary.wiley.com/doi/10.1002/ejsp.1901/abstract

[15] Ibid.

[16] May, Cindy, "The Advantages of Not Saying You Are Sorry," *Scientific American,* July 2, 2013

[17] Keltner, Dacher, *The Power Paradox,* Penguin Press, New York, 201

[18] Keltner, pgs. 129-130

[19] Janoff-Bulman, Ronnie, Werther, Amelie, in A. Nadler, T. Malloy,

and J. Fisher (Eds.), *The Social Psychology of Intergroup Reconciliation*, Oxford University Press, New York, pgs. 145-170

[20] Ibid., pg. 7

[21] Ibid., pg. 7

* As the Supreme Court explicitly stated in the Atwater v. Lago Vista case described on page 208

* As exhaustively detailed in Michelle Alexander's *The New Jim Crow*. We continue to punish criminals long after they have "paid their debt" to society by denying them access to jobs, education, social benefits, voting rights, etc., essentially making them permanently less human than the rest of us in meaningful daily humiliating ways.

[22] hotair.com/archives/2015/10/17/sadly-deven-guilford-probably-got-exactly-what-he-deserved

[23] Janoff-Bulman, Ronnie, Werther, Amelie, in A. Nadler, T. Malloy, and J. Fisher (Eds.), The Social Psychology of Intergroup Reconciliation, pp. 145-170. NY: Oxford University Press, New York. Cited from https://pdfs.semanticscholar.org/aef8/cd5d89a38abd8e6fb891b527054dbc29dcdd.pdf?ga=2.197136425.707620642.1559577704.693824276.1559577704, pg. 4

[24] Ibid, pg. 11

[25] Ibid, pg. 11

[26] Ibid, pg. 12

[27] Tyler, Tom, "Legitimacy and Procedural Justice: A New Element of Police Leadership", U.S. Department of Justice, Bureau of Justice Assistance, March 2014, pg.11

[28] Ibid.. pg. 11

[29] policeforum.org/assets/docs/Free_Online_Documents/Leadership/legitimacy%20and%20procedural%20justice%20-%20a%20new%20element%20of%20police%20leadership.pdf pg. 11

[30] Ibid., pg. 9

[31] Ibid., pg. 12

[32] Ibid., pg. 10

Chapter Ten

[1] www.sscnet.ucla.edu/anthro/faculty/fiske/RM_PDFs/Goodenough_
Moral_Territoriality.pdf

[2] www.psych.nyu.edu/jost/Wakslak,%20Jost,%20Tyler,%20%26%20
Chen%20(2007)%20Moral%20outrage%20mediates%20the%20d
ampening%20effect%20of%20system%20justification.PDF

[3] Ibid.

[4] Ibid.

[5] Ibid.

[6] Ibid.

[7] Ibid.

[8] www.pewtrusts.org/en/projects/financial-security-and-mobility

[9] NPR Interview on "Fresh Air," July 21, 2016

[10] Ibid.

Chapter Eleven

[1] Author Interview

[2] Stamper, pg. 186

[3] Ibid., pg. 212

[4] sfblueribbonpanel.com, pgs. 144-147

[5] Ibid.

[6] ww2.kqed.org/news/2016/07/11/panel-finds-sfpd-code-of-silence-
outsized-influence-of-police-union

[7] *San Francisco Chronicle,* July 12, 2016, pg. A11

[8] Ibid.

[9] www.ebcitizen.com/2016/06/amid-growing-sex-scandal-oakland-
police.html

[10] Van Craen, Martin, Skogan, Wesley, "Achieving Fairness in
Policing: The Link Between Internal and External Procedural
Justice," *Police Quarterly,* July 13, 2016

[11] Stamper, pg. 6

[12] www.whitehouse.gov/the-press-office/2016/07/12/remarks-
president-memorial-service-fallen-dallas-police-officers

[13] Ibid.

[14] Hochschild, Arlie, *Strangers In Their Own Land,* The New Press,
New York, 2016, pg. 135

[15] jpubhealth.oxfordjournals.org/content/27/2/143.full.pdf

[16] Lakoff, George. *Moral Politics,* 3rd Ed., University of Chicago Press, Chicago, 2016, pg. 167

[17] Ibid., pg. 315

[18] www.nytimes.com/2016/01/06/opinion/campaign-stops/purity-disgust-and-donald-trump.html

[19] Ibid., pgs. 297-307

[20] Hibbing, John R., Smith, Kevin B., Alford, John R., "Differences in Negativity Bias Underlie Variations in Political Ideology," *Behavior and Brain Sciences,* 2014 (37), pg. 299.

[21] Miller, pgs. 292-342

[22] Douglas, pg. 8

[23] Lakoff, pg. 159

[24] Hochschild, Arlie, pg. 144

[25] www.brookings.edu/2015/11/25/drug-offenders-in-american-prisons-the-critical-distinction-between-stock-and-flow

[26] www.wsj.com/articles/SB1000142405274870447150457443890008 30760842

INDEX

Abdullah, Kareem, 226
Abuse. See Bullying
Accountability, 72–73, 213
    conservative/liberal dichotomy of, 342–343
    of the many vs. the few, 340–342
    of police, 333–343
"Activists," 134
Acute stress response, 73
Adams, Eric, on public opinion of police officers, 330–331
Adams, Leon, 283
Adams, Mary, 283
Advantageous Comparisons, 202
AFF (Asset Forfeiture Fund), 263
African-Americans
    and being "raced" black, 240, 246, 248
    and black/white relations, 236–238, 244–246, 255, 356
    and Declaration of Independence, 95
    in Ferguson, Missouri, 232–233
    financial problems facing, 215–218
    and "honorary white status," 242–244
    policing of white people vs., 13, 15, 103, 110, 219, 223–224,
        226, 241, 246–247, 250–252, 255, 311, 331
    and racial progress, 219–220, 233
    and racism, 215–217, 226, 241–242, 248
    and respect, 307, 311
    and slavery, 142
    and "stop and frisk," 103
    and white privilege, 236, 240, 246
"Aggressive" (label), 311
Alcala, Joe, 106
Alcoholism, 74
Alexander, Michelle, 13, 35, 109
Amar, Akhil Reed, 141, 143, 144, 147
American Civil Liberties Union (ACLU), 116–117, 232–233
American Dream, 219, 248, 252, 347
American Revolution, 135, 140
Amiel, Henri Frederic, on apologies, 288
Anger, 66

www.ingramcontent.com/pod-product-compliance
Lightning Source LLC
Chambersburg PA
CBHW060305030426
42336CB00011B/954